Time, Innovation and Mobilities

In social theory and sociology, time and travel in technological cultures is one of the new and challenging research topics in the 'mobilities turn'. Yet surprisingly, contemporary practices of mobility have till now seen only limited theorization within these disciplines. By analysing historic and contextualized transit practices, this revealing book argues that travel cannot now simply be reduced to getting from A to B; it is an integrated part of everyday life.

In this area, researching how problems can be identified as dilemmas and reformulated as design problems helps create a new vocabulary, one which will not only change the agenda in the debate on mobility problems in the public domain, but will also suggest new ways of theorizing mobility innovations. In this fascinating book, author Peters:

- develops a conceptual framework to study contemporary transit practices and evaluate innovation strategies;
- offers new insights regarding historic and contemporary design strategies and regarding innovations related to travel in technological cultures;
- gives special attention to electronic timespaces and ICT-based mobility innovations;
- investigates cases of travel in technological cultures, car travel, air travel and cycling in Dutch towns.

An original and provocative contribution to the emerging field of mobilities, this book will become an essential resource for advanced undergraduate and postgraduate researchers and practitioners in the fields of sociology, geography, spatial planning, policy and transportation studies.

Peter Frank Peters is assistant professor at the Faculty of Arts and Culture of the University of Maastricht. He has published on time, mobility and travel in technological cultures. His research is concerned with the debates on public problems related to mobility and the assessment of innovations suggested to solve these problems.

International library of sociology
Founded by Karl Mannheim
Editor: John Urry, *Lancaster University*

Brands
Logos of the global economy
Celia Lury

Visual Worlds
John Hall, Blake Stimson and Lisa Tamiris Becker

Time, Innovation and Mobilities
Travel in technological cultures
Peter Frank Peters

Time, Innovation and Mobilities
Travel in technological cultures

Peter Frank Peters

Routledge
Taylor & Francis Group

LONDON AND NEW YORK

First published 2006
by Routledge
4 Park Square, Milton Park, Abingdon, Oxon OX14 4RN
605 Third Avenue, New York, NY 10017

Routledge is an imprint of the Taylor & Francis Group, an informa business

© 2006 Peter Frank Peters

Typeset in Sabon by Wearset Ltd, Boldon, Tyne and Wear

British Library Cataloguing in Publication Data
A catalogue record for this book is available from the British Library

Library of Congress Cataloging in Publication Data
A catalog record for this title has been requested

ISBN 978-0-415-37072-1 (hbk)
ISBN 978-0-415-58123-3 (pbk)

To Stijn and Bernike

Contents

Illustrations

Acknowledgements

This book originates from my work as a journalist in the early 1990s, when I wrote about the public debate on mobility politics in the Netherlands. Discussions focused on how to curb the increase in car use. By using the concept of travel time, transport scientists and economists were able to explain why this would be difficult, but in their explanations, I missed the cultural aspects of what makes driving a car so attractive. That I have been able to study travel in technological cultures, I owe to Rein de Wilde and Gerard de Vries, who became my thesis supervisors after I moved to the Faculty of Arts and Culture of Maastricht University in 1996. I am especially grateful to Rein, without whom this book would not have been written. His creative comments had a profound influence on how I shaped my argument. Gerard's criticisms on this argument helped to sharpen it in the final phases of writing the book. I would also like to thank my colleagues at the Faculty of Arts and Culture, who have read, criticized and constructively discussed my work on many occasions. In particular I must thank Ruth Benschop, Maarten Doorman, David Hamers, Anique Hommels and Jessica Mesman for their support. I have also greatly benefited from working on research projects with Wiebe Bijker, Maarten Hajer, Bruno Latour, Paul Peeters and Michiel Schwarz. I would like to thank John Law for discussing with me many topics related to the book. Finally, I am indebted to the Department of Philosophy of the Faculty for generously funding the translation, and to Margaret Meredith for her conscientious work in translating the Dutch text into English.

When doing my research, I had contacts with many people and institutions. I am grateful to those who agreed to be interviewed, or who helped me in other ways in finding sources for my research. I also wish to thank David Nathanson of the National Park Service History Collection in Harpers Ferry, West Virginia, Ethan Carr of the Park Historic Structures and Cultural Landscapes Program of the National Park Service and Timothy Davis of the Historic American Buildings Survey/Historic American Engineering Record for sharing their knowledge of US national park history with me. I wish to thank the employees of KLM who showed me how they work on time, and Jaap van de Linde of KLM's Passenger

Services, Daan Nijland and Klaas de Waal of KLM's Operations Control for their hospitality. I would not have been able to write this book without the help of many people in the Dutch Ministry of Transport, Public Works and Water Management, for which I am grateful.

I would also like to thank Uitgeverij De Balie in Amsterdam for granting me permission to translate and publish the Dutch text of the book, first published in 2003. The following institutions I thank for permissions to publish the plates, figures and tables. Figures 3.1 and 3.2 have been reproduced from Don Parkes and Nigel Thrift, *Times, spaces, and places: a chronogeographic perspective* (1980) with permission from John Wiley and Sons Ltd. Figure 4.1 is reproduced from Warren Belasco, *Americans on the road: from autocamp to motel, 1910–1945*, with permission from Warren Belasco. Figures 4.2, 4.3 and 4.4 are in the archives of the National Park Service History Collection and have been reproduced with permission from the National Parks Services' archivist, Tom DuRant. Figures 5.1 and 5.2 have been reproduced with permission of KLM Royal Dutch Airlines. The figures and tables in Chapter 6 have all been reproduced from CROW-record nr 10 *Sign up for the bike: design manual for a cycle-friendly infrastructure* (1993) with permission from CROW, the Dutch Centre for Research and Contract Standardization in Civil and Traffic Engineering.

Finally, I would like to express my gratitude to my parents, Kees and Kitty, for their support and to my friend Louis Stiller, who taught me how to travel. Bernike and Stijn have given me their attention and endurance over the years, for which I am grateful. On one of our cycle tours, my daughter Stijn explained to me the difference between bicycle kilometres and car kilometres, and also why bicycle kilometres are more fun. She is the best traveller there is.

Peter Frank Peters
Maastricht, Spring 2005

Introduction

Travel takes time. And because we experience time as scarce, innovations in the way we travel generally aim at reducing the amount of time a journey takes. In this book, I will challenge the basic assumption underlying this line of thinking, the idea that the time spent travelling can be reduced to a neutral and measured unity which can be saved if we speed up. The core of my argument is that travel not only *takes* time, but that it also *makes* time. In examining everyday travel practices, I argue that travel time can also be understood as the product of situated transit practices. The book's ultimate aim is to provide a pragmatic understanding of the way people actually travel in order to open up new perspectives on both mobility innovations and on the study of travel in technological cultures.

Focusing on travel time takes us right to the heart of three interrelated debates. To start with, there is the public debate on mobility politics and policies. Since the 1970s, mobility problems have been described and analysed within a conceptual framework that assumes the inevitability of increased mobility on the one hand, and the proliferation of problems resulting from it on the other. Along with transportation economists, urban planners, social geographers and traffic engineers, I argue that travel time is of pivotal importance in grasping the character of these problems. Economic and geographical models that explain and calculate travel demand using quantifiable units of time shape the vocabulary at our disposal to discuss mobility problems and their solutions. Yet, as this book will make clear, this vocabulary has its limits when used to explain the success and failure of mobility innovations.

Second, the mobility of people, objects, capital and information across the world is one of the new and challenging research topics in what could be called the 'mobility turn' in social theory and sociology. Academic interest in such 'mobilities' has been more or less implicit in theories of modernization and globalization. Recently, however, greater emphasis has been given to local processes of daily travel, developments in transport and communications infrastructures, and the cultures related to mobility. This book contributes to this emerging field by analysing and studying 'mobilities' as practices of travel. These concepts are in tension with each other.

The word 'mobility' is an attribute of people, goods and information which are in a dynamic state. Thus, the term mobility can denote a marketable commodity, e.g. the products of airlines or travel agencies, but it can also be a subject for statistical analysis, e.g. the total number of kilometres travelled in country, or refer to a policy domain, e.g. transport policies. The word 'travel' has a different set of meanings. It refers not just to a dynamic state, but to a meaningful activity that has a long cultural and social history. It not only engenders a movement in space and time, but also assumes the subjectivity of experiences as well as the intersubjectivity of texts and discourses. The main aim of this book is to analyse systematically practices of travel. In this practice-oriented approach, travel is not reduced to getting from A to B as quickly and as smoothly as possible – the underlying assumption in mainstream transportation research vocabularies on mobility – but instead, travel is treated as an integrated part of everyday life, a 'normal' practice.

As a normal practice, travel has been and still is characterized by solving the duality between planning and contingency, between knowing where to go and solving unexpected problems. Researching how these problems have been identified as dilemmas and reformulated as design problems in five case studies of travel practices helps to create a new perspective on the innovation of mobilities. The practices I examine include 'romantic' walking in the early nineteenth century, the excursions by steam trains and steamships organized by Thomas Cook & Son between 1841 and 1872, car travel to US national parks in the 1950s, contemporary air travel at Schiphol Airport in Amsterdam, and finally, bicycling in Dutch towns and villages since the 1970s. I have based my analysis partly on primary archival sources and ethnographic research. In doing so, my aim has not been to produce an exhaustive treatment of these widely divergent topics, which deserve a book-length analysis in their own right. Instead, my aim has been to draw concepts and ideas from these practices that together form a starting point for creating a new vocabulary for analysing travel in technological cultures and for conceptualizing the innovations that changed it. Central to this vocabulary is the concept of 'passages'. In order to travel, I claim, we need to construct passages that produce a situated relation between time and space. How this is achieved in practice can be described on three levels. As heterogeneous orders, passages assume both material and discursive elements. As planned yet contingent orders, they must be 'repaired' continuously in real time. And as orders that both include and exclude people, places and moments in time, they are inherently political and have to be justified and legitimated. The conceptual framework which unfolds in this book enables us to examine innovations in travel in a new way: how can they be conceived of as passages? How are passages created? What are the politics of these new passages? In designing and innovating passages, travel time is constructed. Shorter travel times can therefore never be a sufficient argument for mobility innovations; instead we should envision different possible passages and present them as argued choices, not between different speeds, but between different 'worlds'.

What sets my approach in answering these questions apart from others is its focus on travel as a problem-solving activity as well as an activity that leads to social problems. Innovation can be expected wherever travellers encounter problems or where their travelling causes problems. Studying travel in a pragmatist register allows the focus of analysis to shift to issues of design. This book argues that, regardless of whether you are talking about the design of visitor centres in American national parks, KLM's Operations Control Centre at Schiphol Airport, or cycle-friendly infrastructure in the Netherlands – all can be viewed as ways of solving dilemmas that arise when passages must be standardized, repaired and legitimated. Putting design at the forefront of the analysis makes it possible to get around the deterministic assumptions underpinning most mainstream transport research. Instead, understanding mobility dilemmas as design problems implies that there is not just one 'best' solution, but many, and therefore makes it possible to debate different design *styles*. This approach opens up new ways of elaborating on the political and normative character (e.g. social exclusion) inherent in mobility policies. Reasoning in terms of passages leads to the 'sociological irony' (Gusfield 1981) that questions the self-evidence underlying most debates on mobility, both public and academic.

A practice-oriented approach to travel and mobility requires an interdisciplinary perspective. In conceptualizing travel from a pragmatic perspective, I have relied upon many theoretical and methodological insights from social theory, human geography, and constructivist science and technology studies. In social theory, travel and mobility have been conceptualized and theorized extensively, leading to concepts like flows, circulations and mobilities. However, in much of the older scholarship in this field, these flows have remained as if black boxed. Flows are presented as explanations for processes of globalization rather than as phenomena that have to be explained (Castells 1996). Mobility has been identified as a stratifying condition in a globalized world, yet without explaining the various ways in which concrete practices of mobility include and exclude 'tourists' and 'vagabonds' (Bauman 1998). Only recently the need for understanding 'mobilities' in modern societies has been translated into research projects focusing on mobilities as an everyday practice and culture. In human geography, processes of time-space compression (Harvey 1989) and the new power geometries they call into being (Massey and Jess 1995) have been theorized extensively, but also without focusing on the actual travel practices that create a 'shrinking globe'. Of seminal importance for the development of my own thinking has been the work by John Urry on travel, tourist cultures and recently mobilities, and Nigel Thrift, who has written on almost every aspect of time-space practices, ranging from early time-space geographical models to recent theories of networked and distributed Time-Space. In developing my perspective on travel practices, I have also drawn extensively on work in the field of science and technology studies. It is surprising to note that a number of groundbreaking books and articles in this field have transportation as their subject. The social construction of technology has been developed by starting to analyse the innovation processes that found their closure in the modern bicycle (Pinch and Bijker 1987). Early formulations of actor network theory were developed in case studies of the failure to build a light electric vehicle (Callon 1986), and of the heterogeneous networks that enabled the Portuguese in the fifteenth and sixteenth centuries to navigate their sea vessels over long distances (Law 1987). Bruno Latour, to whose work I also owe a great debt, has worked out the claim that any innovation process has an unpredictable outcome by recounting the 'death of Aramis', an unmanned Parisian metro that never made it from the drawing tables to the real world (Latour 1996a).

Although the case studies discussed in this book are widely dispersed both historically and geographically, many are situated in the Netherlands. Holland is a good place for anyone studying practices and problems of mobility. It has the third largest harbour in the world (after Shanghai and Singapore) and the fourth largest airport in Europe. It is a small, densely populated country with a very high number of cars per square kilometre. Building new infrastructure invariably leads to lengthy debates in which many interests have to be weighed. The Netherlands faces severe traffic-related environmental problems, one of which is air pollution due to high concentrations of fine dust particles which, according to a recent study, cause 18,000 premature deaths annually. Perhaps the most characteristic feature of Dutch mobility is its bicycle cultures. One of its larger cities, Groningen, has the highest number of bicycles per capita in the world. Yet the number of cycle kilometres in the Netherlands tends to be stable, whereas the number of car kilometres continues to rise every year. This development is usually explained by pointing out that cars are faster than bicycles. Precisely this line of reasoning leads to the main question in my book: how can we speak about mobility innovations without having to fall back on a perspective which compares the old and the new in terms of decontextualized speed or slowness?

An outline of the book

The central question in Chapter 1 is how the innovation of mobilities is addressed within dominant discourses of mobility politics and mainstream transport science in the Netherlands. Beginning in the early 1970s, Dutch politicians argued that increased mobility would lead to a host of future problems, including increased congestion in urban areas, unsafe roads, social exclusion stemming from unequal access to car-centred transport systems and problems related to the quality of life, such as noise, pollution, health risks and urban sprawl. A variety of policy measures aimed at changing people's travel behaviour were suggested, and some were implemented. However, in the long run, the basic social dilemma remained: mobility innovations which benefit the individual traveller lead to societal costs. Economists and transport scientists have used a quantitative concept of travel time to explain *why* mobility continues to increase, and why it is so difficult to change people's travel behaviour. An example of their style of reasoning can be found in the 'hypothesis of constant travel time', which states that within a population the mean daily time travelled is constant. In strong variants of this hypothesis, the constant is taken to be 70 minutes over a long period of time, regardless of culture and country. I will argue that a quantified concept of travel time can be used to render convincing arguments, but only at a price. Innovation boils down to the choice between speeding up and slowing down.

How do the dualities like speed and slowness or 'travelling as in being in transit' and 'travelling as a journey' shape both historical and contemporary narratives on travel time? Chapter 2 addresses this question by describing how the practice of walking changed in the early nineteenth century. The onslaught of new and faster means of transport, especially the steam-powered train, meant that walking could be perceived as 'slow' in a way that it could not have been before. Now that travelling could be fast, moving slowly became a choice that had to be 'legitimated'. The advent of romantic walking reinforced a duality in reflections on the distinction between what could be called 'travelling as being in transit to reach one's destination' and 'travelling as a journey that is a goal in itself'. When seen as merely being in transit, travelling has to be as fast as possible; the journey itself no longer possesses any value. On the other hand, travelling as a journey can be seen as a meaningful activity in itself. Romantic walkers in the early nineteenth century created a 'self' in the act of walking. Their destination was often unclear; they improvised as they went along, reacting to unforeseen circumstances in ways that were perceived as a product of their creativity. Underlying this duality are two different notions of time: time as a linear and fixed sequence of events and time as a progression from past to present to future. To contextualize travel time we have to transcend this dualism and study how travel speed can be the outcome of the actual practices of travel in which situated relations of time and space are produced.

Chapter 3 aims to tackle the question of how it is possible to conceptualize travel time as the outcome of 'passages'. The characteristic experience of modern travel has been summarized in the nineteenth-century phrase 'the annihilation of space through time'. This metaphor, implicitly or explicitly, structures the arguments of Giddens (1990) and Harvey (1989), who, in historicizing the separation of space and time, attempt to explain why modernity is characterized by a constant process of speeding up. But in doing so, both end up in a position that locates the cause of historical change in a quasi-autonomous technological development. Once time and space can no longer be taken as constants, the explanatory power shifts to technological innovations. However, technologies can never be their own explanations. In order to create a contextual notion of travel time, I describe the technologies that 'shrunk the world', not from the spectator's perspective of technological determinism, but from an actor's perspective, which focuses on the innovative work that has to be done in order to make faster travel possible. I reconstruct the actor's perspective in such innovative work by describing the labours undertaken by Thomas Cook to make travel speed 'do-able', which rendered travel times shorter and created a 'smaller world' for his customers. My claim is that, in order to sell travel speed and shorter travel times, Cook had to build passages to his destinations.

Chapter 4 focuses on creating the heterogeneous order of a passage. In the previous chapter, I argued that this order is built out of material and immaterial elements. To answer the question of how these elements are linked in order to render the effect of a swift journey between one place and another, I examine a historical case study on how car travel in the United States affected the design of the national parks. There are many explanations for the relatively short period of time in which the transition from train to car took place in the United States. One underlines the fact that with the car, people could travel when and where they wanted. The ubiquity of car travel can be taken as an effect of passages. What connections had to be made between diverse elements to make places accessible at any time? 'American passages' were created not only out of cars, but also out of roads and highways, gas stations, drive-in restaurants and motels. These passages had to be standardized in order to connect these elements in such a way that 'flow' was the main effect of a passage. As a result, car journeys became more predictable than in the days of the early motorists. Together with the contingencies of travel, stories of hardship and adventure on the road disappeared, only to reappear in narratives and iconography. Next to 'place myths' (Shields 1991), 'travel myths' told car travellers how driving America's 'blue highways' could be experienced as an adventure. American passages not only made new destinations accessible, they also changed them, as is shown in the example of one of the quintessential American travel destinations, the national parks. The dilemma between park use and preservation characterizes the history of National Park Service (NPS) park designs. In the 1930s, park roads, look-out points and park museums were designed to blend into the surrounding landscape. This approach was abandoned in the 1950s when the number of visitors by car rose dramatically. Helping all these people to find their way through the parks quickly became the main objective of the new designs that the Mission 66 programme introduced in 1956. Visitor centres were located near major intersections, providing information enabling visitors to find the major sights. Preserving the wilderness while at the same time circulating an increasing number of cars through the parks not only required material innovations such as visitor centres, but also a constant restyling of the representations and iconography of park nature in 'intermediary landscapes'. This chapter claims that, to understand the creation of passages, it is necessary to study innovative connections between the material and immaterial elements in the heterogeneous order that make swift transportation possible.

The American passages discussed in Chapter 4 show that the predictability of a journey is an important precondition for 'flow'. The car traveller knows what to expect and is therefore in a position to try to reduce the contingencies that can cause delays. Chapter 5 builds on the previous case study by showing how planned passages can be repaired when contingencies do arise. This case study focuses on the work which employees of the Dutch airline carrier KLM must do in order to provide customers with reliable and punctual flights. How do they ensure planes fly on time when the complexity of daily flight operations is increasing? Ethnographic research at KLM's Front Office of the Operations Control Centre at Schiphol Airport provides an answer. If we follow air travellers checking in, we see them moving from the check-in counter, through customs, to the gate where they board the aircraft. During the first part of the journey, KLM employees are able to solve problems and air travellers are disciplined step by step in order to 'fit' into the flight passage. Airport employees see the unpredictable behaviour of passengers as the main reason for disruptions in the flight schedule. The Departure Hall is just one of the locations where a flight passage is constructed. How an overview of spatially distributed actions is created becomes clear in the Front Office of the Operations Control Centre. Here the processes making up the KLM network on the day of operation are continually monitored. If something goes wrong anywhere – whether in baggage handling, aircraft handling, passenger services or elsewhere – this can affect scheduled departure times. This chapter examines two problematic episodes in KLM's Front Office from the perspective of the 'exchange', the material and immaterial resources needed to repair passages and fly on time. In general, innovating 'exchange' is necessary to connect and synchronize the temporal orders that constitute a passage in *real time*.

The aim of Chapter 6 is to examine how passages are related to each other, and to elaborate on the political and normative consequences of these relations. This chapter focuses on urban transport in the Netherlands and how the Dutch government has attempted to design infrastructure promoting the use of bicycles over cars. Unlike KLM's Operations Control Centre, there is no means of centralizing control in the case of people travelling within and through cities. Urban travellers are each other's contingencies, and in urban traffic, space and time are constantly contested. Innovative solutions for remedying the intersection of passages date from the nineteenth century when the traffic landscape was redesigned to create the material and immaterial conditions for the intersection of passages. Different design styles were employed, depending on the degree to which the passages were segregated or integrated. Regulating the crossing of passages entails the use of immaterial elements such as traffic rules. The crossing of passages requires what I call 'ensembles of passages'. Considered from an actor's perspective, such ensembles do not merely distribute already existing speeds, but are constitutive of the differences in speed attained. Instead of the intersection of existing speeds, ensembles produce speed or slowness in the space, time and risk that are exchanged among actors in a traffic landscape. Because the distribution of space, time and risk among travellers is unequal, the design of ensembles is always a matter of politics. This chapter examines such exchanges in the Dutch government's implementation of the Bicycle Masterplan in the 1990s, introduced to encourage the use of bicycles in cities. The centrepiece of this plan was the *Design manual for a cycle-friendly infrastructure*. This chapter analyses the ways in which the *Design manual* answers one of the basic questions which must be asked when designing cycle-friendly infrastructure – do bicycles have to be integrated with or separated from motorized traffic? It argues that the solutions of the designers of traffic landscapes represent a technocratic position. They take the differences in speed between motorized and non-motorized traffic as a given and present a broad range of possible design solutions that aim at 'fine-tuning form, function and the use of infrastructure'. In doing so, they ignore the fact that in the design of crossings and road sections, the politics of passages are always present, either in the way space, time and risk are distributed at the street level, or in the way the design is implicitly or explicitly an expression of the political process. The concept of 'ensembles' makes it possible to formulate a new normative criterion for innovative design. Because there can be no single optimal solution for constructing a traffic landscape, even after fine-tuning the details of any given situation, a good design should present two or three possible solutions which can be compared in terms of the way they distribute space, time and risk and create new 'worlds' (Winner 1986).

Chapter 7 picks up the thread of Dutch mobility politics with which I began. In the age of 'smart travel', new technological innovations are put forward as solutions to what was presented in 1997 as the most urgent mobility problem, congested highways. The Dutch government no longer wanted to be the only actor responsible for solving the problem. They redistributed 'problem ownership' by implementing a technical system that made it possible to tax car drivers for using the road at specific times and places. This system used new locating technologies, with which the position of any car can be determined in time and space. In analysing the eventual failure of this policy scheme, I offer a way in which the vocabulary of passages can be used to theorize the success and failure of mobility innovations. The book ends with a discussion of how, with the use of this vocabulary, problems, innovations and mobilities can be interrelated in new ways.

1   Reasoning with travel time

Introduction

In the main hall of the Traffic Information Centre (TIC) in Utrecht stands a two-metre-high video wall which displays in schematic form all the highways in the Randstad, the central western region of the Netherlands where most of the country's largest cities lie.[1] The Randstad is one of the largest conurbations in Europe, with more than seven million inhabitants and one of the highest number of cars per square kilometre. The TIC's video wall is covered with green, yellow, orange and red dotted lines, which indicate the average speeds of traffic on any given stretch of the region's highways. Green indicates that the traffic is flowing without any obstructions, while red indicates total gridlock. This morning the A16 which runs from Breda to Rotterdam is coloured red. A truck containing hazardous fluids has turned over on the highway, causing a backup that has already grown to several kilometres. The national radio issued a warning to motorists to avoid this stretch of the highway. But backups have already begun to appear on all the highways that connect to the A16 growing to a staggering 400 kilometres by later that morning. Meanwhile, the TIC's traffic manager sits stoically watching how the situation is developing on the screen. He explains that from the control room you can watch a traffic jam come into being, but you cannot intervene to solve it. This is the reason he remains ambivalent about broadcasting urgent traffic warnings that interrupt regular radio programming. 'People want to know that there *is* a traffic jam, but they seldom choose alternative routes. This morning, the A16 is not the only highway which is blocked. The diverting routes are also silting up. Many people will be late for work, but that doesn't seem to matter very much. A traffic jam is something that is not your fault.'[2]

The red dotted lines on the video wall in the TIC control room metaphorically represent congestion, scarcity and stagnation. The computer monitors that sit in front of TIC staff display the emergence of the unwanted delays. The hope of clear traffic flow, taken for granted in television commercials showing cars driving through deserted landscapes, will not be met today in the western region of the Netherlands. The traffic manager who is aware that there *is* a traffic jam, but who cannot do anything about it is like many policy makers who have tried but failed to solve the problem of traffic congestion. The number of car kilometres travelled in the Netherlands has risen every year since the 1950s, and traffic experts predict that it will continue to do so in the future. What can the Dutch government do to solve the problems caused by the increase in car mobility? It could do nothing at all and let the traffic jams get worse, forcing people to look for alternatives, such as taking the train or other means of public transport. But when the former Dutch Minister of Transport suggested taking this approach shortly after taking office in 1994, she caused an uproar among car users all over the country, and little has been heard of her proposal since (van der Malen and Pama 1994).[3] Another solution seemed more reasonable: build new roads to create more space for the growing number of road users. But this approach cannot solve traffic congestion in the long run, because all of the people who decide in response *not* to use their cars and to use alternative means of transport instead, will be encouraged to get back on the road in the future. Apart from creating a 'latent demand' (Fischer 1997), as traffic experts call this effect, there are good reasons for exercising caution in using the limited space available in densely populated areas for constructing new roads to solve traffic congestion. A third solution lay in offering new alternatives for public transport, for example, adding a 'light rail' system in the Randstad. The combination of train and light rail would operate at high frequencies so that travellers would never have to wait very long. But the drawback of this solution is its cost. Some traffic experts also doubt that it would be effective, because cars and public transport are not interchangeable. A fourth option would be to distribute the available road capacity more equally over time by requiring car drivers to pay for road use during rush hours by implementing a congestion charge. Some economists have predicted that this approach would ease traffic congestion significantly. But Dutch transport ministers know from experience that asking drivers to pay for road use through taxes per kilometre driven instead of fixed and fuel excises taxes is like rubbing salt in an open wound. The introduction of a congestion charge has been proposed many times, but never realized.

The traffic problem which is schematized in the Traffic Information Centre's video wall is complex. In the last three decades, politicians, researchers and policy makers have been occupied with making it a topic of both public and parliamentary debate, by analysing it, and by developing instruments to solve it, at least partially. In 2001, the Dutch Ministry of Transport, Public Works and Water Management organized an 'innovation fair', intended to introduce new ideas for building 'roads to the future', as the title of the fair expressed it. When asked for their favourite innovation, visitors to the innovation fair preferred the long distance, unidirectional wind tunnels for cyclists, electronic assistance for car drivers and a radical overhaul of the tax system.[4] There was no shortage of wild ideas proposed to solve mobility problems. But if one looks at the progress that has been made on 'the road to the future' in the Netherlands over the past 30 years, what is striking is the persistent character of the problems and the lack of effective innovations in the proposed solutions. It would be an exaggeration to claim that the Dutch mobility policies have had no positive impacts. The number of traffic fatalities has dropped significantly since 1970. Cars pollute less, and restrictive parking policies in city centres have curbed the ubiquitous presence of the car. But any sceptic will observe that many of the problems caused by increasing mobility still exist. This is especially true for carbon dioxide and other harmful emissions, which continue to create the greatest number of problems in the most densely populated regions. Traffic noise is on the rise, despite the use of technical measures to abate it, such as sound screens along highways. And, because cars have become not only more fuel-efficient but also bigger, heavier and more numerous, fuel consumption is also rising. The different kinds of scarcity resulting from growing mobility remain largely unaddressed despite many innovations. The stagnation in effective innovation is the subject of this chapter. When it comes to mobility problems, the public debate has followed a predictable course, and the politics of innovative mobility tends to get in a jam. But why?

To answer this question and to provide a starting point for my analysis of innovation, time and mobilities, I begin with a short overview of recent Dutch mobility policies. In the early 1970s, the insight that the problem of scarcity could not be solved simply by building new roads gained ground. At the time, both policy makers and transport scientists defined solutions in terms of what they called 'shifts' – shifts from the car to public transport and the bicycle, from physical mobility to electronic mobility such as teleworking, from offices located near highway exits to locations which are more easily accessible by public transport, and from one travel behaviour to another. Transport science and economics have played a crucial role both in the design of transport policies and in explaining their success or failure. In the models transport scientists constructed to compare modes of travel, locations and travel behaviours, quantified travel time proved to be indispensable for creating a comparative perspective (Heggie 1976). In this chapter, I will suggest that arguments and models that rely on measured time have shortcomings for understanding and evaluating proposals for improving mobility problems.

The small margins of Dutch mobility politics

Until 1970, fast-growing car use was not conceived of as a complex, almost insoluble problem in the Netherlands. Far from it: mobility was the cornerstone of a widely held dream of a society which was growing in prosperity and individual freedom of movement. In the 1950s and 1960s, an increasing number of people traded their bicycles and mopeds in for cars. If traffic was related to 'problems', these problems were viewed largely in relation to passenger safety and the need to extend road capacity. Government initiatives for building new roads simply deduced the length of new roads that was needed from the expected growth of car traffic.[5] There were occasional traffic jams, but only at the notorious bottlenecks, such as the Oudenrijn cloverleaf near Utrecht (Buiter and Volkers 1996). New roads and highways as well as urban designs were drawn up to accommodate car traffic. Urban planning often aimed at opening cities to the car by building large throughways that led traffic off the highway into the city centre. To accommodate these changes, more parking space was created, sometimes by filling in old canals. Increasingly, cars tended to dominate the street.[6]

In 1970, the Ministry of Transport issued a report called *Future projection 2000*, which predicted that the number of cars in the Netherlands would reach 7.5 million in 2000.[7] Should the increase in the number of cars lead to problems, the ministry explained, they could be solved by technical innovations, such as cleaner car engines. But studies such as this one had a profound effect on progressive politicians, such as the leading social democrat, Ed van Thijn, who spoke of a 'quantified phantom'. He argued that more attention should be given to matters like air pollution, increased fuel consumption, and the use of raw materials in the production of cars. In the public debate that followed the publication of the report *Limits to growth* (1972), commissioned by the Club of Rome, the growth of mobility in general, and especially car traffic, was considered an issue of scarcity in the Netherlands – scarcity of traffic safety, of space, of clean air and, increasingly, of mobility itself (Meadows *et al.* 1972).[8] In the wake of this debate and the 1973 oil crisis – both of which had a strong impact on Dutch politics – a clear change occurred in traffic and transport policies. Car use should no longer simply be accommodated on the basis of projected demand. Instead, demand should be curbed by new policy measures, such as improving public transport and creating more space for slower modes of transport including bicycling and walking.

In the years following the publication of *Future projection 2000*, Dutch mobility policies were characterized by ambiguity. On the one hand, they authorized the extension of the national network of roads and highways and the decrease of the share of public transport in the total mileage travelled, which resulted in an overall shift towards car use. On the other, the government had succeeded in reducing some of the negative effects of fast-growing mobility. The number of traffic fatalities had dropped from 1973 and continued to decrease. Car engines became less polluting, and fuel consumption per car dropped slightly. The hegemony of the car in the city ended when parking fees were introduced, and metal and concrete posts were installed between roads and sidewalks to prevent parking on the pavement. The deep economic recession that hit the European market in the early 1980s, following the 1979 oil crisis, nearly succeeded in reversing the upward trend of mobility. But from 1986, total car mileage began to climb again. The progressive political climate of the mid 1970s was followed by a 'no-nonsense' approach of successive coalitions between Christian democrats and liberals emphasizing the importance of free-flowing traffic for economic recovery. The problem of congestion rose quickly on the political agenda and the reduction of car traffic was believed necessary to solve it. For the first time, research investigating different types of 'road pricing' began.

In November 1988, the Ministry of Transport presented a draft of the Second Transport Structure Plan, called the SVV II, to the Dutch parliament. It was an ambitious plan which was intended as a guide to traffic and transport policy beyond 2000. The white paper sought a multi-pronged approach that included improving accessibility, mobility and sustainability, also adding several measures directed at changing the mentality of Dutch motorists. Such changes in mentality were to be effected by the release of all sorts of public information. However, while the plan did emphasize the need to increase the use of public transport, it also called for more funding for building new roads. The SVV II had been the product of a policy vision in which the increase of car mobility had once again been accepted as an unalterable fact. But when the white paper was sent to the parliament in early 1989, public opinion was still heavily influenced by disturbing reports about the detrimental effects of acid rain. In December 1988, the public learned about the findings of a major study undertaken by the RIVM, the leading research institute on public health and the environment, which gave a very bleak image of the state of the Dutch environment (Langeweg 1988). The report had been leaked to the press, which had heightened the public's sense of alarm and dismay. Just weeks after the publication of the study, Queen Beatrix reinforced the prevailing apocalyptic mood by pointing out in her annual Christmas radio speech that 'life on earth is slowly dying'. Out of nowhere the environment was back on the political agenda.

The public's dismay about the environment following RIVM's report had a palpable influence on the direction of policy discussions on traffic and transport in the months following its leak to the press. Discussions about reducing auto emissions now targeted the growth rate of car mobility. In parliament, only the right-wing liberal party, the People's Party for Freedom and Democracy (VVD), failed to acknowledge the urgency of taking strict measures to reduce demand for car kilometres. When the VVD opposed the abolition of a tax deduction for travel costs incurred while travelling to and from work in the spring of 1989, the Dutch Cabinet resigned. It was the first government in the world to collapse over an environmental issue. The SVV II was rewritten under the new coalition government between the Christian democrats (CDA) and the social democrats (PvdA). The new government took a stronger stand on the reduction of the increase in car use. It called for halving the expected increase of

70 per cent in car use from 1986 to 2010, which would be achieved through the implementation of a broad range of measures. Most prominent among them were the so-called pricing measures which aimed at making car travel less attractive by increasing its cost. Such measures included higher parking fees in city centres, higher duties on petrol and new road-pricing policies. As a general principle, reducing the future growth of car use by 35 per cent became the cornerstone of many of the mobility policies created in the early 1990s.

The new Minister of Transport, Hanja Maij-Weggen, had the task of implementing many of the new policies aimed at growth reduction. In an interview she gave shortly after taking office in 1989, Maij-Weggen claimed optimistically that the 'tide has never been more favourable for a car-curbing policy'. However, the Dutch parliament ultimately proved to be ambivalent about following through with such policies. Politicians urged that new pricing measures be taken, but a majority always backed out when it came to seeing them through to implementation. Not only in parliament, but also in public opinion, the tide turned once again. In the early 1990s, the apocalyptic vision of the environment gave way to worries about congestion: traffic and transport policy was now perceived as the need to build new infrastructure. The image of the car was no longer that of a main cause of acid rain. Government-sponsored television commercials telling the public that 'their cars could do without them for a day' were cancelled, and travelling by car was reconceived as an integral part of a modern, mobile lifestyle.

The new focus on congestion as the most urgent mobility problem brought road pricing back onto the stage. Road pricing had been off the political agenda for some time but when it returned in 1994, it served a new role. It was now presented as an instrument for relieving congestion in metropolitan areas, rather than for reducing car mobility throughout the whole country. Confronted with tales of growing traffic delays around the four largest Dutch cities,[9] Parliament urged the new Minister of Transport, the liberal, Annemarie Jorritsma, to stick to a tight implementation schedule. As a member of parliament she had opposed road pricing, but as a minister in a coalition government she worked toward its implementation. In a new policy report issued in 1996, *Working together on accessibility*,[10] Jorritsma announced a market-oriented approach to problems related to mobility. The moral appeal to citizens, so characteristic of the debate around 1990, had vanished. Now corporate and public actions were to be understood as governed by an economic rationality, in which choices were matters that could be explained within the vocabulary of rational choice theory, and traffic and transport policies were to be designed according to it.[11]

In marked contrast to 1989, in 1996 the national government no longer conceived of itself as the central directing actor in policy implementation. It was now deemed inappropriate for the national government to monopolize 'problem ownership'. Instead, the national government believed it should embark on 'interactive policy making' in which all policy measures would be negotiated with a range of social institutions representing the public (Hendriks and Tops 2001). Policy making on mobility issues would cease being a matter of changing public behaviour through persuasion and political leadership. The new culture of policy making would be made up of package deals and trade-offs. Creating 'win-win' situations was to be the new objective. The vision behind this new approach was achieving shared goals through continuous interaction with the public. If the government was to build new lanes on a congested highway, it could expect that social organizations and corporations in turn would take measures to reduce demand. Alongside this emerging neo-liberal discourse on traffic reduction and new infrastructure creation, there was a strong belief in technological fixes. If people could not be convinced that it was better for the environment to drive less, technologies could be used to do the job of cleaning and economizing car use.

In 1997, preparations began for a new transport structure plan that would follow up on the SVV II. What had changed since the white paper had initially been presented to the public in 1988? First, the growth of mobility, and especially of car mobility, had been accepted. Mobility was no longer something to be discouraged. It was this change that created a break from policies recommending a reduction in the growth of car use that had been central to SVV II. As the increase in mobility began to be perceived as a phenomenon beyond the influence of politicians and policy makers, all they could do was target its consequences, such as decreasing accessibility, traffic safety and the quality of the environment. The definition of the problems related to mobility growth also changed. No longer did the accent lay on the harm done to the environment. Now the main problem was the reduction of accessibility due to congestion. The government also changed the way it approached citizens. Tactics such as moral appeals to citizens, symbolized in the slogan 'The car can do without you for a day', which achieved their persuasive power from images of dying forests and a warming globe, now gave way to a more businesslike approach, in which the road was viewed as a 'market'. Citizens were now allowed to be mobile, but only at a price. Now the social costs of mobility had to be paid for by individual travellers. Another change was the distribution of responsibility between the national government and the provincial and municipal governments. No longer did the national government want to be the main 'problem owner'. Decentralizing administrative power and responsibilities could, politicians at the national level believed, lead to policies that were better fitted to local situations and needs. Finally, a policy style that was based on the knowledge of experts was traded for a culture of deliberation. Nothing could be achieved politically without public support, which meant that as many social organizations and actors as possible should be involved in the formulation and working-out of policies.[12]

Mobility and social dilemmas

In 1976, the Dutch Social and Cultural Planning Office (SCP) issued the results of a government-funded study of how car use could best be curbed and how social acceptance of this policy could be achieved (Sociaal en Cultureel Planbureau 1976). The report distinguished between three types of measures: those aimed at reducing the number of car kilometres, counter-acting the adverse effects of car use and effecting a 'change in attitude' among Dutch motorists. The first type included a combination of monetary disincentives, urban planning, support of alternative transport modes and encouraging different kinds of car use, such as car pooling. The SCP hoped to reduce the adverse effects of car use by making inner cities car-free, introducing car-free days, making technical improvements to cars and changing traffic rules to benefit slower traffic participants, such as bicyclists and pedestrians. Finally, the SCP thought of influencing the public's attitudes toward car use through information about the necessity of these measures.

The SCP concluded the report with a statement claiming that improving public transport without also implementing disincentives for car use would have only a small impact on the size and place of car use in Dutch society. Influencing commuter traffic would spread congestion over the course of the day rather than over two or three hours. The resultant reduction in congestion would optimize the use of the automobile infrastructure. The report predicted that increasing the costs of owning cars would also have some effect on both car ownership and car use. Increasing the costs of using a car would have a more powerful effect, but the increase would hit those who were the least well off hardest. Technical improvements to cars, however, would not significantly change the problems which the 'car system' caused. And car-free Sundays were only expected to have a limited effect on the amount of car use.[13]

Rereading the SCP report now reveals an interesting development. It shows that almost 30 years after its publication, little has changed, both in terms of the total sum of problems caused by traffic and the proposed policies to counter them. In other words, the political debate on mobility has been more constant than is often assumed. The SCP report lists the increase in the number of cars on the road as the main cause of the sharp increase in car kilometres. According to them, this growth did not occur without consequences. Increased car ownership and car use led to more congestion, more land use, more air and soil pollution, more traffic noise, more use of raw materials and energy, an increased number of traffic fatalities and greater disadvantages for those who cannot afford a car. These are, with some minor variations, the same problems facing Dutch public officials today.[14] Why has it not been possible to solve these problems?

Social psychologists have argued that mobility problems have the character of a social dilemma (Steg and Sievers 1996). A social dilemma is characterized by a tension between the advantages which individuals can obtain in the short run and the disadvantages that follow from the collectivity of individual choices. For example, every individual driver expects to get home faster by taking the car. But collectively their individual needs create traffic congestion which results in the journey taking longer for everyone. For every driving 'internality', the advantages that accrue to individual car drivers, such as flexibility, comfort and privacy, there are 'externalities' or costs that are only partly paid for by individual car drivers. These external costs can be a lack of traffic safety, the emissions of greenhouse gases like carbon dioxide, or the increase in land use and the fragmentation of landscapes.

Traditionally, finding a way out of these types of dilemmas – looking for a balance between individual and collective interests – lies in the domain of the government. One of the themes in the Dutch debate on mobility is the inability to address the social dilemma that modern traffic and transport creates: the tension between individual goods and collective bads. Politicians face this dilemma daily. On the one hand, they take it as their task to facilitate mobility, especially car use, through the construction of roads and other automobile-related infrastructure. On the other, they see it as their responsibility to reduce the societal costs caused by growing mobility. As a result of this tension, specific issues continue to ascend and descend on the political agenda. Social organizations and interest groups have been moderately successful in bringing their points of view to the government's attention. The Dutch media highlights different aspects of the problem. However, although the debate may seem to be fragmented and often contradictory, the chalk lines that demarcate it, as well as its characteristic rhetoric and hang-ups, are surprisingly stable.

Storylines and discourse coalitions

Mobility problems may often have the structure of a social dilemma, but this does not explain why it is so hard to break out of them. Social theorists and policy scientists have argued that what counts as a problem in politics is not a given, but is the result of the social processes of agenda setting. According to Gusfield (1981), drunken driving only developed into a public problem in the United States when it got powerful 'problem owners'. These actors succeeded in imposing their definition of the problem to others, and thus were able to create political momentum. In the definition of a problem, Gusfield argues, political oppositions are covered up or emphasized. A choice of a specific way to define a problem implies that some aspects of social reality are debatable while others are not.

Problem definition takes place in what has been described as a 'discourse'. In his analysis of environmental policy debates in the Netherlands and Great Britain, Hajer uses discourse analysis to study how and why certain definitions of problems became more authoritative (1995). Follow-ing Foucault and authors like Michael Billig and Rom Harré, Hajer takes discourse as 'a specific ensemble of ideas, concepts and categorizations that are produced, reproduced and transformed in a particular set of practices and through which meaning is given to physical and social realities' (1995: 44). Acid rain, the subject of Hajer's book, is an 'interdiscursive' subject, which can only be understood as a collection of discourses, each with its own social and scientific context. 'Consequently a policy document on acid rain may easily involve discursive elements from disciplines as various as physics, tree physiology, terrestrial ecology, mathematical modelling, eco-nomics, accounting, engineering, and philosophy' (Ibid.: 45). The 'commu-nicative miracle' of environmental policy, Hajer argues, is that, despite many variations in the ways of speaking, the participants in the debate understand each other (Ibid.: 46). Mobility, I argue, can also be under-stood as an interdiscursive subject. Viewed from this perspective, we can ask how different actors in the debate understand each other, and how many different expertises are combined in authoritative narratives on mobility. Within and between discourses on mobility, different perspec-tives are created, claims are put forward, and interests balanced. What becomes apparent is that the discourse on mobility within the environ-mental movement differs strongly from that in the car industry: trees and asphalt seldom go together.

Hajer shows how connections between different and sometimes oppos-ite discourses can emerge using two concepts – 'storylines' and 'discourse coalitions'. Storylines are narrative visions on social reality that render a symbolic point of reference to actors which they can use to come to a shared understanding of a problem. The 'car as a cause of acid rain' is a storyline in which the negative environmental effects of car traffic come together: the 'car as a means of taxing people' is about the perceived costs of taxing car use, and the lack of any ground made on reducing bottle-necks despite them. Hajer uses 'discourse coalitions' to show how different discourses can get entangled with one another. They are kept together by the 'discursive cement' of storylines. Discourse coalitions are not the same as political coalitions. Discourse coalitions share a linguistic basis rather than being structured by shared interests. In Hajer's terms, actors use the vocabulary of the others' discourses and feel attracted to, or see different interests being given a voice in, shared storylines. An example is the dis-course coalition between the environmental movement and the organi-zation for traffic safety, in which a lowering of the maximum speed is advocated. This coalition is held together by a storyline that 'cars drive too fast', but the discourses behind them differ. The environmental move-ment's attempts to lower car emissions is one, and the traffic safety organi-zation's aim to reduce the number of traffic fatalities another.

Different storylines and discourse coalitions can be discerned in mobil-ity discourses in the Netherlands. When the Second Transport Structure

Plan was published in 1988, a discourse coalition was created between storylines like 'the car as cause of acid rain', 'liveability' and 'dying forests'. Social groups like environmental organizations and the government succeeded in defining the social problems caused by car use in terms of harmful emissions and other negative effects, such as noise pollution, fragmentation of the landscape and the dangers of auto use. Many politicians argued that the unimpeded growth of car use was undesirable, and that a 35 per cent reduction in its growth was necessary. This aim was laid down in the final version of SVV II, which the parliament passed in 1990. Politicians and civil servants now could be held to a concrete and measurable policy goal. The policy that was developed to reach this goal aimed at a substantial decrease in the growth of car mobility in general. Pricing policies such as road-use levies and tax increases were said to make driving a car less attractive and improve the competitive position of public transport.

In 1994, when a new coalition of social democrats and liberals took office, signs of change began to appear. The discourse coalition between storylines now included terms like 'employment', 'accessibility', 'economic growth', 'infrastructure', 'market approach' and 'technology'. A coalition was forged around these concepts in which mobility was no longer viewed as a fundamental social problem, but instead as a necessary development which entailed problems of adaptation. Of all the adaptation problems, that of congestion rose quickly on the agenda of public and political debate, because traffic jams, it was argued, caused economic damage created by the loss of travel time, which, in turn, cost money. This view was expressed in political opinions in favour of constructing new traffic infrastructures. Arguments for a mobility politics no longer focused on achieving reduction goals, but strived instead to accommodate the demand for mobility at the lowest possible societal cost. The policy of road pricing, which had been presented mainly as an environmental measure, was now legitimated as a means of spreading traffic demand in time and place, rather than reducing demand overall.

Together with other social actors, the Dutch government has tried several ways to influence people's travel behaviour. Government policies have aimed at establishing 'shifts' in the choice of transport, of destination and even of where to live. If people would make different choices – that is, by choosing to travel to work by public transport rather than by car – they would still be mobile, but at a lower societal cost.

We now know *how* subsequent cabinets and other social actors have defined the problems related to mobility, and how changing discourse coalitions appeared and disappeared. But reconstructing the Dutch mobility debate does not point the way out of the conflict which lies at the core in every social dilemma: individual goods lead to collective bads. In other words, a discourse analysis of mobility politics makes clear how the building is structured, but it leaves unaddressed where to look for the exit.

Constant travel time

To understand better how the mobility policy debate became stagnated, the question which must be addressed is *why* people in traffic behave the way they do. Why does the car win out so often over public transport if people are given the choice? What causes urban sprawl? Why are business travellers in more of a hurry than tourists? And why does mobility increase every year? Questions like these have traditionally belonged to the domain of transport science and urban planning. To answer the first, they have studied the differences in travel times between cars and public transport. They have found that, if using public transport takes 1.5 times longer than travelling by car, people will usually choose to use their car. Using this 'transit time factor' (or VF-value), Dutch transport scientists have offered a simple word of advice: if the government wants people to shift from the car to public transport, then it must make sure that trains, buses and metros can compete with the car in terms of travel time (van Goeverden and van den Heuvel 1993). The question of why cities have continued to spread has been answered by pointing to the relation between mobility and spatial planning. The 'action space' of people is determined by the number of destinations they can reach in a specific amount of time. The faster they are able to travel, the more destinations are accessible to them in the same amount of time. For centuries, the size of cities and the distances between cities and villages depended on the maximum distance people could walk in a day. When faster means of transport became available, the 'action space' of people increased, and so did the size of cities (Dijst 1995; Dijst and Vidakovic 1995). Why business travellers are in more of a rush than tourists becomes comprehensible when the time for the former group of travellers is assumed more valuable than that of the second; the 'value of time' for most businessmen is higher than that of tourists, and therefore they are willing to pay more to travel quickly from one place to another (Loos and Kropman 1993; McKean, Johnson and Walsh 1995; González 1997).

These examples show how transport scientists and urban planners have used the concept of travel time to explain 'travel behaviour'. To analyse their style of reasoning, this chapter will look more closely at the last question: why does travel demand tend to increase continually? This question has been at the core of the Dutch public debate on mobility over the last 30 years, and Dutch transport scientists have used the 'hypothesis of constant travel time' to answer it. It is based on the assumption that, on average, people travel a constant amount of time regardless of the means of transport they have at their disposal. In 1977, the Dutch transport scientist Geurt Hupkes used this hypothesis to create scenarios about the future growth of mobility in the Netherlands.

The 'BREVER' law

When the *TP 2000* projections were published in 1970, they provided reasons for progressive politicians like Ed van Thijn to question the desirability of any further increases in car use. Transport scientists raised questions about the *method* used to produce the report's future projections. The linear and exponential character of the *TP 2000* extrapolations were criticized by those in the subdiscipline known as 'critical futurology'. According to these critics, the extrapolations could only lead to the outcome that 'the society of the future would be twice the society of today' (Ministry of Transport 1973: 7). They argued that the type of prognostication used in the report on the future of mobility clouded the debate on the desirability of the future situation which the report had sketched. If the future of mobility could only be sketched in terms of continual growth, what were the options to solve the problems that followed from this scenario? After all, 'the traffic sky was not the limit' (Ibid.: 13). Even the growth of mobility had its limits, the critics argued.

The Dutch transport scientist Geurt Hupkes was one of these critics. In his dissertation, *Accelerate or brake: future scenarios for our transportation systems* (1977), he claimed that 'the transportation needs in the year 2000 are fixed, and the only thing that has to be done, is to work out the plans for the accompanying infrastructure' (Hupkes 1977: 19). Prognoses, he argued, quickly became self-fulfilling prophecies. Building on the concepts used by futurologists including Bertrand de Jouvenel and Herman Kahn, and referring to the *Limits to growth* report, Hupkes concluded that it was better to develop scenarios, which were 'argued and logically coherent descriptions of possible futures, in which a statement on the probability is lacking' (Ibid.: 37). As argued visions of possible futures, scenarios could help in making policy choices because they made their respective consequences explicit. Hupkes developed two scenarios for what he calls the 'transportation system'.

Hupkes believed it was necessary to understand the *mechanism* behind mobility growth in order to construct his scenarios. He was able to describe it by using the hypothesis of constant travel time.[15] Hupkes' argument begins with the idea of an increase in the scarcity of time that is created by the need to do more things at the same time coupled with a reduction in the amount of time spent on any one activity. One of the ways of solving the problem of time scarcity is to travel faster. But while people had indeed begun to travel faster in recent decades, time budget studies indicated that the time spent on sleeping, working, personal care, recreation and mobility had remained more or less constant. Human beings, Hupkes deduced, 'evidently do not feel the need to shorten travel times, nor do they want to reduce the number of journeys [they make]' (Ibid.: 261). Nor do they *'feel the need to expand their travel time or the number of journeys they make, which actually could not be expected for a time use, the utility of which is derived from other activities*' (Ibid., emphasis in the original). Thus Hupkes concluded that

> Human beings evidently have a balancing mechanism at their disposal, the nature of which is not known, but that enables them to fix their average travel time and the number of trips on the same level. The only one of the three dimensions of mobility that has actually increased, is the travelled distance per head, which was made possible by increasing the number of journeys with relatively fast transport systems.
>
> (Ibid.)

What evidence did Hupkes use to support this claim? He himself acknowledged that useful data in the field were 'extremely scarce' (Ibid.: 256). He cited a Dutch study by Vidakovic from 1968, which claimed people living in south Amsterdam spend 68 minutes a day on making trips. Hupkes also refers to other work that argues for a constant travel time but that does not quantify the constant.[16] The main evidence for Hupkes' claim that travel time is constant was *The use of time*, an exhaustive study of time budgeting, published in 1972 by Szalai and Converse. This study was based on some 30,000 interviews with persons living in cities or urban areas in 15 industrialized or industrializing countries, ranging from the United States to Peru (Szalai and Converse 1972). Hupkes summarized four tables of data from Szalai's study in the appendices of his book. One of these was a table of time use on an average weekday. Szalai and Converse found an average of 82 minutes per day for 'mobility'(which Szalai and Converse referred to as 'travel'). Hupkes claimed that this mean was not dependent on the relative wealth of countries or people. 'The level of this constant travel time was . . . on average 1 hour and 13 minutes per day, or 444 hours per year' (Hupkes 1977: 260). Hupkes called the conjecture that travel time is not only constant but calculable on the basis of time budget studies, the BREVER law, the name of which is based on the Dutch acronym for 'constant travel time and trips'. According to Hupkes, this law is valid on the aggregated level of 'the means per head in all transport systems over a period with a specific duration: a day, a week, or a year. The longer the period, the smaller the dispersion of the means per person' (Ibid.).

Having formulated his law of constant travel time and trips, Hupkes was then able to analyse the mechanism which explained the growth in mobility. The fact that people travel faster does not lead to shorter travel times. Instead, travel times are constant and people cover larger distances. That the number of kilometres travelled every year continues to rise must therefore be explained by the increase in the availability of faster means of transport.

According to his critics, Hupkes did not so much formulate a 'law' as an hypothesis about the existence of a statistical constant in daily travel time and number of trips (de Wit 1980; Hamerslag 1998; van Wee 1999).[17] The existence of a constant travel time budget is contested.[18] The degree to which time values of budgeted time are viewed as absolute varies. Among traffic scientists, there are some who support stronger and weaker variants of the hypothesis of constant travel time. There are those, including Hupkes, who find it possible to give the constant an absolute value, namely 73 minutes per day or 444 hours per year. But there are still others who are only willing to defend the claim that the amount of time people spend on travel is *not* related to the transportation system they use (van Goeverden 1999).

Hupkes' claims have spurred debates on the reliability of the data he used, on the policy implications of his findings and on his explanations of the constant. Hupkes himself began to address the last question. Why the average travel time varies only to a small extent, especially between countries with high and low GNPs, is not clear. Hupkes claimed that '[t]hese differences could be expected and now that they are not there, the cause needs to be found. The mysterious reason for the found regularity in time use remains hidden in a black box, formed by humans as biological, physical and psychological beings' (Hupkes 1977: 259).

The scientific literature on transportation shows that until now, it has not been possible to open this 'black box'. There have been only scattered attempts to explain the mechanism behind a constant travel time. Höjer and Mattsson (2000) have suggested that these explanations should be considered with respect to the academic disciplines in which they were produced: biology, economics and the social sciences. Researchers who have sought a biological explanation link the constant to what they call human travel behaviour. The average travel time is constant because people dispose of biological or psychological attributes and mechanisms (hormonal homeostasis or genetically determined behavioural patterns) which ensure that the time spent on travel fluctuates between a minimum and a maximum. Hupkes himself relies on this type of explanation in assuming that people must stabilize certain psychobiological variables (Hupkes 1979), one of which could be travel time. However, how such a psychobiological variable should be studied remains unclear in his argument.[19] Economic explanations of constant travel time use economic utility theories to explain travel behaviour. Hupkes also used this type of explanation. He pointed out that the total utility of a journey is a combination of intrinsic and derived utility. This renders an optimum of about 75 minutes per day (Hupkes 1979: 368). Social explanations of constant travel time are rare. Höjer and Mattsson (2000) refer to the chronogeography of Hägerstrand, which is outlined in Chapter 3. Hägerstrand claims that a normal day for any given person consists of a routine distribution of activities like sleeping, working, eating, personal care and travel. The amount of time people are able to spend on travel is therefore, on average, limited. According to Höjer and Mattsson, this is the only type of explanation that can explain the constant character of travel time budgets and its absolute value, which is calculated as being approximately 80 minutes.[20]

The scientific style of reasoning in transportation studies

Hupkes' use of the BREVER law is an example of the way in which the concept of travel time enables transport scientists to explain people's travel behaviour. Hacking (1985) has argued that theoretical concepts such as 'travel time' or 'travel behaviour' are only given meaning within a specific style of reasoning, showing a loose congeniality with Kuhn's idea of a paradigm (Kuhn 1962). Hacking goes beyond Kuhn in emphasizing the specific ways in which truth claims of propositions are argued for in different scientific traditions. In the BREVER law, the question is not if the hypothesis of constant travel time is true or not, but how it is presented as true or false in the first place. In order to examine this, we have to study the assumptions underlying the central claims in Hupkes' argument.

Assumptions about *time* are of central importance in both Hupkes' scenarios and the transportation sciences in general. Gell (1992) has argued that the vast majority of economic models use a time concept from what he calls B-series time. These are time concepts distinguishing between 'before' and 'after', which are used in creating a linear ordering of events. 'Time is seen as the stable framework within which these predetermined events occur in inexorable order, static, objective and unchanging' (Gell 1992: 180). B-series time underlies the time budget studies by Sorokin and Berger (1939) and Szalai that form the empirical basis of Hupkes' hypothesis of constant travel time. By using clock time, these studies are able to measure the amount of time people spend travelling, and present it as an independent variable in models. A quantified concept of time such as B-series time makes it possible to create a comparative perspective which forms the basis of time budgeting studies such as Hupkes'. To be able to speak of a 'constant' between different countries, historical periods or social groups, time budgets have to be compared regardless of the specific contexts from which they are taken.

In what way can disciplines like transportation science and planning contribute to breaking the stagnation in thinking on mobility innovations? To begin with, it is possible, using the hypothesis of constant travel time, to explain mobility growth in terms of a single behavioural mechanism, whether it is genetically anchored, economically motivated or socially determined. People travel for a constant share of their time. If they are able to travel faster, then they will, on average, travel longer distances, not for shorter periods of time. Technological innovations have made it possible to travel faster and therefore further. If we assume continuing technological and economic progress, the argument goes, then the distance travelled will continue to grow in the future.[21] This type of 'if ... then' argument in which travel time is used forms the basis of countless transportation scientific models.

Transportation science and economics can also indicate *where* we can look for solutions to mobility growth. They show the 'buttons' so to speak that we have to press. This is done once again in the form of hypothetical deductive reasoning. If the growth of mobility is considered to be a problem, then a solution must be found in the *speed* with which people travel. If travelling faster leads to covering larger distances and increasing mobility, then travelling slower means less distance can be covered and a reduction in mobility growth. This type of reasoning can be found in Hupkes' scenarios. After studying a number of 'subsystems', including car travel, air travel, railways, local and regional public transport, taxis and the 'unprotected or soft systems' of walking or cycling, he offered two alternative mobility futures, one which focused on cars and airplanes and one which gave priority to soft systems and public transport. The first scenario

> corresponds with a relatively fast growth of the number of kilometres per person in the car system and air travel, combined with a decrease in slow transport per head and a certain limitation of the use of public transport. In contrast, in [the second scenario] there is a relatively small growth in car kilometres and of holidays to far away destinations like Bali, Bangkok and Benidorm, coupled to a sustained use of slow means of transport at the level of 1972 and some extension of public transport.
>
> (Hupkes 1977: 263–264)

Hupkes' scenarios may enable him to confront policy makers with the effects of their decisions. But they do not address 'the probability of realizing one of both scenarios'. He argues that it

> is the essence of scenarios that they enlighten the choice for the current generation in relation to the future. They are not prognoses. The future is unpredictable, but is formed by the work of mind and hand, instructed by the intuitions of the heart. All of us carry our own responsibility.
>
> (Ibid.)

As a person rather than an analyst, Hupkes chose the slower scenario. Slowing down is better than accelerating. Whether society will follow him in this choice is a matter of politics in democratic societies (Ibid.: 284).

Conclusion

Since the early 1970s, the continuing growth of mobility, especially car mobility, has been seen as an important public issue in the Netherlands. What is good for the individual has to be weighed against the costs for society, such as environmental degradation, the detrimental economic effects resulting from congestion, the deteriorating quality of life in urban areas, the fragmentation of the landscape and the lack of traffic safety. Governments have formulated policies to solve these problems, but without reaching any sustainable solution. Policy analyses explain the persistent character of the problem by the character of social dilemmas. Policies aimed at breaking out of this dilemma have been formulated since the 1970s. Problem definitions change; discourse coalitions and storylines emerge and disappear; new policy instruments are proposed, debated, and in some cases, implemented.

If there is one common denominator that underlies most of the policy proposals put forward, it would be that the politics of mobility in the Netherlands has been a politics of time gains. Building divided highways, ring roads and bypasses around towns and villages, constructing new railways and tunnels, constructing a new runway at Schiphol International Airport, as well as proposing the introduction of national road use levies have found their ultimate legitimation in the shortening of travel times. However multifaceted the debate may be, the primacy of shorter travel times as a main goal is itself not seen as an issue in the debate. Conversely the 'loss' of time, as an effect of traffic jams or delays on the national railways, counts as an important topic that warrants ample attention in politics and policies. In political terms, travel time counts as the ultimate point of reference in judging the expected public support for a position and the feasibility of a proposed policy measure. Travel time is crucial or, as the Dutch sociologist Goudsblom has put it, 'a despot with which people put themselves and others under pressure, a regime' (Goudsblom 1997: 37).

The politics of time gains rests on two assumptions. The first is that time can be gained by speeding up transport systems. The second is that the societal costs and losses that result from this can be balanced by introducing new policy measures such as road pricing. Transport scientists like Hupkes have used the hypothesis of constant travel time to show that this balancing act is flawed. The time people gain by travelling faster is lost in the increase of the number of kilometres they travel. The growth of mobility must be explained from a mysterious mechanism which leads to longer distances rather than shorter travel time, and, as a result, no time is gained in traffic anyway. On this view, the political striving for shorter travel times can only fail in the long run. If one wants to escape from the negative effects of mobility growth, there is only one alternative, namely, to choose a slower scenario.

Of course, this argument is valid only if there *is* a constant travel time. Establishing if it exists must rest in turn on a comparative perspective based on a quantified concept of time: different cultures, social groups and historical periods have to be made equal in terms of the time they spend on travel. This quantification therefore necessarily has to abstract from concrete practices of travel. It is precisely because of this decontextualizing move that traffic scientists like Hupkes pay a price for the validity of their argument. In the end, their scenarios only differ from others in one dimension, namely in the speed of future transportation. As a consequence, they are no longer able to address the political normative consequences of their scenarios. Exactly because the context of travel is erased, the quantified concept of time comes even more to the fore, but without being subjected to debate itself. When gains or losses in travel time are debated, a quantified, decontextualized notion of time is assumed that is never itself brought under examination.

The history of recent Dutch mobility politics underscores the fact that the desirability of shorter travel times is not contested. The unwanted slowness created by traffic jams is an anathema, and discussions about improving the quality of life and traffic safety, and the expected increases of travel time have proved to be powerful counter-arguments. Current transportation studies of travel behaviour offer policy makers the possibility of formulating solutions by choosing slower scenarios. But this style of reasoning cannot explain why people would choose this scenario. The strength of this style of reasoning proves to be its weakness: when we speak about innovation, we only have terms like fast and slow at our disposal. But these terms are problematic if taken out of context, as will be argued in the next chapter, in which discourses on speed and slowness are analysed in relation to time and travel.

2 Narratives on travelled time

Introduction

On the drawing tables of automobile design visionaries, mobility problems were solved decades ago. It is not difficult to sketch the abstract lines of a future car that makes no sound and uses no fossil fuels, does not emit greenhouse gases, needs little room for manoeuvring and will not cause any serious accidents. Such a car would be built out of light materials and powered by solar energy. But its realization would come at a price: speed. The car of a sustainable future could only drive a maximum speed of 60 km/h (37 mph) instead of the 120 km/h (75 mph) we take for granted.[1] In car designs for a sustainable future, progress takes the form of slowness, and this is precisely the reason why it is highly unlikely that it will ever make it from the drawing table to the road. The reason is not that it is technically impossible to build one, but that nobody would want to drive it. The obstacles of a slow car are not technical, but are social, psychological, economic and cultural. Speed is a dominant and pervasive value in Western culture. Other than time and space, however, speed as a concept has not yet been systematically theorized in social and cultural theory (Peters 2000).[2] In this chapter, I analyse speed in relation to travel and different notions of travel time.

Speed and slowness are relational concepts. They have no meaning in themselves, but derive meaning from how they relate two or more phenomena, such as two different ways of travelling. Speed and slowness appear in commonplace accounts about modern mobility as means of describing experiences and problems. The delayed train, the racing cycle boasting 21 speeds, the tranquillity of a Sunday walk in the forest and the dynamics of a flight all cannot be understood without making reference to the speed or slowness of the movement. Speed and slowness are words used to seduce travellers to take the train. The French railway company, SNCF, ran a poster campaign on stations to promote their high-speed trains. The illustration they used showed two pages of a book which had kilometre signs instead of page numbers, a cunning play on the attractiveness of serenity and speed. 'Take your time to go fast', the caption of the image read.[3] Concepts like speed and slowness enable us to make sense of slogans like this one, but also to justify the decisions we make. In discussions about the need to build a high-speed train from Amsterdam to Paris, the argument most often used to justify the billion-euro investment is the expected reduction of more than two hours in travel time. Conversely, debates on mobility issues are usually visualized on television with images of traffic jams, the pre-eminent symbol of slowness and stagnation.

In daily life, we use concepts of speed and slowness without questioning them. But when it comes to understanding change and innovation in contemporary travel, it is necessary to investigate how these concepts are used to answer questions, to give reasons and to justify decisions. In other words, how does the vocabulary of speed, and its opposite, slowness, frame our ways of speaking, thinking and acting in relation to mobilities? To answer this question, I will start by examining an episode in the history of travelling on foot. In the late eighteenth and early nineteenth centuries, innovations in road construction and the advent of new and faster means of transport, especially the train, meant that walking could now be experienced as slow, in the sense that it had not been before (Wallace 1993). Now that travelling could be fast, moving slowly on foot became a choice. The emergence of what could be called 'romantic walking' reinforced a duality in thinking on what had been called 'the art of travel' since the sixteenth century: the distinction between 'being in transit to reach one's destination' and 'making a journey as a goal in itself'. I will then show how this duality of being in transit and making a journey can be traced in various discourses on the role of speed in modern travel. These discourses show why people want to travel fast, but also why slowing down was believed to be more rational. Finally, I take the apparent paradox that travel at higher speeds does not lead to time gains for the traveller as the starting point for an analysis of another duality, that of objective and subjective travel time.

A brief sociology of walking

In December 1801, the teacher and poet Johann Gottfried Seume (1763–1810) left his home in Grimma, near Leipzig, and set out on foot to Syracuse on the island of Sicily. He had a knapsack and some money sewn into his clothes to prevent highwaymen from stealing it. As was customary for the educated elite who travelled, Seume kept a journal of his journey. After his return in August 1802, he wrote *Spaziergang nach Syrakus im Jahre 1802* [A Walk to Syracuse in the Year 1802]. It tells of many hardships, varying from badly signposted routes and shabby inns to unfriendly inhabitants of backward villages, who at one moment told him he 'would be beaten to death a bit'. What was special about Seume's journey for the period was not the destination. In the eighteenth century, Italy was a common destination for noblemen who took the Grand Tour. It was that he travelled part of the distance on foot, not, as was common, by coach and boat. 'When walking, one sees on average more than if one fares' (Seume, Drews and Kyora 1993: 543).[4] Seume was convinced that everything would go better if people would walk more. In his view, someone travelling in a coach had already distanced himself from 'original humanity' (Ibid.). For Seume, the way one travelled mattered in an almost metaphysical sense. He claimed it brought him closer to ordinary people. In 'going on foot', much more was at stake than just the movement from one place to another. Seume wanted to show that walking renders a different journey than travelling by coach.[5] He was not alone. In the second half of the eighteenth century, walking acquired a new meaning, not only in traversing long distances, as Seume had done, but also in making shorter, circular walks.

Walking as a bourgeois practice

When Seume began walking to Sicily, travelling still meant hard and sometimes dangerous work. The difficulties of travel before modernity are apparent in the etymology of the word. The term 'travel' is derived from the French word 'travail', meaning work (Wallace 1993: 19). Travel accounts recounted the discomforts and obstacles that had to be overcome (Brilli 1997; Kaschuba 1991). These were not only related to the bad state of the roads or the discomfort of the coaches, but also to the quality of the inns. Hindrances like these were even worse when travelling on foot. Until the beginning of the nineteenth century, most people seldom travelled for more than one day from their homes (Lay 1992: 20). Life took place on 'time-spatial islands', the boundaries of which were determined by the distance they could cover in one day's walk (Wallace 1993: 25).[6] Between these islands, large tracts of wilderness stretched out that were full of dangers to the traveller on foot, such as highwaymen, treacherous roads and dangerous animals, but also dangers that we now view as unreal, such as ghosts and shadows, will-o'-the-wisps and other supernatural phenomena (van der Woud 1987: 555).[7] Since the late eighteenth century, however, the meaning of travelling on foot had changed. In her extensive study of 'the walk' [*Spaziergang*] as a cultural practice in the late eighteenth and early nineteenth centuries, Gudrun Koenig (1996) reconstructs what she calls the 'anatomy of the walk'.[8] She analyses the changing meaning of walking in the emerging bourgeois society, using travel writings and *Veduten*, relatively cheap etchings of landscapes depicting outdoor social events. These etchings often represented a city or town seen from outside the city walls. Sometimes walking people were portrayed in the open areas surrounding the city. Koenig interprets their clothing, the artefacts they bring with them and their posture. The walk, she argues, is a microcosm of social relations during the period (Koenig 1996: 16).

Koenig argues that walking became the expression of the civil ideal of equality, which is also evident in Seume's writings. While walking was a necessity for the lower classes, the well-to-do and nobility rode on horseback or travelled by stagecoach. Walking was a means by which the wealthy expressed their social status in at least two ways. First, walking for pleasure could be done only by those who possessed leisure, the time during which one could recreate rather than work. Second, walking for pleasure was done in places especially designed and created for walking, like parks and gardens, which were viewed as extensions of the spaces inside palaces. Walking in parks or gardens was a privilege of the wealthy. Only the wealthy possessed leisure. Koenig sees an important distinction between noble and bourgeois walking. For feudal rulers, there was no difference between the inside and the outside, between nature as stage and nature as ceremonial. In walking in the outdoors, they evoked their public role. For the bourgeois, however, different values were at stake in the act of walking. The bourgeois saw walking as recreation, as physical and mental regeneration, as the experience of free, unspoiled nature. Walking for the bourgeois became a new way of presenting oneself in the public sphere (Ibid.: 23).

As the meaning of walking changed, the activity itself moved 'outdoors'. Until the end of the eighteenth century, people walked in specifically designed places like promenades. These were furbished with benches and other places to stop. The kind of shady tree, the choice of pavement – everything – was directed toward the activity of walking. The promenades were an extension of the palace gardens. Their strict architecture revealed an aesthetics that implicated a bird's eye view, rather than a direct interaction with nature. However, the direct interaction with nature increasingly became part of the goal of walking. Walkers left the designed promenades – and the city – and moved out into the open. Koenig notes that the bourgeois walk did not as much reduce the distance to nature as enlarge it. Walking was a daily activity for a large group of people; by walking out into the open, city dwellers created a completely new experience of nature (Ibid.: 31).

According to Koenig, walking became the expression of a different attitude towards time. If someone walked for pleasure, it meant that they had the time to do so. It was a practice through which the new middle class self-consciously expressed the difference between themselves and both the nobility and the lower classes. This difference was also revealed in their tempo of walking. Sauntering had been perceived as idleness, and was rejected on moral grounds in the seventeenth and eighteenth centuries. But at the turn of the nineteenth century, such appeals to a work ethic were relativized. If one could afford it, a slow pace in walking was allowed and even favoured. Many bourgeois walkers even started to read while walking, which some saw as the ultimate snobbery. Others rejected reading while walking because it hampered their interaction with nature (Ibid.: 51).

Walking expressed differences between the classes as well as gender. The length of one's stride and tempo also distinguished men from women. Women were not supposed to walk alone, because it was feared they might not be able to bear the loneliness of nature. Another reason was that women who walked in unfamiliar places were considered suspect, because it was believed that no man would allow his wife to go out for a walk without him. Only at the arm of her husband was a woman allowed to walk, and this posture expressed the dependence of women on men (Ibid.: 44). Where men could go for a free and lonely walk out in the open, the woman always had to be accompanied by others.

The materiality of walking

Koenig explains the rise in the popularity of walking at the turn of the eighteenth century in terms of social and cultural changes following the French Revolution – the emancipation of the bourgeoisie, the discovery of nature as the opposite of new city life and the focus on health and physical exercise. In Koenig's analysis, walking is first and foremost a social practice. Ann Wallace, who has written about the English peripatetic poets like Wordsworth (see also Wyatt 1999), underlines the materiality of walking. She argues that the new understanding of walking for pleasure was linked to a number of changes in material culture at the end of the eighteenth and at the start of the nineteenth century. Two in particular, the transport revolution after 1770 and the enclosure of the British commons are relevant for this analysis.

In using the term 'transport revolution', Wallace refers to transport historian Philip Bagwell's history of transport systems in England from 1750 (Bagwell 1988). Bagwell distinguishes between three phases in the transport revolution, the first of which dates from the decades before and after 1800. Because roads and transport were poor in the eighteenth century, journeys tended to be short. If one had to travel over a large distance, connections had to be improvised, which was a time-consuming, costly and often dangerous undertaking (Bagwell 1988; Vance 1986).[9] An exception was the system of stagecoaches which developed in most European countries in the seventeenth century (Behringer 1990). Coaches travelled along fixed routes, and travel times by coach were shortened considerably because, for example, horses could be changed more often (Brune 1991). By the beginning of the nineteenth century, innovations in road construction improved road surfaces. Better roads meant that stagecoach companies could increase travel speeds significantly. The construction of roads shifted from a local to a national responsibility in the first half of the nineteenth century. France led the way. There 'Le corps des Ponts et Chaussées', founded in 1713, worked on a network of the Routes Nationales, and during the remainder of the *ancien regime*, played an important role in shaping France's national highway system (Vance 1986:

154). Better roads, faster stagecoach services and increased comfort led to a growth in the number of travellers and in the number of kilometres they travelled.

Wallace shows how these developments in transportation technologies gave walking a different social and economic meaning. As relatively fast transportation became available to larger groups of people, the class differences that had been expressed in the act of walking eroded. Walking no longer signified that one did not have enough money to pay for a coach, but that one preferred this means of locomotion above others. A second consequence of the availability of different means of transport was the variation in travel speeds. Until the nineteenth century, the prevailing speed had been that of a walker. Because of bad road conditions, coaches hardly reached higher speeds. In the low countries, barges travelled at the pace of the horses that pulled them. In the new stagecoach systems, travel speeds were raised, and the speed of walking was no longer the measure of all movement. According to Wallace, this differentiation in speeds created a range of 'perceptual frameworks', in which walking acquired its own character. It became 'possible to regard walking as a deliberately selected mode of travel, and to compare its highly legible process with other travel processes' (Wallace 1993: 10).

Wallace credits a second development as having had a great influence on the positive evaluation of walking, the privatization and enclosure of the commons. This development, which had been slowly overtaking open-field agriculture in England since the sixteenth century, accelerated in the mid eighteenth century, and radically changed the character of the landscape. Footpaths which had been 'common' property suddenly disappeared from the maps because they were closed to the public. Walkers in the late eighteenth and early nineteenth centuries were 'by means of walking itself, unenclosing that path, reappropriating it to common use and preserving a portion of the old landscape against change' (Ibid.: 10).[10]

Around 1800, with new roads and new maps of the enclosure, the old, local landscape which had often been experienced by the traveller as hostile and mysterious, slowly disappeared. However, orientating oneself out in the open remained difficult for the traveller on foot well into the nineteenth century, when the unsignposted and, consequently, dangerous landscape changed into a 'space of security', as Scharfe (1991: 20) claims in his history of signposts. Travellers were advised to buy local maps in the cities or villages they passed. These were then glued onto pieces of cloth so that they could be folded (Brilli 1997: 24). Little is known about the equipment that walkers used. However, instructions have been found in contemporary travel guides that were specifically aimed at walkers. Maçzak (1995) examined the advice of an Italian doctor named Guglielmo Grataroli, who was an expert in the field of healthy travelling. He advised travellers on foot to wear a broad belt around the waist to protect the kidneys, belly and breast. He advised wearing thin iron soles for walking in the mountains while, for shorter distances, dry ground leather sandals would do (Mączak 1995: 38). Published travel writings did not typically provide any practical information on road conditions, hotels and inns along roads, customs, formalities or toll tariffs at borders. This changed in the mid nineteenth century, when the first travel guides by Karl Baedeker (1839) were published and the first *Continental Railway Guide* (1847) appeared (Brilli 1997: 21).

Walking as a literary motif

While walking is a recurring motif in the literature of the second half of the eighteenth century, it is even more so in the first decades of the nine-teenth (Wellmann 1991; Albes 1999).[11] In many published accounts on walking, ranging from poems to travel stories, reaching a destination was seen as less important than the activity of walking itself. In his *Confessions*, published between 1781 and 1788, Rousseau reflected on this distinction when he recollected how he used to travel on foot, without the burden of baggage, obligations and business. To his regret, when he grew older, he was not conscious of anything but the necessity to reach his desti-nation and, because of this, he tended to misunderstand the real goal of travel, which is travelling itself. In his analysis of Rousseau's ideas about walking, Van den Abbeele refers to *Emile* (1762), in which Rousseau pointed out to his pupil that people should not travel as if they were couri-ers who only have to reach their destination. 'When all you want to do is to arrive, you dash in a post-chaise; but when you want to travel, you must go on foot' (cited in Van den Abbeele 1992: 113). In his last book, *Reveries of the solitary walker*, Rousseau recorded a series of ponderings he had made during his daily walks. The philosopher preferred 'reverie' in the open air to 'reflection' in his study. This plea in favour of walking fit his philosophy in which he encouraged others to discover their selves in confrontation with nature.

From the end of the eighteenth to the early nineteenth century, the lone-liness, the nature, the inner world of thoughts increasingly became the goals of walking. The writer Karl Gottlob Schelle claimed that walking attained its own codes and rules, and developed into a new art of living. In 1802, the year in which Seume made his journey to Italy on foot, Schelle published *The walks or the art of walking*, in which he reported his own experiences of walking. Schelle's motto was discovering and understanding the small objects and habits of daily life. The purpose of walking was to be found in its aimlessness, and precisely by wandering around without a spe-cific goal, one could observe what had escaped the attention of others (Wellmann 1992). The German word 'wandern' means both 'walking' and 'roaming around'. Both meanings can be found in many *Wanderlieder* or *Walking songs*, of which Wilhelm Müller's 'Winter's journey' (1824) has become the most famous after Schubert put the words to music. Müller's two series of twelve poems describe a young man who, after having been rejected by his love, travels through a wintry landscape which contains many metaphors for the traveller's state of mind. Wilhelm Müller's love of *wandern* as a literary theme was common during the 1820s. The image of a tramp on a lonely road, driven by a curse or who had become enchanted by a loved one, forms a common topos in the German romantic literature. In opposition to *Wanderzwang*, the need to walk, is the *Wanderlust*, the pleasure a writer finds in walking (Solnit 2001). This pleasure is often defined as a form of freedom and contrasted to other, more regulated forms of travel. Rodolphe Töpffer put the freedom of the walker to words in an unpublished manuscript dating from 1843/1844:

> Leave, you are the master: your route is not just the main, dusty road, but also the small paths that run parallel to it, that divert from it, that wind over hills or lose themselves in the thicket; you are not in a driving box, covered with burned leather, but the whole region is in front of you, the plains and the mountains, the forest and the open (cited in Meeuse 2000: 7).

In the course of the nineteenth century, walking and travelling on foot became an accepted and valued activity on which authors and poets such as William Hazlitt, William Wordsworth, Henry David Thoreau, Robert Louis Stevenson and Leslie Stephen have all reflected (Robinson 1989; Wyatt 1999; Solnit 2001). All of these poets believed that the physical act of walking restores the natural and primitive quality of observation, through which one can re-establish contact with both the physical world and the moral order underlying it (Wallace 1993: 13). To the romantics, walking and travelling on foot both created cherished memories and stories, as well as reinstalled a quality in human life that had been lost through the mechanization of travel. Walking had become a way to create a relation, both with one's own inner experiences and with the landscape. From the early nineteenth century, guides for walkers began to appear, pedestrian routes were created and signposted and organizations to promote walking were established. The emancipation of walking took place at a moment when it started to disappear as an ordinary means of getting around (Amato 2004).

Discourses on speed and slowness

Romantic walking, which I have situated in a number of social, material and cultural changes in the decades around 1800, can be understood against the background of a more general duality that lies at the heart of the cultural history of travel: the distinction between making a journey as a goal in itself and the activity of travelling as a means to arrive some-where (Hlavin-Schulze 1998). The journey as a goal in itself derives its meaning from subjective experience, as an act which creates meanings and memories. It counts as a 'rite of passage' that not only moves, but also transforms the traveller, who is destined to return to a home other than the one that was left behind (Van den Abbeele 1992). On the other hand, we find the idea of travel as being in transit from one place to another. Here, it is not the journey itself that counts, but reaching the destination, preferably in as little time as possible.[12] According to Wallace (1993), this destination-oriented travel 'ideally excludes the process of travel, the travail of moving from place to place, and its advocates and practitioners seek to make that process as nearly transparent and unnoticeable as possible' (1993: 39).

As with many romantic writers who wrote on walking, the duality of travelling as a goal in itself and travelling to arrive at a destination quickly acquires a normative distinction between purposeful slowness and mindless speed. In their praise of walking, Rousseau, Seume, Töpffer and Walser expressed a marked contempt for other ways of travelling, which meant initially the coach and later the train. This normative judgment does not seem to have lost its relevance to modern commentators on the history of travelling. In just one example out of many, Daniel Boorstin (1962) describes travel as a 'lost art'.[13] He dates the beginning of the decline somewhere midway through the nineteenth century, when the act of travelling changed as a result of the growing popularity of Thomas Cook & Son. 'This change has reached its climax in our day. Formerly travel required long planning, large expense, and great investments of time. It involved risks to health or even life. The traveller was active. Now he became passive. Instead of an athletic exercise, travel became a spectator sport' (Boorstin 1962: 84). Where travel had once been an art that required knowledge, experience and creativity, modern journeys have become almost automatic, so it is inferred.

Closely linked to these narratives on the lost art of travel are stories about the importance of increased travel speed in travel. If the journey is of no value at all, why spend time on it? This argument takes shape in three discourses that explain the value of higher travel speeds: speed as an inevitable technical development, speed as time related to money and speed as an expression of progress and prosperity.

Speeding up

In a technical-determinist vocabulary, the history of travel can be written as an logical sequence of new technologies of transportation, in which slower means of travelling give way to faster means.[14] In his book *Capturing the horizon: the historical geography of transportation since the transportation revolution of the sixteenth century* (1986), the historian of transportation, Jack Vance, provides an example of this line of reasoning. In exhaustive detail, Vance describes the interaction between 'technologies of movement', the vehicles used for transport and 'facilities', the infra-structures on which they depend, that guided vehicles along geographical lines. He argues that, by the end of the middle ages, a revolution in trans-port began which lasted for three centuries, caused by a series of techno-logical innovations varying from the construction of canals and locks to the development of new coaches and wagons (Vance 1986: 38).[15] As a result of these innovations, Vance argues, the mobility of goods and people increased, which led to new bottlenecks, which in turn were eliminated by further innovations in vehicles and infrastructure. 'During the half millen-nium since the onset of the Transportation Revolution, the creation and relief of stress has been continuous – so much that we have come to expect transportation to continue expanding endlessly and a continuous effort to improve facilities and technology' (Ibid.: 13). Vance identified the trans-ition to the Era of Technological Advance between 1780 and 1830. During this period, there was an emphasis on speed, so much so that it became the distinguishing feature between various forms of transit (Ibid.: 27).

Historians of transportation such as Vance and Bagwell (1988) write the history of travel as a series of 'transportation revolutions' that made travel faster, cheaper and more comfortable. From this technical-determin-ist perspective, the transition from slower to faster forms of transit is explained by the inevitable development of technology itself. For these historians, the steam train's replacement by the electric train, and the Zep-pelin's by the airplane is a logical development. Not only is this technical development independent of other social developments, technologies of transportation form an important driving force behind all social change (Smith and Marx 1994; MacKenzie and Wajcman 1999).[16]

If innovations in transport technology have created the possibility to travel at different speeds, how can we explain that people tend to prefer the fastest alternative? This question has been answered in the prevailing economic discourse which assumes that people maximize their utility by making a rational choice between available options. The argument is based on the idea that people's time is scarce. Since few people can do several things at once, they constantly must choose which activities they are willing to spend their time on. Transport economists have modelled the amount of time people spend on travelling.[17] People travel from A to B because they can maximize utility at B. The utility of the travel time is a combination of the intrinsic utility of the journey itself and its derived utility (Sharp 1981). In welfare economic theory, it is assumed that indi-viduals experience maximum utility from the way they spend their time, and are only willing to deviate from this when they are compensated (financially or in terms of comfort). The key assumption underlying this kind of economic modelling of travel time is that the marginal utility of travel time is usually given a negative value: utility can be maximized at B and not at A, and the more time it takes to get to B, the less time is left for the preferred activity. The more utility that can be derived from the activity at B, the more people are willing to pay for shortening their travel times. Sharp (1981) claims that the negative utility of travel time is the reason why the rationale for innovating transport systems is shortening travel times. 'The most important benefit resulting from the majority of new investments in transportation projects is a saving in transportation time that can be transferred to some alternative and preferred activity' (Sharp 1981: 85).

The preference for speed is also explained in another discourse linking travel speed to progress and prosperity. A historical example of this discourse, which has a distinct cultural-utopian character, is the 1939–1940 World's Fair in New York. Here the historical dimension of speeding up transportation was linked to the utopia of fast travel. Visitors to the World's Fair saw the 'world of tomorrow'. As Grover Whalen, chairman of the organizing committee, expressed it, 'The New York's World Fair will predict, may even dictate, the shape of things to come' (cited in Gelernter 1995: 343; see also Cohen 1989). In the world of tomorrow, people travel faster and farther than ever. At the end of the 'streamlined decade', Ford, General Motors and Chrysler, the three biggest car manufacturers in the United States, represented the past, present and future of travel as a single movement from sandal to rocket (Bush 1975; Lichtenstein and Engler 1992). The popular Futurama exhibition of General Motors, 'Highways and Horizons', which was designed by Norman Bel Geddes, featured a 35,000 square-foot diorama with a giant highway and intersections, the so-called 'Magic Motorways'. Visitors made a 16-minute 'flight' over the miniature landscape in a structure with comfortable chairs that moved slowly, and from which they could look down upon the world of the future. They saw a theme park, mountains, an apple orchard covered by glass, and a city that could have been built by Le Corbusier. The 'Magic Motorways' had 14 lanes. Technicians controlled the traffic from high towers and pear-shaped vehicles reached speeds of 150 mph (Nye 1994: 217). The image of the future that General Motors presented was optimistic, if not utopian. Travelling at higher speeds, without being obstructed by traffic jams, was seen as a condition for a modern, individualist world in which people could determine for themselves when and where they wanted to be. The acceleration of travel was presented not only as a fact, but also as a desirable societal value. In a not so small microcosm, the New York World's Fair exemplified a dominant interpretation of the history and future of travel: faster is better.

Each of these discourses which value speeding up travel offer explanations for shortening travel times. In a technical-determinist vocabulary, technologies of transportation constitute the driving force in a society in which slow means of transport give way to faster forms of transit. In an economic vocabulary, maximizing utility requires spending time, including travel time, as efficiently as possible, the utility of which is usually perceived to be negative. In a cultural-utopian discourse, the faster world of tomorrow is presented as attractive and desirable. Higher travel speeds thus have a distinct surplus value in technical, economic and cultural terms.

Slowing down

Despite the differences in the three discourses introduced above, they are similar in envisioning the history of travel as a history of acceleration. This shared perspective helps to explain people's travel behaviour, their choices for specific forms of transit and the cultural meaning that they attribute to them. Assuming that travel will continue or should continue to accelerate enables us to make predictions about the future of travel and the character and logic of technological transitions, about the increase in future transport demand, and to analyse how utopian images of acceleration and escape from the shackles of time and space give form to stories of progress and prosperity (Dienel and Trischler 1997).

But however consistent and dominant these discourses are, they also have their limits. They create what the philosopher of technology, Ivan Illich, calls 'a goal of high speed', in which the future can only be envisioned as a faster world (Illich, Rieger and Trapp 1998). The conceptual straitjacket of a faster future is a prevailing theme among analysts who, like Illich, criticize the logic of speed and argue instead for slowness. Behind the striving for speed lies the utopian promise of technology that it will save us time. But critics argue that this promise is false. One of them, the German sociologist of industrial relations, Rainer Zoll, pointed out the paradox of time scarcity. 'We save time in the transportation of people, goods and information, we save time when producing and consuming, and even when we eat fast food, yet we have less time than ever. The time gained in the morning is lost in the afternoon' (Zoll 1988: 10–11). Zoll argues that instead of accelerating our lives, we should try to reclaim our proper time (see also Nowotny 1989).

The time saved by delegating activities to accelerating technologies does not stay 'empty', but is used for other activities. Marcel Proust's novel *Remembrance of things past* (1922; 1989 edn), offers a beautiful example of this paradox. One day, the narrator, Marcel, wants to surprise his beloved Albertine, by renting a car and making a trip to two nearby villages. Albertine, who has never made a trip by car before, is surprised that they will be able to visit both Saint-Jean-de-la-Haise and La Raspelière in one day.

> Although she realised that it would be possible to stop here and there on our way, she could not believe that we could start by going to Saint-Jean-de-la-Haise, that is to say in another direction, and then make an excursion which seemed to be reserved for a different day. She learned on the contrary from the driver that nothing could be

easier than to go to Saint-Jean, which he could do in twenty minutes, and that we might stay there if we chose for hours, or go on much further, for from Quetteholme to la Raspelière would not take more than thirty-five minutes. We realised this as soon as the vehicle, starting off, covered in one bound twenty paces of an excellent horse. Distances are only the relation of space to time and vary with it. We express the difficulty that we have in getting to a place in a system of miles or kilometres which becomes false as soon as that difficulty decreases.

(Proust 1989: 1029)

For Albertine, the two villages were 'prisoners hitherto as hermetically confined in the cells of distinct days as long ago were Méséglise and Guermantes, upon which the same eyes could not gaze in the course of one afternoon' (Ibid.).[18] However, Albertine and Marcel do as the new technology enables them to do and visit friends in both villages. Then something unexpected happens. Albertine, who only hours before did not believe that they could visit Saint-Jean and La Raspelière on the same day, suddenly finds herself in a hurry: 'When Albertine had quite finished displaying her toque and veil to the Verdurins, she gave me a warning look to remind me that we had not too much time left for what we meant to do' (Ibid.: 1035).

In *Planet dialectics* (1999), Wolfgang Sachs of the Wuppertal Institute for Climate, Environment and Energy asks where the time goes which has been saved by using the car. Car drivers

do not spend less time in transit than non-drivers ... Those who buy a car do not take a deep breath and rejoice in extra hours of leisure. They travel to more distant destinations. The powers of speed are converted not into less time on the road but into more kilometres travelled. The time gained is reinvested into longer distances.

(1999: 193)

Possessing a faster means of transport creates new possibilities and expectations. The horizon does not come closer; it moves further away.[19]

If speed is a problem, as critics like Illich, Zoll and Sachs argue, then slowness could be the answer. One argument for slowness is to criticize the development of new technologies of transport. Albertine's haste would disappear, the argument goes, if travellers were prepared to take more time for their journeys. Sachs (1999) argues that the development of transportation systems should not be approached from the imperative of acceleration. He believes that, if this were the case, the belief in progress as a continuing decrease in the natural friction of duration and distance will disappear. 'Countless bridges, tunnels, highways, cables and antennae are the heredity of that belief. Instead, the suspicion grows that progress could perhaps also imply deliberately leaving the resistance of time and space unchanged, or even increasing it' (Sachs 1999: 195). But how should we imagine a new utopia of slowness? Longer travel times mean that people will either have to travel shorter distances or spend more time travelling. Instead of heading for the EuroDisney theme park, Europeans who do not live near Paris will choose destinations that are closer to their homes. Working and living at a distance will be less attractive. Shops and other commercial outlets will cease to be viable if located beyond the outskirts of residential areas, where they can now be increasingly found because of the car.

A second line of argument in favour of slowness focuses on its economic consequences. People would be prepared to accept longer travel times if they could liberate themselves from the yoke of economic growth and the pressure of the clock. Jeremy Rifkin (1987) proposes to exchange 'mechanical time' for 'natural time'. Time, he argues, was once anchored in biology and nature, but it has been wrenched from them and confined within the wheels of an automatic machine which now distributes it in 'meaningless ticks' (Rifkin 1987: 65). Rifkin claims that the current tempo of life is not compatible with the rhythms of nature, and the time it needs to renew used resources. In a sustainable society, slowness instead of speed and haste is the underlying principle of experienced time. The invisibly slow tempo of nature should be the guideline of our actions. This means that time is no longer the quantified, marketable, economic unit it is now, nor the imprecise framework of 'earlier–later' it used to be. Ecologically meaningful actions connect to biological and natural rhythms, and thereby restore the subjective experience of time, the proper time that was lost.[20]

Critiques of speed can also be found in reflections on the dystopian aspects of Western modernity. The French essayist Paul Virilio has described the development of what he calls a 'raging standstill'. Because of increasingly faster means of transport and worldwide telecommunications networks, people can be everywhere and thus nowhere in particular. Sitting behind the windshields of our cars or the screens of our computers and televisions, Virilio argues, we physically come to a complete stop, while being handed over to the hallucinating, ever-changing appearances of speed. To Virilio, speed is no longer a vector in concrete space-time, but a form of representation. For him, the 'cadaver-like immobility' that comes as a result is the most threatening aspect of the dystopia of speed (Virilio 1977).[21] The German philosopher Peter Sloterdijk has also linked his critique of speed to a critique of modernity. In *Eurotaoismus* (1989), he claims that what started as a merry mobility at the beginning of the twentieth century has degenerated into an irreversible process of 'kinetic mobilization'. This development, he argues, can be described with the term 'kinethics', in which the conceived possibility of movement is already its justification. His critique of 'kinethic politics' thus takes the form of advocating an ethics of refraining from the lure of speed. He believes that society must sever itself from the false conception of mobilization and regenerate the idea of time. For Sloterdijk, silence, stability and slowness should be seen as the answers to the modern condition of permanent mobility.

Although these pleas for slowness differ substantially, they all share a reversal of the logic of acceleration. If travelling faster will not lead to saving time, but only to travelling over larger distances, to making more visits in one day and more haste, as Albertine and Marcel experienced, then travelling slower will open the way to more rest. Sachs (1999) concludes that people will only save time if they refrain from the speed which seems to enable time to be gained. As de Wilde (1997) argued however, such arguments rest upon a logical mistake known as the reversal of antecedents. In logical terms, what these authors claim is that fast forms of transit result in haste, ergo, non-fast forms of transit will result in non-haste (rest). This kind of argument, however, can only be made valid if it limits itself to the dimension of speed and excludes a priori all other qualities a journey can have. It is only in reducing travel to the dimension of speed that slowness can be the solution to the problems that speed may cause. The effect of this a priori condition of leaving out the specificities of concrete travel is that both positions mirror each other in their basic assumption, namely that speed is the defining characteristic of any kind of travel. Because they mirror each other, both positions render a 'closed future'. In the case of speed, the innovation of mobilities can only be thought of as forms of acceleration. The success and failure of transport systems are thus measured in terms of the gains in travel time they generate. Solving problems basically means eliminating 'bottlenecks' and decreasing the friction of transit. The history of travel is written as a development that has only one direction. The coach, the train, the car, the airplane are all seen as progressive stages in a continuing process of acceleration. The case for slowness is based on the same logic. The future is viewed as the reversal of the dominant picture. By introducing slower cars, more bicycles, more walking, the world will return to a more restful state.

The two positions not only mirror each other in that they reduce travel to the dimension of speed, they also share the need for a quantified notion of time. This measured time is used to construct a timescale that is necessary to distinguish between fast and slow ways of travelling. What are the consequences of using a quantified timescale for comparing modes of travel? The sociology of walking described above suggests that comparisons based on quantified time are of limited use in understanding the reappraisal of walking in the early nineteenth century. The contempt of Seume, Rousseau and Töpffer for the stagecoach and their pleas for walking imply a comparison of two ways of travelling within a frame of reference in which time is not quantified but experienced and valued. Discourses on speed and slowness need a quantified notion of time, but they cannot be reduced to it. Stories of technological and cultural progress, or its converse, are based on other concepts of time as well. We must examine the category of time itself, and the different ways it relates to travel, in order to understand the complex temporalities in these narratives of travelled time.

Contextualizing travelled times

It has become a cliché that time does not exist as a singular category. Time can be clock time, natural time, nuclear time, cosmic time and even glacial time (Macnaghten and Urry 1998). It can be seen as duration, speed and intensity, as finite and infinite, as change and continuity, as rhythm and measure and as a quantitative unity and qualitative experience. As living beings, our bodies react to a plurality of hormonal rhythms and, at the same time, are interwoven with a range of other biological time frames. As Adam (1990: 16) has argued, thinking about different concepts of time without using dualisms has proved difficult. The dualism in the opposition between objective and subjective time has been debated and criticized over and over again yet, for the clarity of my argument, I will take it as the starting point in my discussion of travelled times.

Objective time is given without any reference to human beings (Goudsblom 1997). Time exists whether there is or is not anyone to observe it. The ascent and descent of the sun and the moon, the rotation of the earth, the half-life of radioactive atoms and the dissolution of a sugar cube in a cup of coffee are events which take specific amounts of time to transpire. Subjective time is customarily considered a phenomenon which exists in an individual's sense experience or, as Kant viewed it, as a subjective category of the intellect that precedes sensory perception. Subjective time is both more familiar to us and more complicated. Our lives take place in changing temporal 'horizons', as landscapes which constantly change, just as one views a landscape from the window of a train. People experience the passing of time differently, and no one experiences one hour in the same way as he or she has the previous ones.

The distinction between objective and subjective time underlies many categorizations of time. The anthropologist Alfred Gell (1992) claims that it is possible to detect, 'amid the turmoil of conflicting voices, two opposed tendencies, which will be labelled the A-series view and the B-series view' (1992: 151).[22] Gell takes these labels from an article by the British philosopher McTaggart published in *Mind* in 1908. A-series propositions distinguish between past, present and future. B-series propositions distinguish between earlier and later.[23] The A-series notion of time is subjective in that it assumes an observer, for whom there exists a past, present and future. The B-series is objective in that the relation between earlier and later does not depend on the perception of an observer. As McTaggart argues, the statement that Caesar died before Queen Victoria is true, regardless of the moment it was uttered. The statement therefore expresses B-series time. The claim that yesterday it rained in Amsterdam can only be verified if we know when it was stated. It thus belongs to A-series time that entails so-called tensed statements that are fundamentally dependent on an observer and a context (Adam 1990: 20).

The distinction between A-series and B-series time concepts has consequences throughout the human sciences, Gell claims, in economics, sociology, geography and anthropology.

> Very roughly, A-series temporal considerations apply in the human sciences because agents are always embedded in a context or situation about whose nature and evolution they entertain moment-to-moment beliefs, whereas B-series temporal considerations also apply because agents build up temporal 'maps' of their world and its penumbra of possible worlds whose B-series characteristics reflect the genuinely B-series layout of the universe itself.
>
> (Gell 1992: 154)

Gell lists different aspects of A- and B-series time concepts. When we conceive of time as the passing from past to present to future, as in the A-series, it is dynamic. The basic outlines of understanding time in this way can be summarized as 'passage' and 'becoming'. Change is a result of 'coming into being' that is experienced in memory, observation and expectation. As such, an appropriate schema for understanding time is the human consciousness of the passage of time. When we understand time by distinguishing between earlier and later, as in B-series time, it is not dynamic. Its basic outline is that of 'being' and 'four-dimensional space-time'. Pastness, presentness and futurity, Gell claims, are not real characteristics of events but arise from our relation to them as conscious subjects. The idea of 'becoming' is therefore not an objective phenomenon, as change can only be understood as the 'variation between qualities of a thing and the date at which these qualities are manifested by that thing' (Ibid.: 157).

How can we relate A- and B-series time to different notions of travel time? The approaches to traffic congestion discussed in Chapter 1 clearly relied on a B-series conception of time. Hupkes' differentiation between a slow and a fast scenario depended upon using clock time as a fixed frame of reference. As such it could be used to create an aggregated level of comparison between groups of people, countries and historical periods. How could travel speed be understood with an A-series conception of time? Nathaniel Hawthorne's 1851 novel, *The house of the seven gables*, offers a clue. The two main characters, Clifford and Hepzibah, travel by train through the eastern parts of the United States. While they looked out of the window, 'they could see the world racing past them'. But Clifford noticed that life was unfolding within the train life itself:

> It seemed marvellous how all these people could remain so quietly in their seats, while so much noisy strength was at work in their behalf.

Some, with tickets in their hats (long travellers these, before whom lay a hundred miles of railway), had plunged into the English scenery and adventures of pamphlet novels, and were keeping company with dukes and earls. Others, whose briefer span forbade their devoting themselves to studies so abstruse, beguiled the little tedium of the way with penny-papers. A party of girls, and one young man, on opposite sides of the car, found huge amusement in a game of ball. They tossed it to and fro, with peals of laughter that might be measured by mile-lengths; for, faster than the nimble ball could fly, the merry players fled unconsciously along, leaving the trail of their mirth afar behind, and ending their game under another sky than had witnessed its commencement. . . . Old acquaintances – for such they soon grew to be, in this rapid current of affairs – continually departed. Here and there, amid the rumble and the tumult sat one asleep. Sleep; sport; business; graver or lighter study; and the common inevitable movement onward! It was life itself!

> (Hawthorne 1965: 273–274)

When the train reached a solitary way-station, the travellers leave the car.

A moment afterwards, the train – with all the life of its interior, amid which Clifford had made himself so conspicuous an object – was gliding away in the distance, and rapidly lessening to a point which, in another moment, vanished. The world had fled away from these two wanderers.

> (Ibid.)

This fragment from Hawthorne's novel suggests that the understanding and experience of speed and slowness while using an A-series time concept does not only depend on the position of one observer, as was the case with Proust's Albertine. Clifford and Hepzibah's train was observed from different positions at the same time; a multiplicity of speeds which corresponds to a multiplicity of observers. To compare the speed of transit in terms of A-series time, the position of the observer in relation to other observers must be made explicit. Because the perception of speed in A-series time depends on the relative positions of the observers, there can be no single shared observer's perspective, and therefore differences in speed can never be absolute as is the case in B-series time.

The use of the terms fast and slow thus assumes an inherent conception of time that is either B-series or A-series. Chapter 1 showed that the hypothesis of constant travel time, which relies on B-series time, is characteristic of a style of reasoning which can be found both in the economics of transportation and transport planning and the policies which rely on them. This chapter has argued that the dualism of speed and slowness, as it is found in the history of travel and in a number of discourses on modern travel, also relies on A-series time, the travelled time of the romantic walker. The pianist and musicologist Charles Rosen argued in his book on the early romantic style in music that '[r]omantic travellers delighted to look back to perceive the different appearance of what they had seen before, a meaning altered and transfigured by distance and a new perspective' (1995: 236). It is precisely the walking pace that enables a traveller to notice the changes in the landscape and thus create the travelled time of memories and stories. As an analytical framework of travel time, the A- and B-series are valuable, but to get a better understanding of travel time we also have to transcend their inherent dualism and find out how these conceptions of time are present in everyday travel practices.

Travel practices and time practices

In his essay *Time* (1988), the sociologist Norbert Elias considers time to be neither a given objective framework that has no relation to the context in which it is experienced nor a subjective experience. Rather it is seen as a sociocultural construction which helps people orient themselves in the world. Human beings are able to relate two or more types of events, and this in turn enables them to take one of these events as a frame of reference, for example, the burning of a candle or the changing quarters of the moon. The social use of time is the product of an individual's ability to construct instruments such as the mechanical clock with which they can compare the duration of other events with that of a frame of reference (Elias 1988; Tabboni 2001). Elias' conception of time comes out of a long sociological and anthropological tradition reaching back to Durkheim. Within this tradition, time has been studied 'in the manifold ways it becomes salient in human affairs' (Gell 1992: 315). Historians have researched the development of determining time, not as establishing time as a given entity, but as an activity which led us to calculate with time (Aveni 1989; Barnett 1998; Borst 1990; Dohrn-Van Rossum 1996; Goudsblom 1997; Howse 1980; Landes 1983; Lippincott and Eco 1999; Wendorff 1980). Anthropologists like Evans-Pritchard, Lévi-Strauss and Clifford Geertz have studied the practices of timekeeping in non-Western cultures to establish the ways in which our time awareness is culturally conditioned (Fabian 1983; Levine 1998; Östör 1993). Sociologists have argued that calendars and schedules, as timekeeping devices, are not only meant to coordinate and synchronize social life, but also to control it and to exert power over others (Fraser 1987; Hassard 1990; Lash and Urry 1994; Nowotny 1989; Schmied 1985; Urry 1995, 2000a; Young 1988; Young and Schuller 1988; Zerubavel 1981). Such a view underpins the argument that the new division of labour which came with industrialization in the nineteenth century also led to new practices of timekeeping (Thompson 1967; Glennie and Thrift 1997).

For these scholars, the question of what time *is* is no longer relevant. Instead they ask how time is used by people in concrete situations as a *means* to solve practical problems of orientation and synchronization in social life. Time in this corpus of work both entails and transcends the dualism of A- and B-series time, and is viewed as historical, social and cultural time. On this view, time is intersubjective and precipitates everyday practices. The geographer Nigel Thrift has researched the question of what it means if we take these everyday practices as foremost in our accounts of time (Glennie and Thrift 1997; May and Thrift 2001; Parkes and Thrift 1980; Thrift 1996).[24] The points he makes about the nature and experience of social time are of seminal importance to my own argument, as I propose to analyse travel time as a form of social time. Thrift claims that if we want to make sense of the construction of time practices, we have to pay attention to four interrelated domains. The first has already been identified by Elias, and concerns manmade, biological and cosmological timetables, calendars and rhythms. Next, a sense of time is shaped by and enacted through various systems of social discipline which could be broadly secular or religious. A sense of time, thirdly, emerges from a variety of instruments and devices. These are not just sundials and clocks to measure the passage of time, but also the video recorders and refrigerators we use to order and shift in time activities like watching a television programme and drinking milk.[25] Finally, a sense of time emerges in relation to various texts that set out particular understandings of time (May and Thrift 2001: 4–5).

> Thus, the picture that emerges is less that of a singular or uniform social time stretching over a uniform space, than of various (and uneven) networks of time, stretching in different and divergent directions across an uneven social field – think for example of the uneven dissemination of the mechanical clock through the fourteenth and fifteenth centuries or of the railway time in the mid to late nineteenth century.
>
> (Ibid.: 5)

Within this conceptual framework, we can now understand romantic walking around 1800 as both a new travel practice and a new practice of making sense of the travel time that resulted from it. Bourgeois walking practices cannot be separated from the new social contexts in which the middle class experienced them, such as in their association of leisure with social status. Also, new walking practices had to fit into social regimes that ordered woman to walk only when accompanied. Romantic walking has a material dimension of new instruments and devices as well. New vehicles and new roads, the enclosure movement and changes in the landscape all contributed and made possible the appearance of a romantic walking practice during the early nineteenth century. Finally, romantic walking was represented in texts as a form of travel that was superior to driving in a coach, because the slowness of walking underscored the point that reaching one's destination was of less importance than making the journey itself. In the practice of walking, travel and time co-evolved.

Conclusion

In common language, concepts like speed and slowness enable us to make sense of our world of movement and mobility. In ordinary life no one questions their meaning, yet these relational concepts urgently need to be analysed if we want to study the nexus of travel, time and innovation. I began my investigation of the vocabulary of speed and slowness with the example of a slow car that would solve the problems caused by fast transportation, a line of reasoning that can be found in the work of transportation scientists like Hupkes. Technically, making a slow car would not be difficult. In our world however, slowness is an anathema. One way of situating this anathema historically and culturally is to trace the idea of the contrast between speed and slowness in the emerging practice of romantic walking in the decades around 1800. Another is to outline a variety of discourses on the relation between travel and speed.

In the late eighteenth and early nineteenth centuries, the activity of walking underwent changes in meaning and practice which together constituted it as a means of locomotion that was intended to be slow. As I have shown, the rationale behind this change can be found in the interaction of social, material and narrative elements. In romantic walking, a dualism which is integral to the history of travel returns: travelling as a means to reach a destination quickly and making a journey as a goal in itself. This dualism also underlies a number of discourses on the relation between travel and speed: the technical-determinist discourse on the development of new transport technologies, the economic discourse which explains why people prefer travelling fast and a cultural-utopian discourse which identifies speed as an important value in Western culture. These discourses are mirrored by others which focus on the detrimental effects of speed, and argue for slowness as a way out of what Virilio termed a 'raging stand-still'.

Underlying both the duality of speed and slowness and that of travel as transit and travel as journey is a third duality, which can be related to the underlying concept of time. Following Alfred Gell, I have used A- and B-series time to distinguish between two ways of creating the comparative perspective on travel that the use of words like fast and slow implies. When we speak in terms of B-series time, we are forced to decontextualize time, reducing 'travel time' to measured time. We can then compare between ways of travel in terms of absolute speed or slowness. In contrast, A-series time leads to a variety of observer-based positions from which multiple travel speeds can be experienced simultaneously. Comparing different means of travelling implies a context of concrete situations. If we want to understand the role of time in everyday travel practices, we have to transcend the dualism of A- and B-series time and study how travel time is constructed *within* practices of travel. This is not to say that a perspective on travel time relying wholly on a B-series approach, such as in mainstream transport science, is less true. Each perspective renders a different type of temporal understanding of the problems of modern travel and, consequently, leads to different views about how to solve them. Thus these categorizations have yet another heuristic goal. They enable us to distinguish between different styles of reasoning about time, innovation and mobilities. What sort of time is foregrounded depends upon the specific interests and research questions of the researcher.

My argument would be that, when comparing different forms of transit and travel, it is not possible to rely solely on either the decontextualized framework of measured time or the countless time frames of subjective experience. I have said that time practices change in relation to practices of travel. The travel time on which I will elaborate in the following chapters takes this approach. In the next chapter, I will work out a style of reasoning about travel time that foregrounds the relations between travel practices and the multiple and situated times that emerge from them. To do so, it is necessary to show how travel time can be historicized in relation to new practices of travel. The history of the travel agency Thomas Cook & Son in the late nineteenth century shows how rendering travel times shorter required numerous innovations. I will make clear that the acceleration of travel in the days of Cook cannot be adequately understood by focusing only on steam trains and steamships.

3   The passages of Thomas Cook

Introduction

On 7 October 1852, the frigate *Pallada* set sail from the Russian port of Kronstadt for Nagasaki on a diplomatic mission to establish new trade relations with Japan. On board was the 40-year-old writer, Ivan Goncharov, who had written several short stories and a novel, and would become famous for his novel, *Oblomov*. Goncharov, hired as the admiral's secretary, had been asked to keep an official account of the ship's journey around the world. In his spare time during the long journey, Goncharov wrote letters to his friends back home as well as several short essays, which he published after his return to Russia in a collection entitled *The voyage of the frigate Pallada*.[1] In one of his letters, Goncharov told a friend how sailing impressed him.

> Many people take pleasure in it and see it as a proof of man's dominion over the stormy element. I see it quite oppositely as a proof of his inability to master the sea. Look closely at the setting and trimming of the sails, the complexity of the apparatus – this network of rigging, ropes, cords, ropes' ends and twine in which each member has its special purpose and is an indispensable link in the general chain. Consider the number of hands setting the system in motion. And yet how imperfect is the result of all this ingenuity! The time of arrival of a sailing ship cannot be fixed, there is no contending with a head-wind nor any reversing should the ship turn aground; it is as impossible to turn about at once as it is to stop dead instantly. In a calm the ship drowses, in a head-wind she tacks, that is zigzags and cheats the wind, but only a third of the distance she sails is directly ahead. And a period of several thousand years has elapsed while inventing every sail and a century for every rope. In each rope, in each hook, nail and plank you read the history of those instruments of torture by which mankind has won the right to sail the seas with a fair wind. In all there are up to thirty sails, one for each puff of wind. Perhaps it is beautiful to look at a ship broadside or with her white sails set, gliding

over the boundless mirror-like surface of the waters as if she were a swan, but when you find yourself inside that impassable web of rigging, then you see in sailing, not a proof of ascendancy, but rather the abandonment of all hope and victory.... Some people think that there is less poetry in a steamer, that her lines are not so clean and that she is ugly. This is mere unfamiliarity: had steamers existed for several thousand years and were sailing ships a novelty, the popular eye would find more poetry in the fast, visible impetuosity of the steamer on which a weary crowd of people does not rush about from side to side trying to humour the wind, but on which man stands idle with arms folded, quietly conscious that beneath his feet the imprisoned power of steam matches the power of the sea and obliges storm and calm alike to serve him.

(Goncharov 1965: 27)

Goncharov's description of his experiences aboard the ship nicely captures the enthusiasm about the progress which enabled a sea traveller to wrest control of nature in the mid nineteenth century. The steam engine had ended dependence on wind and currents. Travel, it seemed, had become effortless. As the steamship sliced through the swells of the open sea, the steam train glided over the vast expanse of the land with a speed that only decades earlier had been unimaginable. Machines like steamships and steam trains which travel great distances unhindered by the contingencies of nature had become the quintessential metaphor for modernity itself.

The term 'modernity' has been defined in many ways. The sociologist Bauman (2000) sees the changing relation between space and time as the defining aspect of modernity, the 'difference that makes the difference'. According to Bauman, modernity began when time and space became separated from concrete and localized domestic practices 'and so become ready to be theorized as distinct and mutually independent categories of strategy and action' (2000: 8). Those who could travel faster could cover and conquer a greater area, map it and subsequently control it. Bauman argues that the force that drove time and space apart, making it possible to cover larger distances in less time, was the technology of vehicles which were able to move faster than people or horses.

Modernity was born under the stars of acceleration and land conquest, and these stars form a constellation which contains all the information about its character, conduct and fate. It needs but a trained sociologist, not an imaginative astrologer, to read it out.

(Ibid.: 112)

The ideas of sociologists like Bauman support the claim made in the previous chapter that practices of travel co-evolve with changes in the way that multiple times are engendered in everyday practices. As the new machines of modernity forged time and space into two independent categories, they created the notion of travel time as a measurable quantity. So if we do not want to understand travel time as a given, or as an independent variable in explanations and models of travel demand, but as a concept which is itself problematic, we should examine sociological accounts of modernity, space and time. In doing so, this chapter begins by outlining the time-space geographical models of Hägerstrand and Janelle. In these models, travel time is related to space, but because Hägerstrand and Janelle rely on a B-series conception of time, their accounts abstract travel time from concrete travel practices. In the work of Anthony Giddens and David Harvey, the historicity of the concepts of time and space is linked to the advent of modernity. Like Bauman, they analyse the separation of time and space as a modern phenomenon that has its origin in technological developments such as the diffusion of the mechanical clock or the advent of fast means of transport and communication. To examine in more detail how new practices of travel were related to new time-space practices, I examine Thomas Cook's travels. As will become clear, new technologies like the mechanical clock or the steam train cannot be taken as sufficient explanations for the rise of new practices which enabled the acceleration of travel time. When Thomas Cook offered a trip around the world to his customers in 1872, he could only do so after he had created 'passages' through which they could travel unhindered.

Drawing lines though space and time

A traveller like Goncharov can be viewed as writing lines through time *and* space. His journey around the world took two years. Relating travel time to distance requires a different conceptual framework from that which has been offered by transportation scientists like Hupkes. Chapter 1 showed that Hupkes did not refer to space at all in his account of travel time budgets. He determined how long people travelled, but he did not need to know what their destinations were to make his argument. Viewing travel time as the duration of a journey, as the relation between space and time, belongs to the domain of transportation geography and has been studied by the geographers Torsten Hägerstrand and Donald Janelle.

Time-space geography revisited

At the European Congress of the Regional Science Association held in Copenhagen in 1969, Torsten Hägerstrand argued that geographers should be concerned not only with space but with time as well (Hägerstrand 1970).[2] He proposed a space-time model which could account for the 'life paths' of individuals (Figure 3.1). By adding an axis denoting time to a two-dimensional graph denoting space, he created a three-dimensional graph which could account for the movement of people through space and time.

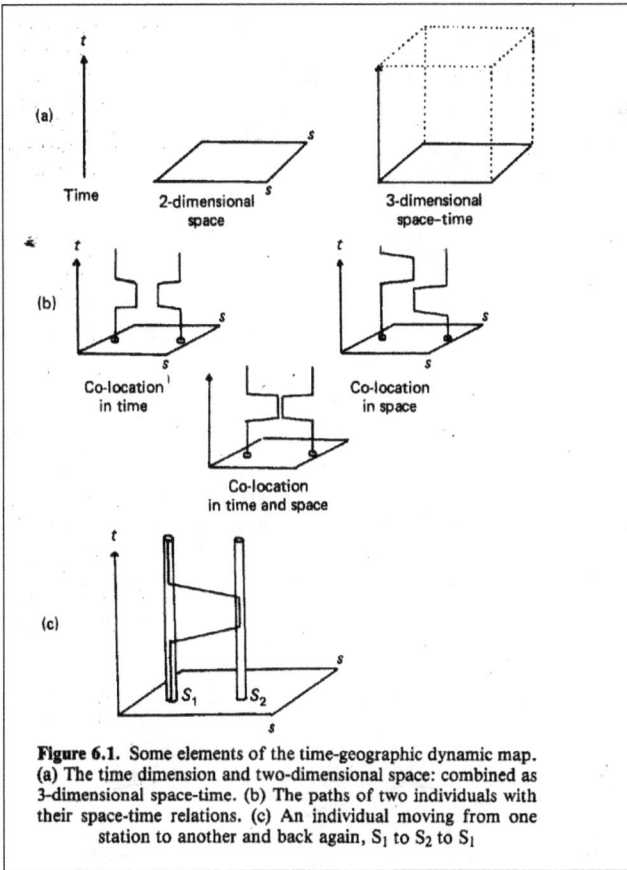

Figure 6.1. Some elements of the time-geographic dynamic map. (a) The time dimension and two-dimensional space: combined as 3-dimensional space-time. (b) The paths of two individuals with their space-time relations. (c) An individual moving from one station to another and back again, S_1 to S_2 to S_1

Figure 3.1 Hägerstrand's model of three-dimensional space-time. Figure (a) denotes three-dimensional space-time. Figure (b) graphically depicts the movement of two individuals through time and space at the same time, at the same place and at the same time and place. Figure (c) depicts an individual moving through time from one place to another and back again (source: Parkes and Thrift 1980: 245).

Hägerstrand argued that human activity is subjected to a number of 'constraints' which stem from an inability to be at two places at the same time: (i) that the time which people have to do something is finite; (ii) that most people cannot perform more than one task at a time; (iii) that movement through space always goes together with movement through time; and (iv) that two people cannot be at the same place at the same moment. Interactions between moving individuals form time-spatial 'bundles' that coincide with concrete locations such as houses, streets, cities and states, which

Hägerstrand calls 'stations'. For example, the last graphic depiction in Hägerstrand's three-dimensional model of space-time shown in Figure 3.1 could represent the spatio-temporal paths of two individuals who meet in a café. Each travels through time, represented by their place on the vertical axis, from a different location in space, represented by their location on the two horizontal axes, to the same location at the same time, represented by the meeting of the two lines. They remain at the café for a certain amount of time, represented by the vertical parallel lines in the same location in space, and then return to the locations from which they originally came.

Hägerstrand's model allowed him to show that individuals do not simply move freely through space and time. Instead they move in what he calls prisms, time-space boundaries, which create a spatio-temporal order and which are akin to the 'cells of one single day' in Proust's account of Albertine's car journey. A prism represents the sum of all the imaginable paths of an individual with a given form of transport. Hägerstrand argued that faster means of transport had greatly enlarged an individual's time-space prism by allowing them to travel greater distances in the same amount of time. Thus, someone who is walking moves in a different prism than someone behind the wheel of a car (see Figure 3.2). Albertine learned that if she took a car, she could visit friends living in two different villages

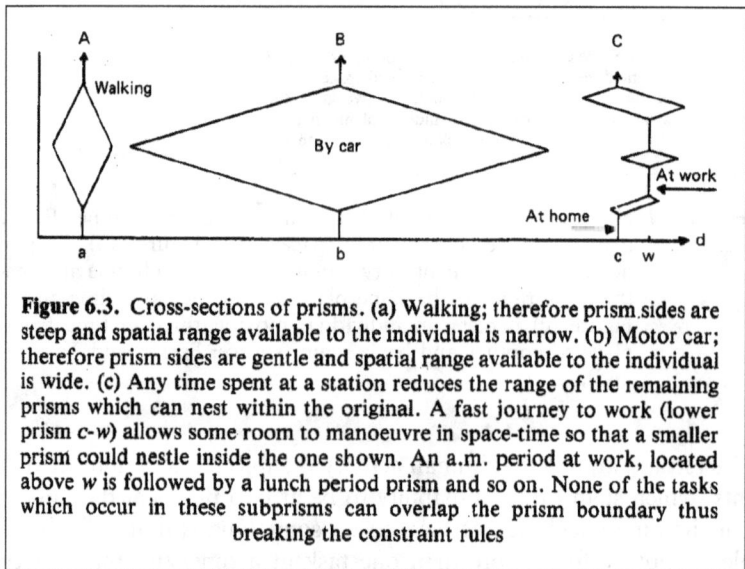

Figure 6.3. Cross-sections of prisms. (a) Walking; therefore prism sides are steep and spatial range available to the individual is narrow. (b) Motor car; therefore prism sides are gentle and spatial range available to the individual is wide. (c) Any time spent at a station reduces the range of the remaining prisms which can nest within the original. A fast journey to work (lower prism c-w) allows some room to manoeuvre in space-time so that a smaller prism could nestle inside the one shown. An a.m. period at work, located above w is followed by a lunch period prism and so on. None of the tasks which occur in these subprisms can overlap the prism boundary thus breaking the constraint rules

Figure 3.2 Hägerstrand's graphic depictions of prisms, comparing travel by foot (a) with travel by car (b). Diagram (c) represents the effects of time spent at any single place within an individual's space-time boundaries (source: Parkes and Thrift 1980: 249).

on the same day, whereas if she had walked or travelled by coach, she could have visited only one.

Hägerstrand's time-space graphs have an alluring simplicity. They depict lines though time and space that every individual creates in the act of travelling which reveal that such movements are always bounded in space and time. But, like the economists and transport experts, Hägerstrand's three-dimensional models of the spatio-temporal order depend upon a quantified conception of time. This is clear in Figure 3.2, in which the travel times of a person walking and a car driver are kept constant. Only by considering clock time as a neutral common denominator can Hägerstrand argue that an individual who is travelling by car has a larger time-space prism than someone who has chosen to walk. It then becomes possible to claim that car drivers travel faster than persons who walk by comparing the distances both covered in a constant span of time.[3]

Time-space convergence

The geographer Donald Janelle proposed another way to relate the duration of a journey to the distance covered. In 1968, he coined the term 'time-space convergence'. When the time it takes to get from one place to another decreases, it results in a time-space convergence. If the amount of time increases, it produces a time-space divergence (Janelle 1968; see also Janelle 1991).[4] Janelle considered technological innovations in transportation and communications as the main reason why the last two centuries have been characterized by a process of gradual time-space convergence. He views technological advances in mail delivery, air travel and telephone connections as exemplary of how various 'space-adjusting technologies' have led 'to the convergence of places' (Janelle 1991: 53). Janelle illustrates this process with a journey from London to Edinburgh. He calculated that the average time-space convergence between these two cities between 1776 and 1966 was 28.84 minutes each year. He arrived at this number by subtracting the travel time in 1966 (280 minutes) from the travel time in 1776 (5,760 minutes), and dividing the result by the number of years which had passed (190). In 1658 a stagecoach needed 20,000 minutes (two weeks) to cover the distance between London and Edinburgh. In 1850, a journey by train took 800 minutes. Since the 1960s, a car was underway less than 400 minutes. The airplane took about 200 minutes – a 100-fold reduction in travel time since 1658 (Parkes and Thrift 1980: 292).

Janelle's notion of time-space convergence can also be understood, in reverse, as a divergence between any pair of destinations. This is the case, for instance, if the travel time between two cities increases as a result of congestion. Furthermore, convergence does not have to be equal in both directions. It can account for the fact that the journey by boat from Astrakhan to Gorki on the Wolga River takes twice as long as when one sails in the opposite direction, because Gorki is upstream from Astrakhan (Ibid.: 296).

In a building, we can speak of time-space convergence when the upper floors can be accessed faster than before as a result of constructing an elevator.

Both Hägerstrand and Janelle offer frameworks for comparing different ways of travelling. Whereas Hägerstrand keeps *time* constant in his prisms, Janelle's conception of time-space convergence and divergence depends upon keeping the *distance* between two places constant. However, these frameworks for conceptualizing the relation between space and time are one-dimensional. They can account only for how fast or how slow travelling is between two places. Hägerstrand's car driver is faster than someone who is walking because a person riding in a car can cover a larger number of kilometres in the same amount of time. Janelle's traveller between London and Edinburgh is faster because he or she can cover the distance in less time.

Hägerstrand's and Janelle's framework require two further comments. First, by keeping time or space constant in comparing different means of travelling, time and space are conceived of not only as two distinguishable entities, but also as entities whose dimensions are measurable. Second, in using such comparisons, there is no choice but to characterize the development of mobility in terms of speed as a relation between measured time and space. In their conceptions of the relation between time and space, technological advancement creates a 'shrinking world', in which individuals can increase the size of their time-space prisms. This process flows only in one direction, namely faster. That their representation of the spatio-temporal order has received little criticism underscores the general acceptance of the three 'faster' discourses which were discussed in the previous chapter. Its wide acceptance is also associated with an experience that is broadly considered to be characteristic of modernity – the annihilation of space through time.

Modernity and mobility

Goncharov and his contemporaries marvelled at the speed of steam trains and steamships. They expressed wonder and admiration by pointing out that the new, faster means of transport would make the world a smaller place. In 1840, the Victorian philosopher, John Ruskin, wrote that 'no change of pace at a hundred miles an hour will make us one wit stronger, happier or wiser. The railways are nothing but a device to make the world smaller' (quoted in Swinglehurst 1974: 11). The German poet, Heinrich Heine, compared the invention of the steam train to that of gunpowder and the art of printing. After the opening of the Paris and Orléans rail line in 1843 he wrote:

> What changes must now occur, in our way of looking at things, in our notions! Even the elementary concepts of time and space have begun to vacillate. Space is killed by the railways, and we are left with time alone. . . . Now you can travel to Orléans in four and a half hours, and it will take no longer to get to Rouen. Just imagine what will happen when the lines to Belgium and Germany are completed and connected

up with their railways! I feel as if the mountains and forests of all countries were advancing on Paris. Even now, I can smell the German linden trees; the North Sea's breakers are rolling against my door.

(quoted in Schivelbusch 1986: 37)

Expressions such as the 'annihilation of space and time' and 'the shrinking world' were common nineteenth-century characterizations of the experience of mechanized travel. Journeys which used to take days now only took hours. The walls of space and time that had once been so absolute now seemed to be levelled. The railroad's triumph of conquering distance is expressed in an inscription at New York's Grand Central Station: 'The Devourer of Space and Time'.[5]

Karl Marx used expressions of progress that must be understood in the context of his analysis of the importance of fast transportation of goods in a capitalist society. In *Grundrisse* (1858, 1973), he reflected on the role of transport and communication in the circulation of capital. The more production depends on exchange value, the more important it becomes to create the physical conditions necessary for exchange. In opening up markets around the world, capital, 'from its very nature', needs to annihilate space through time to minimize the time it takes to transport goods from one place to another. The more developed the capital, the more extended the markets in which it circulates become, and the more capital strives to expand the market, which creates an even greater annihilation of space through time.

Separating space and time

For sociologists and human geographers who study modernity, nineteenth-century metaphors of a 'shrinking world' and 'the annihilation of space through time' are still useful for historicizing concepts like space and time, and for explaining why modernization cannot be separated from acceleration. The sociologist, Anthony Giddens, has brought space and time into the heart of social theorizing. In *The constitution of society* (1984), he argues that reflecting on human actions is meaningless without working out how these actions are organized in time and space. Many sociologists, Giddens claims, take time and space as settings for action and use, without realizing it, a concept of time that goes back to the clock time characteristic of modern Western culture. However, Giddens claims that time and space are not givens, but are at once the condition for and the outcome of human actions. Actions get their meaning in the interactions between people, and these interactions are situated in a spatio-temporal context. According to Giddens, the time-space geography of Hägerstrand offers the possibility of visualizing the topography of this spatio-temporal context, but it wrongly takes clock time as an unproblematic dimension. ' "[C]lock time" should not be accepted simply as an unquestioned dimension of the construction of topographical models, but must itself be regarded as a socially conditioned influence upon the nature of the time-space paths traced out by actors in modern societies' (Giddens 1984: 132–133). Thus *how* time structures social life and at the same is the outcome of it does not become clear in time-space geography.

In *The consequences of modernity* (1990), Giddens examines the concepts of time and space from a new theory of modernization. In his view, the classical sociological theories of Marx, Durkheim and Weber are inadequate because they explain modernity through the development of a single process. The dynamics of modernization cannot be reduced to capitalist production relations (Marx), nor to the rise of an industrial order (Durkheim), nor to processes of rationalization and bureaucratization (Weber) (Giddens 1990: 7). All of these perspectives partially explain what Giddens calls 'the extreme dynamism and globalizing scope of modern institutions' (Ibid.: 16). Giddens argues that modernity's dynamism proceeds in three steps:

> the *separation of time and space* and their recombination in forms which permit the precise time-space 'zoning' of social life; the *disembedding* of social systems (a phenomenon which connects closely with factors involved in time-space separation); and the *reflexive ordering and reordering* of social relations in the light of continual inputs of knowledge affecting the actions of individuals and groups...
>
> (Ibid.: 16–17)

In premodern societies, Giddens contends, people lived within close proximity of each other; information travelled as fast as the fastest means of physical transportation could carry it. There existed what Giddens calls a high *presence-availability*.[6] Human interaction presupposed that somebody was physically present. Place and time were one; 'when' was linked to 'where'. The key event triggering the separation of space and time was the mechanical clock and its gradual diffusion into all segments of society. The emergence of clock time and the standardization of time over large physical space, and, ultimately, the whole world, led to a greater uniformity in social organization.[7] Giddens deals at length with what he calls the 'commodification of time' in his earlier work (Giddens 1981). With the expansion of capitalism, time, just like money, develops into a uniform standard for the value of all things. In Giddens (1981), time as lived time, as the bearer of lived experience, appears as quantified and marketable duration (Ibid.: 131). This 'emptying out of time' is a precondition for the 'emptying out of space', in other words, the separation of space and time. The rise of modernity creates a new space in which human interactions are possible with *absent* others. This separation of space and time – the fact that human action can be lifted from a concrete context and reorganized over large distances in space and time – is what Giddens calls *time-space distanciation*. It is precisely this separation of space and time, he claims, that enables them to be recombined in new ways. The schedule of a railway company can be seen as an instrument which reorders time and space in such a way that the coordination of trains, passengers and freight becomes possible (Giddens 1990: 20).[8]

The historical development of modernity which Giddens depicts from the 'emptying out of time' has an epistemological consequence. From the perspective of Hägerstrand and Janelle, it is possible to compare travel in terms of fast and slow, as long as one is kept constant. Giddens agues that this is possible only *after* both dimensions are disconnected in the historical processes of modernization. In other words, the fact that it is possible to speak of speed and slowness as abstract relations between space and time can be explained from the same cause that explains the dynamics of modernity, namely the invention and diffusion of the mechanical clock.

Compressing space and time

In *The condition of postmodernity* (1989), David Harvey also takes the separation of time and space as the decisive characteristic of modernity. He argues that in premodern societies, the experience of time and space was strongly bound to traditional agrarian, cultural and religious orders. This changed in the seventeenth and eighteenth centuries, when man became viewed as occupying an empty time and space. Newtonian physics reinforced the notion of time and space as abstract categories, as 'containers' of events. Places were increasingly viewed as parts of a space that was more or less homogeneous as a result of new practices, such as constructing networks of coordinates on maps. Harvey argues that a comparable shift also occurred in the temporal dimension. The invention and gradual social diffusion of the mechanical clock created a social time that could be used as a universal measuring rod 'alongside' events.

While Giddens treats the emergence of clock time as an explanation of the dynamics of modernity, Harvey argues that it remains unknown why this dynamic has the character of an *acceleration*. 'The general effect, then, is for capitalist modernization to be very much about speed-up and acceleration in the pace of economic processes and, hence, in social life' (Harvey 1989: 230). Harvey takes the Marxist dictum of the 'annihilation of space through time' as a precondition for capitalist production. The expansion of capitalist modernization leads to acceleration. Central to this process are technical developments such as transportation and communication. Harvey takes Europe's economic collapse after 1848 as an example. The collapse, he contends, was caused by speculation on railroad construction, and was solved when technological innovations made it possible to accelerate the circulation of capital (Ibid.: 264). He claims that such innovations, and the acceleration of production and consumption they engendered, changed the *experience* of space and time. These changes made the world seem smaller, which Harvey called 'time-space compression'(Ibid.: 240).

Harvey believes that it was transport and communication technologies that led to a smaller world. Before 1840, the highest average speed that coaches or sailing ships could attain was 15 km/h. The steam locomotive cut the globe in half. Steam-powered trains could attain speeds of 90 km/h and steamships 50 km/h. By the 1930s, the world became even smaller with the introduction of the propeller plane. And in the 1960s, jet aircraft made it only a fraction of the world in 1500. The history of capitalism can be written as one single, long-term investment in the capturing of space through the development of transport and communication technologies.

> The expansion of the railway network, accompanied by the advent of the telegraph, the growth of steam shipping, and the building of the Suez Canal, the beginnings of radio communication and bicycle and automobile travel at the end of the century, all changed the sense of time and space in radical ways.
>
> (Ibid.: 264)

Building on Kern (1983), Harvey stresses that the phases in crises and accelerations in the circulation of capital effected crises in the *experience* and subsequent *representations* of space and time. Fragmentation became the key experience. Ford's use of the conveyor belt in his River Rouge plant in 1913 fragmented workers' tasks and led to new divisions of labour in time and space that were organized around making production a process of 'flowing'. Time was accelerated by fragmenting the spatial order of production. In the same year, the first radio signal that could be received all over the world was broadcast from the Eiffel Tower, 'thus emphasizing the capacity to collapse space into the simultaneity of an instant in universal public time' (Harvey 1989: 266). The 'now' fragmented into a myriad of spatially dispersed events. For Harvey, modernist developments in the arts and literature – the novels of James Joyce which used new codes, significations and languages, the music of Schönberg and others which lacked a tonal centre, and the cubist paintings of Picasso and Braque – can be seen as examples of the fact that Fordist economics had not only accelerated space and time, but also compressed and fragmented them (Ibid.: 266–267). Harvey is able to explain Janelle's time-space convergence by pointing at the expansion of capitalist circulation. He speaks of 'compression' rather than of 'convergence', because London and Edinburgh are closer not only in measured travel time, but also in the *experiences* of people.

A spectator's perspective on innovation

Travel time as the duration of movement through space can be understood as the relation between space and time. Geographers like Hägerstrand and Janelle have developed a conceptual framework to describe changes in this relation. By reducing space to time, or time to space, Hägerstrand and

Janelle created a perspective in which two ways of travel can be compared on the abstract level of speed. But their approach does not add anything conceptually to Hupkes' account, which takes the hypothesis of constant travel time as a point of departure. Thus these explanatory frameworks add no new elements in accounting for the growth of mobility.

According to Bauman, if we want to find explanations which contextualize and historicize the concept of travel time, we should consult a good sociologist who can read 'the stars of acceleration and land conquest' (Bauman 2000: 112). This 'reading the stars of acceleration and land conquest' is indeed what the sociologist Giddens and Harvey, as a human geographer, have done. They have shown that transport scientists like Hupkes and geographers like Hägerstrand and Janelle were only able to use the quantitative B-series conception of time after it had been extracted from premodern contexts in the process of modernization. When conceived of as clock time, travel time only acquires meaning again when it is linked to space in concrete situations, for example in a railroad company's train schedule.

Yet Giddens' and Harvey's analyses are also problematic. Both conceptualize the separation of time and space as a historical process that is characteristic of modernity. Thrift (1996) argues that this is a dead-end street, because using the term 'modernity' reinforces the finalism and technical determinism in their accounts of time, space and acceleration. Sociologists tend to see modernity as 'a period of acceleration, which marks a decisive break with a slower, more stable past, a period of remorselessly constant renewal in which the experience of "the ephemeral, the fugitive, the contingent" (Baudelaire) becomes increasingly and jarringly apparent' (Thrift 1996: 164). Thrift's critique of this conception of modernity is aimed at the representation of history as a progressive process of temporal coordination, standardization and regularity, a process which is moreover concentrated in one single part of the world, the West. For Thrift, temporal precision for example is not a historical process which has any clear direction (that is, towards ever-increasing precision), but can only be understood within specific practices in which it is more important than in others (Glennie and Thrift 1997).

Giddens and Harvey find the *cause* for the changes they describe in quasi-autonomous technical developments. For Giddens, it is the invention of the mechanical clock, cartography and the land register. Harvey adds to these technological innovations in transport and communications:

> The turnpikes and canals, the railways, steamships and telegraph, the radio and the automobile, containerization, jet cargo transport, television and telecommunications, have altered space and time relations and forced new material practices as well as new modes of representation of space. The capacity to measure and divide time has been revolutionized, first through the production and diffusion of increasingly accurate time pieces and subsequently through close attention to the speed and coordinating mechanisms of production (automation,

robotization) and the speed of movement of goods, people, information, messages, and the like.

(Harvey 1996: 240–241)

Technological-deterministic explanations are characteristic of many sociological and social geographical accounts of space and time. The acceleration of society, and with this, the changes in time and space, are viewed as an *effect* of technological developments. While one cannot deny that jet planes have shortened travel times from Europe to the United States and altered the meaning of time and distance, these approaches view the world as it is seen through the eyes of Goncharov. For Goncharov, the frigate *Pallada* is a painful illustration of human impotence, whereas the steamship represents progress in science and technology. Goncharov shares Giddens' and Harvey's idea that the steamship is the *source* of innovation in modern societies rather than its *product.*[9]

If we see technology as the source of innovation, it is as if we, like Goncharov, perceive the steamship as an unmoved mover 'on which man stands idle with arms folded, quietly conscious that beneath his feet the imprisoned power of steam matches the power of the sea and obliges storm and calm alike to serve him' (Goncharov 1965: 27). In opposition to Goncharov's spectator's perspective, we could take the perspective of the *Pallada*'s seamen. Goncharov continued the fragment with which this chapter opened thus:

> In vain did they take me to see how beautifully the sails bellied out to leeward and how the frigate, heeling over on her side, clove the waves and scudded along at twelve knots.
>
> 'A steamer won't go like that,' they said to me.
>
> 'But, on the other hand, a steamer goes all the time.'
>
> Woe to the seaman of the old school whose whole mind, science and art, backed by his self-esteem and ambition, are centred in the rigging. The conclusion is foregone. Sails are for small ships and manufacturers of modest means, all other ship-owners have taken to steam.

(Ibid.: 28)

The old school seamen see the movement of both the sailing vessel and the steamboat from an *actor's perspective*. They realize that to get a boat moving, whether it is a sailing vessel or a steamship, a lot of work has to be done. Contrary to what Bauman claims then, more than a sociologist is needed to read the modern constellation of 'acceleration and land conquest'. To put it in more general terms, the technical artefacts that appear from a spectator's perspective as a stable *explanation* for the changes in time and space, appear from an actor's perspective as the result of a complex interweaving of social, economic and technical relations. The presupposition that technology can never form its own explanation is at the core of science and technology studies developed over the last 25 years. If technologies do not evolve as a result of some necessary or inner logic, the question then becomes why they attained the *actual* form they did (Bijker and Law 1992: 3–4). In other words, if the steamship cannot be seen as the prime mover of the innovations that changed Goncharov's world, how should we then study and theorize them?

The innovations of Thomas Cook

In *Economies of signs and space* (1994), Lash and Urry argue that the modern world is inconceivable without new forms of long-distance transport and travel. But insofar as commentators on the sociology of travel pay any attention to these new forms of travel, Lash and Urry argue, a technological determinism is present in their work, as if people almost naturally would chose the latest and therefore superior travel technology. Yet

> [a]s important as new transportation technologies have been, it is organizational innovations which have, in certain cases only, ensured that the new technologies have been economically successful and culturally emblematic of the modern world.
>
> (Lash and Urry 1994: 253)

In order to show that long-distance travel must be organized, they describe the emergence of organized tourism as it can be reconstructed from the history of the travel company Thomas Cook & Son.[10] In order to make my own argument on the co-evolution of practices of time and travel practices, in this section I follow their account of Thomas Cook's innovation, which itself is based primarily on Piers Brendon's exhaustive study of Cook and his company (1991), and add to it an account of Cook's journey around the world.

Teetotalism and railwayism

George Stephenson completed the first locomotive, named *Locomotion*, for the Stockton and Darlington Railway in 1825. On 27 September 1825, Stephenson drove *Locomotion* on a journey to transport a load of coal and flour over a distance of nine miles. On the nine-mile excursion, he attached the first passenger car in the world named, appropriately, *Experiment*. The coach, which passengers entered from the rear, contained rows of seats on either side with a long table running down the middle, resembling a horse-drawn bus. The first railway operators in Great Britain saw the railways mainly as a means of transporting goods such as coal (Vance 1986: 197). They also intended to transport passengers, but their expectations on this front were low. Against all expectations, the railway journey from Darlington to Stockton became a success. Railway companies soon realized that passenger trains would be a necessary addition to freight trains if they were going to exploit the railways profitably. Passengers saw the steam train mainly as a fairground attraction – understandably – because in many cases they stood straight up in open 'bathtubs' and got covered with ashes from the locomotive's chimney (Swinglehurst 1974: 8). Travelling by train quickly became popular. The railways offered recreation to people who were not used to travelling any further than the nearest market or other destinations within walking reach. The price of stagecoaches was far too high. But before the train could gain popularity, a lot of work had to be done, and it was done in large part by Thomas Cook.

On 9 June 1841, the 33-year old Cook was walking from his house in Market Harborough to a temperance meeting in Leicester, when he got the idea that would change the world: 'a thought flashed through my brain – what a glorious thing it would be if the newly developed powers of railways and locomotion could be made subservient to the cause of temperance' (cited in Brendon 1991: 5). The distraction that the railways provided was in Cook's mind a means of strengthening progressive and democratic forces. His proposal was received enthusiastically by his fellow teetotallers. Special tickets for an excursion were printed and sold, and on 5 June 1841 a crowded train travelled from Leicester to nearby Loughborough and back.[11] The excursion served as a demonstration for teetotallers. Spectators were waiting at every bridge and, when the train arrived in Loughborough, it was greeted by a group of enthusiastic supporters. After three hours of speeches, Cook could close the meeting by shouting: 'One cheer more for Teetotalism and Railwayism!!' (Brendon 1991: 8; Lash and Urry 1994: 261).

The excursion to Loughborough and back was the first in a long series of such excursions which Thomas Cook would organize. According to Brendon (1991), Cook's strength lay in the fact that he not only recognized the possibilities for recreation that the train offered, but also succeeded in making train travel affordable for large groups of people. Trains may have appealed to the public's imagination, but most people continued to think that travelling by train was both expensive and difficult. The benefits of train travel were something which had to be learned, and Cook was influential in achieving this. In 1842, a Railway Clearing House was founded to bring some order to the chaos created from the myriad small, fiercely competitive passenger railway companies, which had made it difficult for an ordinary traveller to choose from the variety of tickets and lines on offer. By the early 1840s, a specialist was needed to organize travel arrangements and bargain for the most favourable tariffs. Thomas Cook became this specialist. He negotiated the least expensive tickets with railway companies along the routes his passengers wanted to travel (Lash and Urry 1994: 262).

Cook realized that passengers needed a reason to go somewhere and have something to do when they got there. To achieve this end, Cook linked the journeys to Edinburgh he organized in 1846 to the image of the rugged highlands of Scotland which Sir Walter Scott had evoked in his novels and poems. In doing so, Cook created what Shields (1991) has called 'place myths', myths about specific places created out of stories and images which give people a reason to visit them.

> During the late eighteenth and nineteenth centuries numerous other place-myths were created. They became attached to particular kinds of social space, spaces that could only exist with large numbers of visitors. The character of such spaces became the object of a tourist's curiosity, who travelled to them 'to gain a view'.
>
> (Lash and Urry 1994: 266)

In the 1850s, Cook's tours to Scotland became such a success that the Scots began to view his passengers as a 'clan' of their own. The passengers Cook brought to Scotland were given priority in Scottish coaches and hotel owners gave Cook's guests the best rooms in an attempt to attain his approval.

The 1851 World's Fair in London, the Great Exhibition, is another example of how destinations could be created. No less than six million visitors visited the exhibition in the Crystal Palace at Hyde Park. Cook arranged the journeys of 165,000 visitors to London's Great Exhibition, only 25 years after the first passenger trains began to run in Great Britain. Three days after its opening, the first issue of *Cook's Exhibition Herald and Excursion Advertiser* was sold for one penny. As Cook wrote in the first issue, he wanted his '*Excursionist*' to be a 'practical worker more than a sentimental traveller' (cited in Brendon 1991: 61). He used the journal to advertise his travel packages, recommend new excursions and announce new routes as well as cultivate a 'habit of travel' among his readers. It featured a wide variety of advertisements for temperance hotels, steamship companies, but also for handy travel equipment such as Bailey's Air Cushion, which 'reduces the effects of vibrations on the nervous system', and Walter's Railway Convenience, which 'can be worn invisibly and with the greatest comfort and safety' (cited in Ibid.: 80).

Four years later, when the World's Fair was in Paris, Cook again arranged travel arrangements for Britons to visit it. The journey to Paris proved more complex, however. Cook had to arrange the connections between the different railway and shipping companies, book hotels and restaurants along the way, ship luggage, as well as provide information for travellers. After 1855, not only Paris, but cities like Brussels and Cologne, and, after 1860, the Alps and Italy became Cook travel destinations. In each of these destinations as well as in Scotland, Cook exploited myths that had been created about them by romantic authors like John Ruskin. But his organized tours also caused considerable unrest among the London establishment, who considered his passengers vandals, 'mental patients' and sometimes even 'the hordes of Cook' (Lash and Urry 1994: 263).

Thomas Cook went to considerable effort to find out when and where his travellers had to change trains en route to prevent them from losing any time waiting for connections. He made agreements with hotels and restaurants along the routes and sometimes had dinners served on the station platform so that his customers could depart more quickly. Brendon even quotes Cook reporting that at Dijon, where the train stopped for ten minutes, 'a dinner of some eight or nine courses was served and well-eaten' (cited in Brendon 1991: 80). Cook also arranged that his passengers' baggage was transported independently of them so that they would not have to carry their heavy suitcases on board.[12]

After the 1860s, Cook began to organize trips to Egypt and other destinations in the Middle East. And by the close of the century, the company owned a fleet of 20 Nile boats. Wealthy Britons sailing down the Nile on one of these boats exemplified how Cook's clients viewed the local populations of the places they visited. Leaning over the railing, with Egyptian cigarettes in their hands, British travellers looked out over the water at the locals working along the shoreline. Cook saw it as his duty to protect his clients from the less pleasant aspects of daily life in the countries they visited. Yet to many tourists, the reality in Egypt caused them to experience what today would be called a 'culture shock' (Ibid.: 134). From 1865 on, the London office of Thomas Cook & Son offered travellers the opportunity to buy tickets from different railway companies in Europe. His local staff would ensure the reliability of the links in the chain at all intermediate stations. Cook created letters of credit called Circular Notes, the precursor to the traveller's cheque, which could be exchanged at banks within Cook's network (Ibid.: 163). He also created hotel coupons which travellers could purchase before departing that enabled them to stay in hotels along the route (Lash and Urry 1994: 263).

A journey around the world

In 1872 Cook realized one of his dreams, a trip around the world. The journey became possible in part because of the construction of the Suez Canal, the establishment of shipping lines from the west coast of the United States to Japan and China, and the completion of the first transcontinental railroad in the US on 10 May 1869, at Promontory Summit, Utah. Cook, who was now 64 and still curious to see North America, India and the Far East, made a journey around the globe, accompanied by a touring group, only to realize that it was considerably easier than he had thought. While en route, he sent letters to *The Times* and *Leicester Papers* which give a matter-of-fact impression of the undertaking (Smith 1998). In contrast to Phileas Fogg and Passepartout, the main characters in Jules Verne's *Around the world in eighty days* (1873), Cook travelled from East to West.[13] Apart from 'hard gales and strong head winds' (Smith 1998: 10) during the Atlantic crossing, it was a relatively smooth journey. He stayed in New York for five days, 'quite sufficient for general purposes of sightseeing' (Ibid.: 11). He travelled by train to San Francisco, stopping in

Niagara Falls, Detroit, Chicago and Salt Lake City. While crossing the American prairies, Cook saw 'Prairie fires on all sides, antelopes, wolves, and Indians [who] kept us in a state of almost constant excitement' (Ibid.: 13). The Indians, he wrote, friendly, though 'armed to the teeth', 'gave evidence of friendship by cheers and actions, waving of caps and other signs of mirth' (Ibid.). However, Cook found the Rocky Mountains disappointing, but the Sierra Nevada was 'no mistake' (Ibid.: 22).

Cook wrote approvingly about travelling in the United States in his letters. He found the train compartments comfortable, although 'the admixture of strangers and sexes [is] very repulsive to the English traveller' (Ibid.: 18). 'The open cars meet the necessities of long journeys far better than the sectional and boxed-up system of English carriages' (Ibid.: 16). Cook found the baggage arrangements to be perfect. A Baggage Express Company picked up the suitcases, coffers and chests from the hotel. On the platform a brass identity tag was attached to each piece of luggage and a corresponding brass check was given to the owner. When approaching each destination, the Baggage Express Company employee walked through the train to collect the brass checks from departing passengers, gave them a receipt, collected their baggage and brought it to their hotel. Cook was also very content with the so-called 'lie-over ticket', a ticket to the final destination, allowing passengers to interrupt their journey at any station.

From San Francisco, Cook's touring group sailed by steamer to Yokohama. While underway he had plenty of time to write letters which were handed over to a passing ship on the open seas and sent via the United States to London. Cook was especially interested in the temporal effects of passing the time meridian. In his second letter to *The Times* he wrote:

> In a week or ten days more we expect to reach the 180th degree of longitude, when London will be under our feet, and a day will mysteriously drop from the calendar. But this going round the world is a very easy and almost imperceptible business; there is no difficulty about it.
>
> (Ibid.: 23)

As they pass the meridian, Cook's group of excursionists go to sleep on Friday, 17 November and wake up on Sunday, 19 November. Explaining this puzzle, Cook wrote to a friend:

> on reaching the 180th degree of longitude we are at the antipodes of Greenwich, and London time is 12 hours in advance. We then take a leap of 24 hours, leaving Greenwich 12 hours in our rear; but crossing the meridian line we put back our time an hour for every 15 degrees, and by the time we reach London the clocks and time will have righted themselves.
>
> (Ibid.: 26)

As positive as Cook's writings were about Yokohama, Osaka and Nagasaki, where his touring company bought porcelain vases, condescension was the general feeling about Shanghai:

> Narrow, filthy, and offensive streets, choked and almost choking bazaars, pestering and festering beggars in every shape and hideous deformity.... I do not think that the coolies who wheel residents about in barrows got much 'cash' from our party.
>
> (Ibid.: 31)

After 24 hours in Shanghai, the company boarded a coastal steamer to Hong Kong, but had too little time there to get a good impression of the city and Canton. In Hong Kong, they boarded the *Mirzapore* and headed to Singapore, and then sailed from there to India, where they landed in Calcutta, and there commenced a month-long journey to Serampore, Agra, Cawnpore, Lucknow, Delhi, Allahabad, Jubbulpore and finally Bombay.

From Bombay, Cook's travellers sailed on the *Hydaspes*, a beautiful steamer from the Peninsular and Oriental Line, to the Red Sea, and then on to the Suez Canal. Cook achieved his goal. Now he knows the route around the world, where to get train tickets and where the best hotels are. The journey from Egypt back to London has become a routine affair for his firm.

> I feel that I have mastered the anticipated difficulties of the route; I shall know how to advise inquirers as to time, expense and accommodation of all kinds; and the full details I shall give to the public for the guidance of those who follow, as I do not contemplate a second tour round the world. After 32 years of almost incessant travelling, with the view of making travelling easy, cheap and safe for others, I ought to 'rest and be thankful' that no evil has befallen me.
>
> (Ibid.: 47)

Constructing passages

The world was doubtless smaller for Thomas Cook in the 1870s than it was for Goncharov 20 years earlier. For Giddens and Harvey, the experiences of actors such as Cook form a starting point for their analyses of the separation of time and space, and the acceleration that is the basis of time-space compression so characteristic of capitalist modernity. Cook's experiences travelling, which started with a local excursion in 1841 and ended with a journey around the world, can be used as evidence to support the claim that the world became smaller because of the introduction of technical innovations such as the steam train and the steamship. I argue, however, that an alternative to such technical-determinism can be found by reconstructing the actor's perspective and studying the innovations Cook had to introduce to make the world smaller. Cook's undertaking is not imaginable without railways and steamers. But his tours also show that the means of transportation available to his passengers or the construction of new infrastructure, such as the transcontinental railroad in the United States or the Suez Canal, in themselves, cannot explain why so many people began to travel over large distances. Cook sold excursions, but he had to find ways to market quick transit as a product in order to do so. He had to construct what I call 'passages'.

Making a journey assumes the availability of both a spatial and a temporal order. The word 'passage' conveys both aspects, as it simultaneously refers to a span of time, the passing of time and to a space that is traversed.[14] A passage is simultaneously a duration and a way through. Where geographers like Hägerstrand see space and time as 'carriers' of a movement – a traveller writes lines through the emptiness of Euclidian space and time. The transit of people and things, however, implies a spatio-temporal *order* in which time and space cannot be separated.[15] In this meaning, the term passages can also be seen as an implicit critique on the 'separation of time and space' that Giddens and Harvey describe. We can think of travel as the active construction of passages as spatio-temporal orders in at least three ways: as creating heterogeneous orders; as planning and repairing these orders; and as including and excluding people, places and times from these orders.

Passages as heterogeneous orders

In a book on the spatial order of the Netherlands between 1798 and 1848, the Dutch historian Auke van der Woud (1987) defines order as 'an abstract concept with analogies like cosmic order, social order, economic order, juridical order' (1987: 16). The term assumes an inner coherence and design – whether this has been caused consciously by humans or not. 'The spatial order is made up of more than just material elements and contains, in addition to human-made elements, such as bridges, a polder's[16] water level, cities and sea walls, the unformed, the grown, and beside that which has been built, that which is decaying, that which is measurable and weighable, the relations that change between space and time, speed and slowness, mobility and stagnation' (Ibid.).[17]

The idea of space and time as related in a heterogeneous order can also be found in an article by the sociologist, John Law, in which he describes Portuguese sea journeys in the fifteenth century as products of 'negotiations' between the heterogeneous elements in a network that enabled their oceanic transits (Law 1987). Sailing ships were part of that network, but so were the wind, sea currents and the King of Portugal's opinions. Associating entities that range from people, through skills, artefacts and natural phenomena is the work of what Law calls 'heterogeneous engineers'. This work 'is successful if the consequent heterogeneous networks are able to maintain some degree of stability in the face of the attempts of other entities or systems to dissociate them into their component parts' (1987: 129). Following this early formulation of actor network theory, the construction of passages can be defined as the ordering of heterogeneous entities in such a way that a situated relation between time and space is produced. The passages that Cook realized thus assume an ordering that is heterogeneous and complex. It does not only encompass material elements like trains, signals, stations, lie-over tickets, brass identity baggage checks, hotels, steamers and hotel coupons, but also immaterial elements, such as teetotallers' ideals, place myths and colonial prejudices.

Planned and contingent orders

The spatio-temporal order of passages is planned and predictable, but also unpredictable and contingent. Passages can be made in advance, such as in the case of Cook's journeys, which were advertised in brochures, which themselves were linked to infrastructures and schedules, as well as in the case of place myths and travellers' expectations about destinations, which worked together to form the 'journey to Scotland'. But passages are also continuously confirmed or changed in the real-time activity of travelling. In Thomas Cook & Son's travel brochures, all Scotland tours were equal, but every traveller to Scotland made a different journey. The expression 'to take passage' used for travelling by packet boat contains both meanings. One bought a crossing, but it only began at the moment one actually stepped aboard.

The spatio-temporal order of a passage has to be continuously maintained. One of the ways Cook got people to travel was to reduce the uncertainty and contingency underway. Someone who travelled with Cook never had to feel lost in a strange world. Cook ensured that local agents and employees were stationed all along the routes. *The Man from Cook's*, a modest functionary wearing a Thomas Cook's cap, who assisted travellers when boarding a train, became legendary. Innovations like the hotel coupon, the baggage system and traveller's cheques were not only a way to accelerate a journey, but also to reduce its uncertainty for the British traveller. From his first excursions on, Cook realized the importance of travel guides and handbooks. In these, travellers found practical information about the locales they were to visit, its facilities like shops and restaurants, and its local habits. By describing a destination at great length, Cook could reduce the uncertainty for the traveller.

However, more and faster trains led to new contingencies. Whereas it was usually inconsequential if someone arrived a few minutes late to a stagecoach, it became a problem when travelling by train. When railway operations became more complex, and the number of travellers increased, it became more important to organize travelling as temporally precise as possible. To create reliable schedules, departure and arrival times had to be calculated to the minute.[18] This led in turn to more temporal precision in scheduling trains and a growing demand for good watches. Analyses of the use of watches in the nineteenth century illustrate this interaction: the timepiece created the conditions for its own diffusion – as travelling was reorganized in time, someone lacking a reliable watch would inevitably miss the train (Draaisma 1993: 81).

Inside and outside the passage

The concept of passages assumes an inside and an outside. In the spatio-temporal order which is necessary for travel, people, places and moments in time are either included or excluded. The passages of Thomas Cook made the world smaller, but not for everyone. For most of the Egyptians who the British saw from the railings of their Nile boats, the globe was as big as it had been in the days of the pharaohs. In Britain as well, travelling over large distances remained something for only the lucky few. The speed that became possible within Cook's passages was affordable only to a minority. When Thomas Cook died in 1892, approximately 20 tour groups – totalling less than 1,000 excursionists – had made the journey around the world (Brendon 1991: 151). While Cook's trips around the world may have been possible for the very few, his shorter tours did make travelling more available than ever for the emerging Victorian middle class. This was especially true for women. There are countless travel accounts of well-to-do women from this period enjoying Cook's excursions (Grewal 1996).

The spatio-temporal order of the passage guarantees a fast transit, but not everywhere or always. This becomes evident when examining Cook's personal around-the-world itinerary and that of his world-travelling customers. As Withey (1997) shows, the route which both Phileas Fogg and Thomas Cook travelled – London, New York, San Francisco, Yokohama, Shanghai, Hong Kong, Singapore, Calcutta, Bombay, Suez, London – was the only one for several decades. Withey argues that this itinerary was taken because the scheduled routes of large steamships and railway companies were an immediate expression of Western influence in the Middle East and Asia: 'Most travellers hopped from one outpost of the British Empire to the next, with the American dominated Japanese ports, and, for the more adventurous, French Indochina, thrown in' (Withey 1997: 272). The speed that Cook could offer his clients on their journeys around the world was the product of a spatio-temporal order that was formed not only out of fast trains and ships, but also out of the political topography of colonialism. If world travellers were to visit countries like Japan and China at all, they saw little more than the ports, where they, in the wake of Cook, stayed in luxurious Western hotels, and paid attention primarily to the well-known sights, only to avoid contact with the often unpleasant local reality. As soon as one left the standard itinerary, the spatial and temporal order of transit changed radically. If one wanted to travel from the US to Australia or New Zealand, one had to sail to Honolulu, then wait for the first ship going south, which could take weeks. Despite Cook's many innovations, an unequivocally shrinking world remained out of the question.

Conclusion

It is now possible to speak about travel time in a different way than as the *duration* of a journey measured in clock time or as the abstract relation between space and time proposed by geographers such as Hägerstrand and Janelle. The B-series conception of time on which their explanations of the spatio-temporal order are founded is itself the result of a historical development, which has been described by Giddens and Harvey as 'time-space distanciation' and 'time-space compression'. This chapter has argued that these concepts, and the related topos of the 'annihilation of space through time' which dates from the mid nineteenth century, have an important drawback. Although they contextualize and historicize the relation between space and time in any given transit, in these accounts historical change is reduced to the invention and diffusion of the mechanical clock or the development of transportation and communication technologies.

To escape this reductionism, in this chapter I have argued that the technologies which Giddens and Harvey use to account for the separation of space and time – the mechanical clock, steamships and steam trains – had themselves to be made part of a network of innovations. If we consider these technologies not as spectators, as Goncharov did, but instead as actors, we are able to describe the *work* that formed these networks of innovations. The travel company of Thomas Cook can be credited with much of this work. As a heterogeneous engineer, Cook made passages. New means of transportation were not a sufficient precondition for Cook to offer his customers fast journeys. Enough travellers had to be mobilized to keep prices low; negotiations about the tariffs offered by different rail companies had to be made; arrangements had to be made with hotel and restaurant owners; place myths had to be invented; there had to be travel guides in which Cook's destinations were described; and Cook had to place employees all along the route to solve problems, making it possible for his passengers to continue travelling. As situated relations between time and space, the passages of Cook imply an order which contained material as well as immaterial entities. Cook's company tried to reduce the uncertainty and unpredictability of travelling, but a more exact gearing of the elements in the passage could also cause new contingencies. Travel time in Thomas Cook's day was measured with increasing precision, which left less room for slowness and contingency. The passages of Cook made it possible to travel faster, but not for everyone, and not to every imaginable place or at every moment.

Whereas a B-series notion of travel time abstracts from concrete transit practices and therefore creates a decontextualized notion of speed, the concept of 'passages' makes it possible to consider travel time as the *outcome* of these very transit practices. If we want to speak about mobility innovations in a language game that not only contains notions such as 'acceleration' or 'beaking', it is necessary to study how passages are created, maintained and justified in concrete practices of transit, and what their consequences are. Each of the following three chapters considers an aspect of the construction of passages.

4 Roadside wilderness

Introduction

The photograph in Figure 4.1 was taken in 1902 when cars were still a curiosity in the United States. It shows a man sitting behind the wheel of a Toledo on the edge of the Grand Canyon. There is no road in sight, nor any other sign of human civilization. How he got there is not clear, but the scene conveys an air of normality. It suggests that he simply got in his car and drove there, right to the edge, where he could look out over the vast canyon. His elevated gaze expresses control, power and individuality. In the first decades of the last century, countless Americans must have believed what this picture so vividly suggests: the car provides the freedom to go anywhere whenever you want. The great attraction of the car in the 1920s and 1930s was the idea that people could go places where the railroads could not take them, that they could choose not only their own itinerary, but their own tempo as well. Trains, which had once been praised for their reliability and speed, were now experienced as a coercive rather than a liberating means of transport. The first generation of car travellers considered the slow speed of their car as an advantage, because it enabled them to enjoy the landscape at ease and up close, instead of watching it rushing by from behind the windows of a speeding train. In 1907, the American writer Edith Wharton wrote that the car brought back 'the romance of travel' by 'freeing us from all the compulsions and contacts of the railway, the bondage to fixed hours and the beaten track, the approach to each town through an area of ugliness and desolation created by the railway itself' (cited in Withey 1997: 335).

In the United States, the transition from the train to the car took place in the first decades of the twentieth century (Belasco 1979; Belasco 1982; Goddard 1994). In 1910, American railroads still transported more than one billion people each year. Twenty years later, one out of every two Americans owned a car, and the railroads' share of the total number of kilometres travelled had fallen sharply. By 1930, the car had become the dominant means of transport, not only in, but also between, cities, at the expense of public transport by train, electric tramways and the subway.[1]

Figure 4.1 Photograph of a man in a Toledo parked at the edge of the Grand Canyon, Arizona, 1902 (source: Belasco 1979: 9).

The relatively short timespan in which this transition took place is often explained by reference to the qualities of car travel that the first generation of American motorists preferred: freedom and flexibility, not only in a geographical sense but in a temporal sense as well.[2] From the actor's perspective of the innovator, it is not obvious that we can view this complex development as a transition from one means of transport to another. This chapter argues that the individual freedom and flexibility in movement that car travel engendered should not be taken as an *explanation* for the changing practices of travel in the first half of the twentieth century in the United States, but, on the contrary, they should be analysed as the *outcome* of complex and interwoven practices of spatio-temporal ordering. To understand travel flexibility both geographically and temporally, one has to study the practical achievements in finding design solutions to problems that had to be solved in order to create 'flow'.

The chapter has three parts. It begins by exploring the character of American passages through the tension between standardization and contingency which characterized perceptions of car travel in the 1920s and 1930s, and the subsequent development of standardized roads and road services. It will then reconstruct how these standardized passages were linked to the quintessential American tourist destinations of that period, the national parks. In examining this association, it will become clear that journey and destination cannot be separated; the design of the national parks has always been related to the passages that made them accessible. Finally, the chapter will analyse the way that design problems created by the steadily increasing number of visitors to the parks were solved by the National Park Service's Mission 66 programme, which lasted from 1956 to 1966.

American passages

In the previous chapter, I reconstructed the perspective of Thomas Cook, who created new passages for his customers by innovating travel practices. In this chapter one central 'heterogeneous engineer' is lacking, and I therefore introduce the actor's perspective in a different way. As a thought experiment, one could think of creating new American passages as one big imaginary design commission. What had to change in order to render a destination's accessibility almost immediate in the way that American car drivers desired? In order to answer that question, I elaborate on the conditions that must be fulfilled if one wants to make a long-distance car journey: owning a car, having good roads and being able to refuel your vehicle, eat something and stay some place for the night.

Fordism

To drive in a car, as the early car traveller shown in Figure 4.1 did to get to the edge of the Grand Canyon, people must be able to afford one. In popular accounts of the history of American automobility, Henry Ford is usually credited as helping achieve this goal for most Americans.[3] Until Ford introduced the conveyor belt in car manufacturing in 1913–1914, cars were made in more or less the same way on both sides of the Atlantic Ocean. Highly skilled mechanics put cars together from a range of parts. They worked for a long time on a single car which is why the price was relatively high. All this changed in 1910 when Ford opened his Highland Park plant in Detroit, itself an impressive example of modern industrial technique, although having more than one storey made it unsuitable for conveyor belts (Flink 1990: 48). After a restructuring of the factory in 1913, moving assembly lines were introduced and an increasing number of car parts were built on these lines. When the supply of the assembly lines threatened to deluge the end assembly, a moving belt was built for the chassis. The time it cost to put together a chassis was reduced from twelve and a half hours to two hours and forty minutes. The principle of the assembly line was perfected in the Ford River Rouge plant, located along the Rouge River west of Detroit, which opened its doors in 1916.

Ford's rationalizing and standardizing of car production led to lower prices and increased sales, which meant that a growing number of Americans could afford to own a car. The greatest diffusion of automobiles in the United States took place between 1912 and 1923, when the number of motor vehicles went from one million to 13 million (Vance 1986: 499). In 1923, half of American households owned a car and President Warren Harding declared that 'the motor car has become an indispensable instrument in our political, social, and industrial life' (Ling 1990: 125). In the same year, *National Geographic* published a special edition about the car industry, in which it was calculated that, if all 13 million cars already on American roads were lined up, single-file on the Lincoln Highway, which stretches across the country from the Hudson River to the Golden Gate Bridge, it would consist of five rows (Schlesinger and Israel 1999: 2).

Fordist production is an important explanation of the quick diffusion of cars in the United States in the early twentieth century. But Ling (1990) argues that cultural and political developments also played important roles. Many American travellers disliked the big railway companies because, in their attempts to monopolize regional routes, they focused too much on their own interests rather than on the needs of their customers.[4] Between 1910 and 1920, Ling argues that the influential Progressives, an expanding group of young, middle-class, well-educated men, came to see to the car as a means of solving the problems of the city. Cars allowed urban dwellers to live outside the city, which reduced the population density in city centres that was believed to have led to both poverty and slums. Thus the car transformed not only the city, but the countryside as well when it became an indispensable part of daily life (Berger 1979; Kline and Pinch 1996). But for many country dwellers, the end of spatial isolation also meant the end of trusted values and social institutions. Local, closely knit communities gave way to more businesslike ways of cooperation. Even in the early 1920s, in many rural areas, a car was seen as a necessity rather than a luxury (Berger 1979: 215).

Driving on the open road

Cars needed roads to drive on. An important counterforce to the diffusion and use of cars in the 1910s and 1920s was the bad state of the roads. As in many European countries, responsibility for maintaining roads in the US lay with the local and regional governments. The maintenance of roads was seen as a chore, and few through roads existed. If one wanted to travel longer distances, the train remained the only option. While lobbying for the improvement of dirt roads began in the late 1800s by cyclists (Vance 1986: 497), by the 1910s, what had become known as the Good Roads Movement had gained political momentum when the owners of new Ford automobiles discovered they could hardly go anywhere without getting stuck in the mud:

Touring in an open car, with meager springs and little padding, on rough roads was an arduous, bumpy, drafty ordeal. All early accounts detail the trials of soft mud, tortuous mountain rocks and grades, perpetual dust, lost directions, and mechanical breakdowns.

(Belasco 1979: 30)

Apart from car owners, it was the car makers who, by organizing testing journeys over long distances for their new models, told politicians about the bad state of the roads. Then city governments began to argue for better roads. Restoring and improving regional roads with federal monies became the tried and true way of winning the people's vote. Huey Long, the governor of Louisiana, exemplified how a policy to build new roads could win elections (Patton 1986).

In 1913, the Lincoln Highway, the first through road running coast to coast was opened, connecting New York and San Francisco (Hokanson 1999). In 1916, the Federal Aid Road Act was passed and, shortly after World War I, the federal government began providing funds to improve regional and interregional roads. From the early 1920s on, more and more local and regional roads were chosen to be part of a nationwide network of through highways.[5] Making these regional highways into through roads which traversed the country, however, required the introduction of uniformity. To achieve this, all the regional roads which formed a through road were given one route number. All north–south through roads were given uneven route numbers, which spanned from U.S. Route 1, which ran along the Atlantic coast, to U.S. Route 101, which ran along the Pacific coast. Even numbers designated east–west roads, which began with U.S. Route 2, from the eastern Canadian border to Seattle and end with U.S. Route 98, which ran between Florida and southern California.[6]

Vance (1986) divides the development of American roads into five phases, the last of which spans the period when the US Interstate highways were constructed, which lasted from 1954, when President Eisenhower made public the first plans, to 1991, when the system was completed. The history of the American Interstates can be viewed as a process of standardization over very large distances. Their design and construction was largely an affair of the federal government, which financed more than 90 per cent of the construction costs. The federal government framed the design specifications and decided that they should be the same all over the country. Shortly after Eisenhower signed the bill legislating the construction of the Interstate, the Bureau of Public Roads, the predecessor to the Federal Highway Administration, and the American Association of State Highway and Transportation Officials, determined the design standards that would be used. The aim of these was to ensure that the Interstates would be safe and have a 'pleasing appearance' (Lewis 1997: 136).

The design of the standardized route sign that would designate Interstate highways was discussed for more than a year. More than 100 different designs were proposed, including circles, triangles and squares and the contour of the US, until finally the 'federal shield' in three colours was decided upon (Ibid.). The numbering of the Interstates reversed the system that had been used to number the through highways in the 1916 Federal Aid Road Act. North–south Interstates would have odd numbers that ascended from west to east, where Interstate 5 followed the west coast and 95 the east. East–west Interstates got even numbers, with 90 crossing the nation at the top and 10 at the bottom. If choosing a logo and a numbering system for the Interstates proved difficult, deciding on what colour the road signs should be was even more involved. Members of the American Association of State Highway and Transportation Officials recommended a universal system of white letters on a green background. But the new federal highway administrator, Bertram Tallamy, preferred white letters on a blue background. The conflict was resolved by constructing a three-mile-long test road down which 100 motorists were asked to drive 60 miles per hour. They drove past three road signs with the text *Metropolis Utopia EXIT 2 MILES*. A total of 85 per cent of the drivers chose the green signs and Tallamy had to swallow his words (Ibid.: 137).

The US Interstate Highway System was designed as a homogeneous network of roads running over enormous distances.[7] Anyone who understood a road sign in one place could understand them anywhere along the Interstate. In the change from local roads at the beginning of the century and the local and interregional highways during the 1920s and 1930s, to the Interstate Highway System begun in the 1950s, the geographically unique identity of roads gradually gave way to an identity that was based on the national network of which they were a part.

Fill 'er up

Once on the road, drivers must be able to refill their tanks. Together with drive-in restaurants and motels, the gas station became an icon of American roadside culture. The gas station quickly became part of the mystique of the unbridled personal freedom created by the car.[8] At the gas station motorists could refill their tanks and continue their journey. In his 1944 history of the motor age in America, David L. Cohn suggestively phrases the sense of freedom refuelling could give car drivers:

> 'Fill 'er up?' is a thoroughly American phrase. It suggests endless abundance and open-handedness. It is characteristic of a continental people whose life is geared to the car – a free-and-easy people to whom mobility is of the essence of living. ('Look for us next Sunday, Bill. We ought to get there by dinner time. It ain't over two hundred miles.') It is a phrase that could have been invented by no other people.
>
> (Cohn 1944: 263)

In the first half of the twentieth century, the American gas station developed into one of the first places of standardized consumption. Oil companies like Standard Oil, Gulf and Mobil commissioned architects like Frank Lloyd Wright, Walter Dorwin Teague and Norman Bel Geddes to design gas stations that could be built in large numbers. Not only was the architecture of their gas stations standardized, but their logos could be seen all across the country – an orange disc, a flying horse or a dinosaur. Every detail was aimed at gaining immediate recognition from the road by motorists who had come from afar (Wilson 1992: 33). In their study of the American gas station, Jakle and Sculle (1994) investigated the ways in which oil companies developed the marketing strategy of 'place-product-packaging'. Central to this strategy was the idea that services had to be standardized in space and time. Symbols, logos and standardized images were used to indicate to travellers that a specific place was connected to a specific product. This marketing strategy, first applied to gas stations in the 1910s, was later adopted by fast-food restaurants and motel chains. The standardization of roadside commerce became so pervasive that some critics feared its continuation would result in a 'placelessness' which would make it impossible to distinguish localities from each other (Jakle and Sculle 1994: 19–20; Kunstler 1994).

Oil companies had other strategies to attract customers as well: for example, issuing road maps that emphasized not the sameness of locations, but their geographical differences. Introduced in the 1910s, these road maps not only provided the practical information necessary for drivers to orientate themselves and find the right road in an unknown part of the country but, from the 1930s onwards, they also encouraged motorists to discover America by car. Yorke and Margolies (1996) have reconstructed the history of American car travel from early US road maps. Maps from the 1920s often showed a man and woman driving through the country-side together under an orange sun – the Gulf logo. A 1927 map issued by Standard Oil depicted the motorist as a pioneer travelling to new territory in a covered wagon. In the 1930s, the covers of road maps used dynamic lines as visual signs of speed and energy. Also in this decade, map covers featured a woman alone behind the wheel for the first time. The gas station on these maps was depicted as a safe and friendly haven for the female driver. In the 1950s, they began to show the natural beauty of the American landscape. Pictures of popular national parks, such as Yosemite National Park in California, showed a patriotic image of the nation while encouraging car drivers to hit the road again after wartime gasoline rationing was over.

Drive-ins

Like the gas station, the drive-in restaurant underwent a process of standardization and franchising. In the 1920s, restaurants like the Pig Stand began to appear on highway edges. Its founder, J. G. Kirkby, a business-man from Dallas, Texas, was the first to serve people meals *in* their cars. He got the idea when he realized that 'people in cars are so lazy that they don't want to come out of them to eat' (Heimann 1996: 14). The predecessors of the first highway restaurants were roadside stands. Car drivers could pull over and eat at roadside stands, but they had to get out of their cars, which meant a delay. Other entrepreneurs followed the Pig Stand's example and invented new ways to get the food from the kitchen to their mobile customers. Because drivers could remain in their seats in their often open cars, the Pig Stands and their competitors were especially popular in the more sunny parts of America, notably California and Texas.

These initial car restaurants also used standardized designs for their stands, such as the hexagon structure of the first Pig Stands, which was followed by circular designs. To attract the attention of the car drivers, these restaurants placed large signs along the road – signs that were to have the same function as the standardized logos used by the oil companies. Uniformity in the restaurants' appearance was not the only goal. The menus were also designed to be uniform in each location. This enabled customers to be sure they knew what to expect at each restaurant. But standardizing the menus also reduced the amount of time needed to prepare the meals. The Pig Stand became a success with its Coca-Cola, roasted pig meat and ham sandwich combination. Other popular items on the menu were hamburgers, hot dogs, 'homemade' pies, ice cream and regional specialities like chili, tacos and pizzas (Ibid.: 22).

Drive-ins became a beacon for hurried and hungry motorists who did not want to spend the time needed to get out of the car to eat, but preferred to be served by 'car hops' – young women dressed as walking trademarks – who brought their meals to their cars. It was on the elimination of the car hop – the human chain that linked the driver to the restaurant – that the McDonald brothers, who had opened their first restaurant in 1937 in California, based their new roadside restaurant design in 1948. The McDonald brothers calculated that the process of producing meals could be rationalized, and thus speeded up, if car drivers were willing to leave their cars and get their hamburgers inside. 'A production line preparing the reasonably priced ten-cent burgers, fifteen-cent French fries and twenty-cent malts was installed, with paper replacing dishes and fingers replacing silverware. The meal was bagged in a speedy twenty seconds' (Ibid.: 114). Other innovations included a new kitchen layout with steel furniture that could be cleaned easily, the preparation of food in advance and a new division of labour based on carefully synchronized teamwork (Clark and Staunton 1989: 96).

By 1952, the McDonald brothers had sold their first million hamburgers. Two years later, they hired Ray Kroc to transform their restaurants into a national chain and, in 1961, Kroc bought the chain. The McDonalds' idea of luring drivers back inside, however, was taken over by other restaurants so quickly that, by the 1960s, the last authentic drive-ins had disappeared. Roadside restaurants switched to fast-food, self-service or take-home meals. Service inside the car did not return until the 1970s, when the drive-thru service was developed, a logistic strategy in which the motorist orders at the beginning of a special car lane and collects his meal at a window at the end of the lane.[9]

Home away from home

In his detailed history of American camping by car, Belasco (1979) describes the rise of 'Auto Camps' in the 1920s, and the emergence of a new travel industry centred around 'motels', which spanned the period between 1910 and 1945. In the 1910s, hundreds of thousands of middle-class families travelled through the country, camping alongside the road, every night in a different place, cooking over a wood fire and sleeping in their car or tent. Some described this new practice of travel as 'gypsying', a romantically coloured rediscovery of true travel after trains had come to symbolize standardized transit with regular timetables and fixed routes.[10] Car campers opposed what Belasco calls the 'monopolistic rail-hotel complex', and liked to compare their car with the old fashioned stage-coach.

According to Belasco, the growing number of car campers led to problems for the small towns and regions they visited. Car campers littered the roads, quarrelled with the locals and became ill from drinking polluted water. By 1920, local communities started to limit auto camping to special, free 'auto camps' to counter these problems. Many car campers welcomed the convenience of official campgrounds. Camping out in the open was by comparison uncomfortable and time-consuming. To compete with the rising demand for campgrounds, municipalities began to offer ones with facilities such as electric light, hot showers and central kitchens. The shift to commercially orientated auto campgrounds became solidified when these extra facilities became too expensive and free campgrounds attracted unwanted visitors, such as road tramps, looking for a place to stay for the night. The motel industry was born, Belasco argues, in 1925 when commercial campgrounds began offering more and better services. They offered 'cabins' for tourists who wanted more luxury and comfort, with towels, sheets, heaters and even water pipes. By the 1930s, former hotel owners improved the service even further in their 'cottage camps' (Belasco 1979: 4).

Jakle, Sculle and Rogers (1996) describe the rise of the American motel industry as crucially dependent upon franchising chains, place-product packaging and standardization. The relatively benign term 'motel' – first used in 1927 by Arthur Heineman, the originator of the Milestone Mo-Tel in San Luis Obispo, California – was only one of many names, such as Motor Court and Cottages, Tour-o-tel, Trav-o-tel and Plaza Court to remain in use by the 1950s. The motel's distinct architecture and spatial layout developed out of the anarchistic auto camps, and included the familiar criss-cross pattern of cabins and the U- and L-formed buildings, both of which enabled visitors to park their car in front of their room (Jakle, Sculle and Rogers 1996: 36).

In the years following World War II, the basic logic of the architecture could be seen in more and more places. In 1952 the first Holiday Inn Hotel Court was opened in Memphis, Tennessee.[11] Kemmons Wilson had discovered during a vacation journey the previous year that many places lacked convenient and cheap accommodation. He started a motel chain based on the principle of franchising with Wallace E. Johnson, who produced prefabricated houses. Entrepreneurs who joined the new chain were allowed to use the Holiday Inn logo, enabling them to profit from national advertising campaigns (Flink 1990: 304). The architecture of Holiday Inn motels was regulated by strict specifications. Both the shape (the L- or U-form), the number of storeys (two), the location of the swimming pool and the office, and even the thickness of the walls between the rooms were standardized. Holiday Inn also standardized its 'room-geography', which meant that when a traveller entered a room, he or she could be sure that they would look more or less the same. The position of the luggage rack, the size of the drawers and the layout of the bedroom and bathroom were fixed (Jakle, Sculle and Rogers 1996: 270). Just as important as the motel's design was its location along the road and which road was chosen. Howard Johnson instigated special standardized criteria in which regional commuter patterns, traffic censuses and the distances to major nearby destinations, known as 'draws', were specified. This ensured the motel's recognizability from the road. Motel owners were anxious to find out the proposed routes of new highways in order to buy land near exits. Franchising local motels and using prefabricated structures to build new motels added to the industry's standardization. Margolies (1995) argues that this minimized the effect of unpredictability that travelling over great distances had generated. The use of well-known logos and trademarks, smooth access from highways, and predictable designs and layouts pointed the way to a 'home away from home'.

Making miles

For the first generation of American motorists, travelling by car over long distances had been an adventure. Motorists had no idea what they would encounter on the road. When travelling by car, they had to develop the knowledge and skills to solve various problems that might arise while underway. Technically, cars were still far from perfect and often broke down. Roads were in notoriously bad condition, and there are many photographs of T-Fords standing up to their axles in mud. Road signs designated local destinations. Places to buy gasoline or to eat and sleep were scarce, and car travellers had to make detours to find them. In other words, to get anywhere, the first car travellers had to do a lot of work. It was not without reason that they saw themselves as explorers and felt like the pioneers who had gone west in previous decades. The ability of motorists to solve problems resonated with the ideals of self-reliance and individuality formulated in the nineteenth-century Transcendentalist philosophies of Ralph Waldo Emerson and Henry David Thoreau.[12] Motorists travelled differently from train passengers. They saw it as an advantage that they sometimes did not cover more than 20 miles in an hour. The slow pace gave them enough time to see the details of the landscape.

In the 1920s, when the number of cars on the road rose quickly and a national network of through highways was built, car travel changed. As Belasco (1979) has shown, instead of slowly meandering through the country, motorists became obsessed with the idea of covering as many miles as possible, from which the popular phrase 'making miles' came. A car camper in the 1920s wondered why making miles had become an obsession:

We have vowed to curb this impulse. Just why a person should travel miles to see Niagara Falls only to remain about one hour and fail to get a full appreciation of this wonder of nature, is more than I can understand. Yet we have all been guilty of this very thing.

(cited in Belasco 1979: 87)

From the 1920s on, the unpredictability of travel caused by unreliable cars and bad roads was increasingly seen as a discomfort rather than as part of the adventure. Besides new roadside facilities such as gas stations, drive-in restaurants, which sold simple and affordable food, and numerous campgrounds and motels made it possible to stay on the road longer and cover more miles.

As a 'heterogeneous engineer', Thomas Cook was able to offer his customers fast and reliable passages because he 'negotiated' between the elements that formed their spatio-temporal order. But the American motorist no longer needed Cook. Where the British travel agent synchronized connections, selected hotels, offered traveller's cheques and had employees all over the world ready to help in case something unexpected arose, in the United States, the unpredictability of car travel was reduced by the uniformity of and connections between all entities in the passage. Instead of *the Man from Cook's* there to point the way and answer questions, motorists could rely on the logic of the standardized networks of roads and accompanying facilities. These made car travellers more independent than ever. They did not have to buy train tickets because they owned a car. They did not have to make reservations in luxury hotels because they could stay in motels along the road. They no longer ate at restaurants which required a change of clothes for dinner, but went to drive-ins where the food was prepared as quickly as possible and could be consumed without even leaving the car. Standardizing the elements in the passage made it possible for car travellers to *anticipate* what they would encounter on the road. They could, so to speak, 'travel forward in time'. Increasingly, the sense of adventure that had characterized the first years of car travel was giving way to a shared expectation of being 'on the road'.

Standardization in American passages has two meanings. In the first sense, standardization refers to the infrastructure which makes entities within passages equal and attuned to each other. The road signs on the highway and Interstates, the oil company logos on gas stations, the taste of hamburgers and the layout of motel rooms all removed differences in the ordering of passages. In the second sense, standardization refers to the connections between entities in the passage that make the 'flow' of cars possible. In 1910, hotels were not very well equipped to answer the needs of the first car travellers. They were situated in city centres, close to railway stations to accommodate train travellers. They maintained unwritten dress codes that were hardly conducive to the practice of driving a long day on dusty roads. They were not directly connected to roads for cars. Likewise, train travellers were little helped by a motel built near a town's access road. Standardized networks of roads reduced the friction of muddy roads, and motorists could continue driving without having to solve problems constantly. The American car traveller could experience the uniformity and interconnectedness between the different elements in passage as a 'flow'.

It is important to note here that standardization cannot only be understood in its spatial effects, but also in its temporal consequences. When roads, gas stations, restaurants and motels were made interconnected, the span of time during which motorists used these facilities was standardized as well. Old-style city hotels were equipped to host people for weeks, if necessary, whereas motels were designed to provide just a night's accommodation for most motorists. Better roads, road maps and road signs made it possible to find a destination without having to search for it, or ask people where to go, and thus helped to standardize travel time between destinations. In terms of the temporal ordering, the production of hamburgers at McDonald's was analogous to Ford's conveyor belt. The time it took to prepare a meal was standardized to the time it took to eat it. These modern American passages led to new ways to use and experience time on the road, a time practice that cannot be characterized simply in terms of faster or slower transit speed, or even in terms of the experience of 'making miles'. New temporal orders emerged as a result of these couplings and interconnections. The forced tempo of train travel was replaced by a new type of forced tempo produced by the interplay of temporal orders that resulted from the standardization of entities in different domains. When 'on the road', time became as monotonous as the road on which one travelled.

The standardization of passages in both senses made it possible for motorists to anticipate problems that arose while on the road, and thereby to create 'flow'. But it also led to new tensions. As the contingencies and frictions of car travel that the first motorists sought disappeared, car travel became less of an adventure. Motorists knew precisely what to expect from a Standard Oil gas station, a McDonald's drive-in restaurant and a Howard Johnson motel. How then did the myth of the adventurous 'open road' survive? I argue that new travel myths appeared which can be understood as analogous to how place myths function culturally. Shields (1991) argues that place myths act as guiding metaphors which provide '*a set of rules of conduct and procedure* for practices and regimes of thought' (Shields 1991: 256). The standardized emblems, logos and icons, and free road maps that customers could get at gas stations not only helped guide car travellers to their destination, they also helped create new representations of self-reliance and adventure that were characteristic of early motoring. The road signs which identified all 1,926 state highways – white shields with black numbers – became a powerful cultural icon, which can still be seen in the example of the mythologized Route 66 (Wallis 1993). In the 1940 film *The grapes of wrath*, the Oklahoma farmers heading west for work viewed the road shield as a symbol of their hope of a better life at the end of the road in California. Not only road shields, but also drive-in restaurants and the motels stood as powerful emblems of a mobile lifestyle which has been depicted in countless 'road movies' (Eyerman and Löfgren 1995; Cohan and Hark 1997).

This tension between 'flow' and 'myth' or, to put it differently, between standardization and identity, is not only characteristic of American passages, but also for the destinations that such passages made accessible. When 'being on the road' hardly felt like an adventure, and when reaching a destination as quickly as possible was all that counted, it became even more important that the destination was adventurous. The archetypal destinations in the United States – the national parks – owe their very existence to their unique character. But how could the parks be designed as adventurous and foreign destinations, and still be connected to the passages which made them accessible? This was the design problem that the National Park Service faced after its foundation in 1916.

Designing the national parks

One of the most striking features of the national parks in Arizona, Colorado and other western US states for a first-time European visitor is the contrast between the desolation of places like the Grand Canyon, Zion National Park and Bryce Canyon, and the easy, almost casual way in which these places have been made accessible to visitors. Well-maintained and easy roads bring the visitor to the entrance gate, where a park ranger hands out a map that shows the roads, trails and sights. Here, accessibility is not only a matter of physically transporting people into the park, but also of offering ways to see and interpret the landscape once inside it. Every park has a visitor centre that offers practical facilities as well as many visual representations of what is to be seen outdoors. For example, in Zion National Park, a special place is marked where visitors can stand if they want to make a copy of the well-known photograph of the famous cliff, White Throne. After parking their cars in one of the many parking lots, visitors will find clearly marked trails that lead those wanting to see nature on foot into the backcountry. In the parks, nature has been carefully staged to give the visitor the experience of unspoiled wilderness.

National parks as travel destinations

From the moment the United States Congress established Yellowstone Park in 1872 as the world's first 'national park', the design, use and management of American national parks has been intertwined with the transit practices that make these often remote wilderness areas accessible. Popular accounts of Yellowstone claim that the idea for the park originated during a discussion among a group of explorers who were sitting around a campfire in 1870. Instead of allowing the area to be used for private purposes, they argued that the landscape should be preserved as a public park. But as Alfred Runte claims, although politicians quickly adopted their proposal and signed it into law, their motivation was not as altruistic as it may have at first appeared. At the time, the Northern Pacific Railroad and its financier Jay Cooke were planning to extend the railroad's tracks west from the Dakota area to Montana. Completion of the extension would make Yellowstone 'speedily accessible' to tourists, giving them a monopoly over tourist traffic in the region (Runte 1990: 17).

A 'pragmatic alliance' (Runte 1990) between upper class preservationists and western railroad moguls, eager to boost passenger traffic, constituted the foundation of almost all the national parks that were created in the first half of the twentieth century. Railroads were not only crucial in winning congressional support for new parks, like Glacier National Park in Montana, they also led the way in the building of many tourist facilities, including big, luxurious hotels. Initially, travel to the national parks was long, and the first roads through the parks so difficult and arduous that visitors usually remained in them for a long time. As a consequence, hotels and other tourist facilities were usually built within their boundaries.

In 1900, the idea to set aside land for national parks had to be defended against other forms of exploitation, notably the extraction of valuable resources like wood. The arguments offered in defence of the parks were often made in economic terms: the parks would be long-term 'magnets for tourist dollars'. The 'See America First' ad campaign at the beginning of the twentieth century urged wealthy American tourists to spend their money in the United States rather than in Europe. Another reason to make the nature in the parks accessible was that visitors were also voters, and politicians believed they could win more of their constituency's support by protecting the parks. The National Park Service was established on 25 August 1916 to regulate the national parks and national monuments under a directive

> to conserve the scenery and the natural and historical objects and the wildlife therein and to provide for the enjoyment of the same in such manner and by such means as will leave them unimpaired for future generations.

This directive presented the service with a dilemma between park use and conservation, the choice between conservation and use that recurred throughout its history.

Parks are for people-in-automobiles

For Stephen Mather, who became the first director of the National Park Service in 1917, it was clear that the railroads would be replaced by cars as the chief means of transport to and within the parks. He forged what Flink (1990) calls a second 'pragmatic alliance' between the park service and organizations that represented the interests of car drivers and the automobile industry. Mather welcomed cars in the parks. He recognized the political power of car manufacturers, the American Automobile Association, and the growing number of tourists. He was convinced that broad public support was indispensable in obtaining the tax revenues necessary to create and maintain the parks, and for creating a counterforce to the increasing pressure of private companies and government agencies to exploit the parks' natural resources for commercial purposes (Flink 1990: 172).[13] It was the conservationist and former park ranger, Edward Abbey, who captured the spirit of this policy in 1968 by rephrasing the well-known park service slogan 'Parks are for people' to 'Parks are for people-in-automobiles' (Ibid.: 173).

The Federal Highway Act passed in 1921 and the institution of gasoline tax in 1919 enabled state and federal governments to build and maintain a network of new roads by 1929.[14] The new roads made even the most remote parks in the western United States accessible for visitors travelling from the east. The National Parks Highways Association had outlined and marked a route connecting all the national parks. Stephen Mather, the director of the National Park Service viewed the Park-to-Park Highway, which consisted of 6,000 miles of state and local roads, as an important means of turning the western national parks into a coherent and modern park system. 'Connecting the parks, as well as managing them all according to consistent policies, were essential steps in transforming the federal scenic reservations into a modern park system' (Carr 1998: 147).

Cars and roads brought people to the parks, thus transforming the parks into popular destinations for American holiday travellers. This development also influenced the designs of the park service's landscape architects. The National Park Service's use of architects underlines the continuity between large city parks, such as Central Park in New York, designed by Frederic Law Olmstedt in 1870, and the national parks. Both city parks and national parks were carefully designed places where people could recover from the stress of modern life. Whereas city parks had been designed to bring nature to city dwellers, the establishment of national parks made it possible for city dwellers to take their cars to nature.

Mather believed incorporating park villages, buildings, roads and walking routes into the surrounding landscape was the most important aim of landscape design. '[V]ista thinning, locating trails and roads, screening objectionable views, placing utility wiring underground, and improving the campgrounds were important tasks carried out by landscape engineers' (McClelland 1997: 162). In the 1920s and 1930s, the national parks' design followed what was known as a rustic style, which sought to minimize the visual impact of built objects in the parks by using materials from the surrounding landscape, thereby harmonizing handrails, vista points, bridges and built structures such as museums with the nature surrounding these manmade objects.[15]

The need to harmonize built structures in the parks with the natural world created a dilemma for landscape designers and park engineers. On the one hand, they saw it as their duty to remove dangerous curves, sharp bends in the road and steep inclines, which are characteristic of mountainous roads. Car drivers wanted to drive safely and comfortably, and drivers in the parks were no exception. On the other hand, park roads had to be built in such a way that their disturbing influence on the surrounding wilderness was minimized. Roads had to have curves that 'flowed with and lay lightly on the land'.[16] In the 1920s, the principles of road construction in parks were still strongly influenced by the ideas which the garden designer and horticulturalist, Andrew Jackson Downing, had formulated in the nineteenth century. One of these was to make circular drives in gardens and parks. National park designers adopted this principle in building loop roads in parks, such as Yellowstone's Grand Loop, which create flow by enabling the circular movement of vehicles through the parks. The loop roads fit the needs of national park designers to create 'flow' through the parks so well, that they emerged at every level, from the park as a whole to campgrounds, as a means to control traffic (Ibid.: 178).

Between 1933 and 1940 the National Park Service received 220 million dollars from several New Deal institutions. These funds were used mainly to rebuild and repave park roads, and to construct impressive 'scenic roads', such as the Zion–Mount Carmel Road and Tunnel, the Wawona Tunnel and Road in Yosemite and the Going-To-The-Sun Highway in Glacier National Park. These roads featured vista points, traffic signs, road signs, softened curves, parking lots and new plants and trees that helped to embed them into the surrounding landscape. As Carr put it, these features were 'intermediary landscapes', carefully designed to mediate between the American car tourist and the nature of the national parks (Carr 1998: 92).[17] Such intermediary landscapes were the product of a culture that valued the car as a means of getting everywhere and of preserving unspoiled nature as an icon of a powerful national identity closely linked to the ideals of freedom and individuality.

Mission 66

The strategies used to create access to the national parks for motorists did not remain without consequences. After World War II, easy access to the parks was increasingly seen as threatening the parks' existence. Between 1947 and 1957 the number of cars in the United States rose from 37 million to 67 million (Vance 1986: 499), mirroring the postwar prosperity of the American middle class. The combination of higher incomes, higher standards of living, more leisure time and an increased mobility led to sharply growing numbers of visitors to the national parks, which had become popular, 'democratic' holiday destinations.[18] In 1955, a total of 55 million people visited the parks. During the same period, the amount of tax money the federal government spent on them decreased. Reacting to the growing unease about the deterioration of the park system, the journalist and outspoken conservationist, Bernard De Voto, argued in a 1953 *Harper's Magazine* article that parks like Yosemite and Yellowstone should be closed.[19] More critical articles appeared over the next couple of years, in which some authors suggested spending more money on 'our crumbling parks' while others emphasized the importance of improving the facilities in 'the country's shrines'.[20]

Conrad Wirth, who became the National Park Service's director in 1955, claimed that 'the public [was] loving the parks to death' (cited in Sellars 1997: 181), and saw it as his main task to solve this problem. In his autobiography, Wirth recounted how one Saturday evening in February 1955 he got the idea of how this could be done. Instead of focusing on annual budgets for maintenance and exploitation which could easily be cut, he thought the National Park Service should develop a 10-year plan which Congress should accept as a package (Wirth 1980: 239). The following Monday morning, Wirth set up two committees to make plans for what he called Mission 66, a name which expressed a sense of mission as well as pointed to the year 1966, when the National Park Service would celebrate its 50th anniversary. The committees asked all national parks to make an inventory of the problems they faced and to estimate the extra costs they would need to solve them.

Following a year of preparatory investigations and planning, Mission 66 was presented to President Dwight D. Eisenhower on 27 January 1956 during a Cabinet meeting. After Eisenhower responded positively, the project was officially launched during the second 'Pioneer Dinner' held on 8 February 1956 in Washington, DC.[21] More than 700 guests attended, including members of Congress, senators, leaders of conservationist organizations, representatives of tourist organizations and staff of the many national and state parks. The dinner, which featured roasted buffalo meat from South Dakota, was hosted by the Home Secretary Douglas McKay and the American Automobile Association. The menu's cover showed three 'motoring pioneers' in Yosemite around 1900, an indication of the important role the car had played in the formation of the park system. In a table speech, Edwin S. Moore, member of the California State Automobile Association, proclaimed that

> Our interest in the national parks goes back to the beginning of the park system when we were successful in having the park areas opened to the motoring public. How do we preserve these areas and at the same time provide adequately for their use and enjoyment? This would seem somewhat of a contradiction. Nevertheless we think it can be done, and we think it must be done.[22]

In the brochure for Mission 66, called *Our Heritage*, the National Park Service emphasized the importance of the park system as a 'national resource' which greatly contributed to the American way of life and the national economy. The mission's main task was phrased as 'the National Parks are neither equipped nor staffed to protect their irreplaceable features, nor take care of the increasing millions of visitors' (NPS 1956: 5). The park service expected the number of visitors to increase from the then 50 million annually to 80 million by 1966. Mission 66 spelled out an eight-point plan for improving the parks, which included an increase in park staff, the improvement of staff facilities, land purchases to consolidate existing parks and create new ones, the reconstruction and improvement of park roads, and the building of *visitor centres*. Mission 66's task thus essentially entailed adapting the parks to the expected growth in the number of visitors, all of whom came by car, without irreparably damaging the nature inside the parks. An image from a 1956 issue of *Our Heritage* (Figure 4.2) clearly reflects Mission 66's plan.[23]

The tension between wilderness and access was not new in the history of the parks. Thomas Vint, the most important landscape architect for the park service from the 1930s to the 1950s, used the term 'wilderness' to designate an area where he wanted to prevent the construction of new roads in the parks. His master plans identified different 'zones' in the parks, each of which served a different function, such as 'wilderness', 'research', 'sacred' and 'developed'. Mission 66 stood in this tradition. The question of how zones should be qualified depended largely on whether cars should be allowed in them (Carr 1998: 197). There had to be good

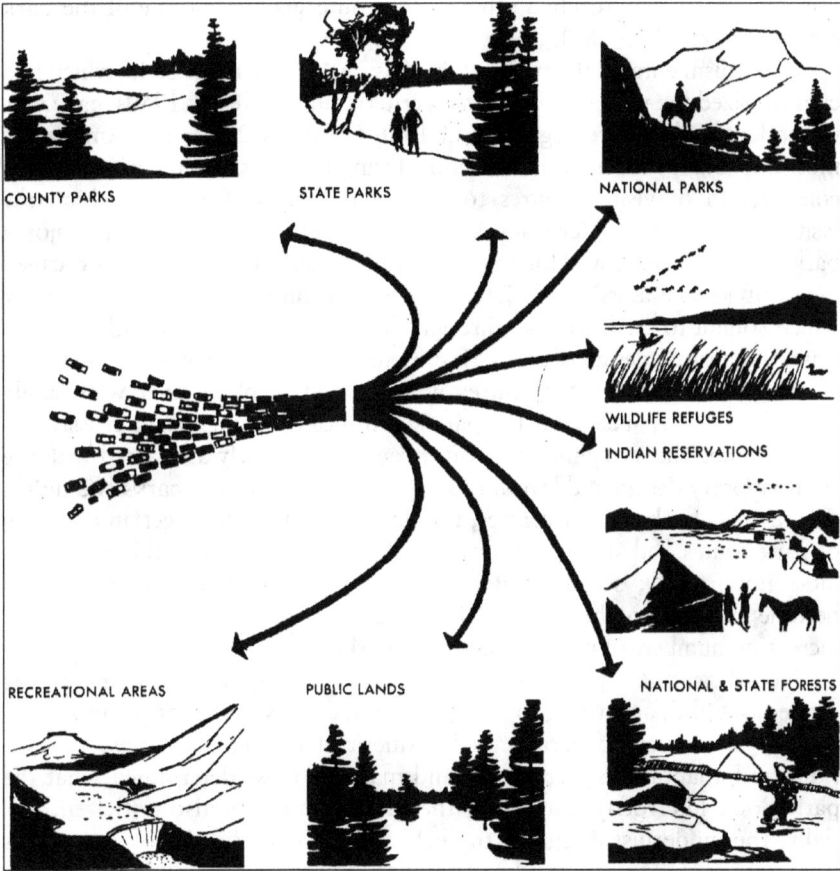

Figure 4.2 'Parks are for people-in-automobiles' (Edward Abbey in 1968). The image is taken from the NPS brochure *Our Heritage*, issued in 1956, and depicts one of the main tasks of Mission 66, accommodating cars in the parks (source: NPS 1956).

visitors' facilities to preserve the parks, which Lon Garrison, one of the Mission 66 managers, called the 'paradox of protection'. One of the central principles underlying the Mission 66 programme was the idea that the impact of large numbers of visitors could be regulated by making certain areas accessible through good roads, paths and other facilities. Building good facilities would not harm nature, but, on the contrary, protect it.[24] For Wirth and Garrison, the difference between 'roadside wilderness' and 'true wilderness' was not a matter of principle, but of organization. In one of the brochures published during the Mission 66 period, the park service used the expression 'accessible wilderness' for areas that could be reached after a 10-minute walk from one of the park roads (Sellars 1997: 187).

Modernism entered the parks with Mission 66. The rustic style, which had characterized the park service's design criteria until the early 1950s, gave way to modern architecture beginning in 1956 (Allaback 2000: 10). Among the most important modernist innovations during the Mission 66 period was the construction of visitor centres to replace museums. The idea behind the visitor centre was to offer visitors all the information they needed to enjoy a park in one place. It was for this reason that visitor centres were also called 'one stop service units' (Ibid.: 21). The visitor centres were part of a strategy which sought to guide visitors through the national parks efficiently. In contrast to the rustic design of the park museums, which were often located close to the main sights, visitor centres were located at places that were easily accessible by car, such as at the park's entrance or at important crossroads. The planning theory behind the visitor centre was closely associated with the contemporary design and layout of shopping malls, business parks and industrial areas.[25] In the visitor centres, tourists should be able to get an overview of park routes and sights, the location of different services, exhibitions and, most importantly, see an audiovisual presentation, a feature which had become popular in the 1950s. These were all ways to accommodate the increasing numbers of people visiting the parks.

The Mission 66 programme was active during the 10 years it was carried out and, according to Sellars (1997), counts as one of the most successful government programmes in American history. Countless innovations and adaptations were made and many of these determined what the parks look like today. However, the programme was also criticized. Initially, the modernist design of the new visitor centres and look-out points were attacked. During the 1960s, conservationists and wilderness advocates criticized the park management philosophies behind Mission 66 because they were considered a danger to the preservation of nature (Sellars 1997: 185). Some critics observed that the parks had been submitted to a process of 'urbanization'. An article which appeared in the *National Parks Magazine* stated that 'engineering has become more important than preservation, creating wide, modern roads similar to those found in state highway systems and visitor centres that looked like medium-sized airport terminals' (Ibid.: 186–187). A vivid example of the modernist design to come under fire is Clingman's Dome Tower, built in 1959 in Great Smoky Mountains National Park, located in the Appalachian mountains in North Carolina and Tennessee (see Figure 4.3). A paragon of modernist architecture of the period, its spiralled tower was hated by some, who considered it an intrusion into nature. Its concrete structure did not blend into the surroundings and was reminiscent of a highway ramp. The changing gaze of the visitor walking to the tower's top imitated the visual experience of driving on a parkway.

Figure 4.3 An artist's impression of Clingman's Dome Tower in Great Smoky Mountains National Park from the 1950s. The tower is still in use (source: McClelland 1997: 471).

Circulation and representation

Thomas Cook cultivated place myths about the Scottish Highlands by referring to Sir Walter Scott's novels. He was convinced that people reading these novels would want to see the rugged mountains with their own eyes once given the opportunity. But such stories are not only imma-terial elements that can be used to create passages; they are created in the act of travelling as well. Auto campers who met each other on the road exchanged stories about road conditions, repairs they had to make on their cars and the best places to stay. When travelling by car became easier and more predictable, not much could be said about it. The Interstate Highway System became a domain of boredom, fuelling the wish to reach destina-tions as quickly as possible. The destination had to be 'different' from the uniformity one experienced on the road, but it should nevertheless be con-nected to the 'flow' that was created by these standardized passages. To meet this double requirement, a different environment had to be con-structed between the highway and the wilderness, or in broader terms, between culture and nature. The results were hybrid landscapes that func-tioned as the 'middle landscapes' which Leo Marx has described as ones which bridge the technological and the pastoral ideals (Marx 1964).

Thus not only was the physical landscape redesigned in a modernist style, the *representation* of wilderness became increasingly designed as well. As Nye (1997) observes, in creating destinations like the national parks, there is always a combination of the techniques of transportation and representation. In claiming that there is no 'innocent eye', he emphasized that any site, however unspoiled it may seem, is viewed through the lens of a powerful visual culture (Nye 1997: 5). As already argued, both the ideas of the American park and landscape designers were influenced by nineteenth-century English landscape architecture in which the aesthetic, picturesque qualities of nature were foregrounded (Bunce 1994). In the 1920s and 1930s, the design of the parks was dominated by the visual rhetoric of the 'vista point'. Cars not only brought visitors to these look-out points but, if they drove through the parks in a car, the nineteenth-century landscape painting itself was set in motion. The tourist's gaze became dynamic: the landscape was projected as a film on the windscreen of the car. In the design of park roads and the parkways which led to them, which can be considered as a sort of extended national park, this film was directed down to the smallest of details.[26]

> [Landscape designers] designed curves that restricted speeds to thirty-five or forty miles an hour and placed those curves in a way that organized the long looks. Since the road follows mountain crests for most of its length, distant views tended to be views down over deep valleys and countless ranges receding into the blue distance.
>
> (Wilson 1992: 36)

It is no coincidence that during the era of Mission 66, park designers not only sought new designs for physical structures, but also new *representations* of wilderness. As explained above, the problem facing park designers was perceived in terms of how to create 'flow' inside the parks, thus preventing waves of new visitors which could harm nature. On a material level, the goal of quicker circulation was partly achieved by building modern visitor centres, look-out points and parking areas that were no longer judged according to the extent that they were 'embedded' in the surrounding landscape, but according to their efficiency in leading visitors to the main sites. This philosophy of what could be called 'democratic access' required fast circulation through the parks via the main sites. To achieve this goal, however, material innovations proved insufficient. The experience of being in parks had to be restyled. What was considered to be the unique character of a park or a place had to be expressed in stylized representations or images. For example, the clearer it was to visitors at Yosemite Valley where the most beautiful places were located, the easier their tour through the park would be, and the shorter their stay on the valley floor.[27]

During the Mission 66 era, the road became an important technique in directing the visitor's gaze as well as in organizing the sequential order and tempo in which the park sights followed each other. The loop roads ordered the landscape in clear spatio-temporal sequences in such a way that visitors were not so much directed into nature as to pass by it. In the 1958 *Handbook of Standards for National Parks and Parkway Roads*, the National Parks Services director Conrad Wirth explained that roads had become the 'principal facilities for presenting and interpreting the inspirational values of a park' (Patin 1999: 55–56). Just like the highways and roadside restaurants and motels, the National Park Service incorporated both a spatial and a temporal logic into the design of its parks. They bear a striking similarity to Disneyland, which opened in 1956 in Los Angeles, which was also the year that Mission 66 was launched. As Bryman (1995: 100) suggests, Disneyland's design was aimed at controlling and standardizing the movement of visitors into and through the theme park. Its spatial configuration, which featured Snow White's fairy-tale castle as an 'attention magnet' halfway through the park, led visitors from the park's entrance to its interior. Visitors were taken in small cars to each of the park's attractions, which enabled Disney to control the amount of time people spent on each one, which in turn made it possible to allow larger numbers of people into the park each day. Mission 66 park designers acknowledged that it would only be possible to direct the increasing numbers of visitors through the parks *and* to preserve nature by shortening the span of time that people spent in them. Walking through the parks, which can take several days, was the privilege of a very small minority – less than 1 per cent of visitors. The majority spent much less time. A recent study has found that the average time a tourist stayed in parks has decreased from several days 100 years ago to less than 12 hours in 1990.[28] For example, at the South Rim of the Grand Canyon visitors spent on average less than four hours.

Figure 4.4 shows a stylized image of a visitor centre which appeared in one of the Mission 66 brochures. It can be viewed as an example of the 'intermediary landscapes' created during the Mission 66 period, a place where visitors could see what they had already seen on countless photographs and other representations of the American wilderness.[29] Because the visitors to the parks were familiar with these images, they already knew what to expect from their visit to them. There was no need to stay longer than the park managers (and conservationists) thought necessary in order to have a 'wilderness experience'.

The passages outside the parks were not the only ones to have been created as standardized spatio-temporal orders. So too were the passages inside the parks. Journey and destination could no longer be separated. When the smooth transits to national parks that car practices created led to an increasing number of visitors, threatening their existence, the passages which brought people to the parks were continued within them. The same design principles organizing 'flow' on the roads outside the parks were used to manage visitor circulation and create roadside wilderness within them.

In the 'intermediary landscapes' at the boundary between the American passages and the wilderness which they made accessible, the promise of

Figure 4.4 A highly stylized illustration of a visitor centre with a vista point, which appeared on the cover of *Mission 66 in action* published in 1959. The imagined landscape emphasizes the wide openness of nature in the western United States. The meandering road behind the visitor centre directs the reader's gaze into the wilderness, while the white mountain just beyond it is depicted as a snow-covered peak, an iconic image of the wilderness (source: Allaback 2000: 31).

unspoiled nature created by countless images and other representations was efficiently maintained. Through the stylings of illustrations and images, visitors learned what to expect, and thus did not have to stay longer than park planners and conservationists believed desirable. During the Mission 66 era, a new type of passage was created which led people efficiently to the 'wilderness' and back home again. This was achieved by styling and standardizing the destination and the collective images of it. This innovation resolved, at least for the time being, the tension between use and conservation which had existed since the early years of the park service and became more urgent in the 1950s with the dramatic rise in the number of visitors.

Conclusion

We can now interpret the photograph at the beginning of the chapter in a different way. Before the driver got to the edge of the Grand Canyon, he probably had to do a lot of 'work' to reduce the friction of primitive car technology, bad roads and the lack of services along the way. During the first decades of the twentieth century, this work became increasingly delegated to standardized networks of highways, gas stations and restaurant and motel chains. Not only was the production of cars organized in a Fordist and Taylorist manner, the car journey itself changed from an uncertain and adventurous undertaking to an event that was predictable and efficiently organized. Standardization provided the connections between the heterogeneous elements in multiple networks, rendering the 'flow' which every car driver could depend upon, making it possible to get anywhere at any time. The flexibility and freedom of the car can thus be shown not as an inherent characteristic of a single technology, but the result of numerous interconnected innovations.

Passages have effects that are contingent. The heterogeneous order that renders a fast and predictable journey is never finished, but has to be repaired continually. Thus, once created, flow leads to new problems. This chapter has examined how such contingencies arose and were solved in the national parks. On the one hand, the parks had to be connected to the passages which made them accessible. On the other, this connection did not mean that the parks lost their uniqueness as individual places of nature and wilderness. In trying to find solutions to this design problem, the National Park Service had to manoeuvre between the exigencies of 'democratic access' and the values of unspoiled nature. The Mission 66 programme illustrates that the design of the parks was never stable. The National Park Service was constantly forced to renegotiate between access and preservation. Park planners had to adapt the parks' design to the increasing numbers of visitors by building visitor centres directing people to the main sites in a short amount of time. Circulation was the main way of preventing the parks from being inundated by cars. From the 1950s on, such circulation was achieved by adapting the material layout of the park design, and restyling representations of nature. The national parks became places that the vast majority of people could get to easily but, precisely because of this, only spent a short time there.

What can be concluded from the history of Mission 66 about the ways in which new passages for the car reconfigured the dimensions of space and time in the national parks? The Mission 66 programme can be read as a continuing process of solving design problems in which at least three tensions existed. First, both Mission 66 and the history of national parks in general reveal a tension between *passage* and *place*, which stems from the fact that the way a destination is made accessible cannot be separated from the design of the place itself. This intertwining of the design of access and the design of place is a curiously under-researched subject in cultural geography and social theory. As this chapter has shown, one goes to a different park when travelling by train than when travelling by car. As the phrase 'roadside wilderness' in one of the Mission 66 brochures suggests, the chief design problem facing architects was how to connect two different worlds. They resolved this dilemma by designing intermediary landscapes. It was in these landscapes that the freedom and flexibility of car access to the parks was constantly renegotiated in terms of the need to preserve the parks' wilderness. These intermediary landscapes were also designed according to different styles: the rustic style of the 1930s worked from different assumptions about how to solve the tension between use and preservation than the modernist design of Mission 66.

Second, there is a tension between *material* and *narrative* design elements in the design strategies developed by park designers. This tension can be found both in passages and in intermediary landscapes. The long and laborious journeys, like the ones the early American motorists made, could be turned into adventure stories precisely because they were contingent and unpredictable. When American passages became more standardized and thus less adventurous, stories of living on the road gave way to what could be called 'travel myths', as the mythology surrounding Route 66 today shows. Here, the signs used to standardize the road system became powerful cultural icons. In the parks, the same dialectic was used by park designers to create flow and circulation through the parks. As the number of visitors who came to the parks increased, they had less time to create their own wilderness adventures within them. Instead, the wilderness experience reappeared in the form of standardized and, often visual, narratives. Experiencing nature in a short time required new representations of the unique character of the parks.

The third tension is that between *space* and *time* in design. The case of Mission 66 makes it clear that designing space cannot be separated from designing time. When creating intermediary landscapes, park designers created specific zones of both spatial and temporal access to the parks. Their goal was to circulate visitors through the parks in less time than could be done using rustic designs. This meant that each visitor could stay in the park for a shorter time. In order to achieve this goal, they had to reconfigure space and time, not by simply speeding up the cars, but by redesigning the wilderness experience both on a material and a narrative level. Because car passages are spatio-temporal orderings, the national parks had to be designed not only as landscapes, but as timescapes as well (Adam 1998).

Flexibility and freedom in car travel are complex achievements. When talking about 'reconfiguring space and time', it is necessary to think of it in terms of contextual and relational dimensions that are the *effects* of the ways passages and places are designed. Thus one must look into the dilemmas and problems that occur in the design process. Urry (2000b: 59) has pointed out the dual character of automobility: 'it is immensely flexible *and* wholly coercive'. This chapter builds on this claim. Taking the design of passages and places as a starting point, it can be argued that the opposition between the corridor-like journeys by train and the individual and flexible journeys by car is not as strong as it may at first appear. Ironically, the photograph of the driver at the Grand Canyon's edge made in 1902 depicts the sort of freedom that had become illusory for the vast majority of visitors who went there in the 1950s and after. The design strategies of Mission 66 made their journey to the South Rim as predictable, if not as coercive, as the train schedules the first motorists disliked so much.

American passages not only changed the activity of car travel in the United States, but also the roadside landscapes and destinations which they brought within the car traveller's reach. Motorists could 'look ahead' in time and know what to expect both on the road and at their journey's destination. The tension between the predictable and the unpredictable returns in the design problems that follow from the need to connect the heterogeneous elements in a passage. But there is still another tension that exists in passages. Even if a traveller knows what to expect from his or her journey and the journey has been planned from A to Z, at any moment contingencies can arise that inevitably lead to a delay. Readjusting and repairing the spatio-temporal order of the passage in *real time* is an achievement that will be dealt with in the next chapter.

5   Airborne on time

Introduction

In an airport, everything revolves around time. It is the sitting and sauntering time of passengers who are waiting until boarding begins. It is the
departure time for the pilot of a Boeing 747-400 bound for New York,
whose slot time links its take off to traffic congestion in the upper airways.
It is the time that ground engineers need to repair a damaged engine. It is
the time needed to load the 90,000 litres of kerosene that a plane burns on
a mid-range intercontinental flight. The time used to structure the myriad
logistic processes in and around an airport, is Universal Time (UTC), the
time of the Greenwich meridian located at longitude 0, and the international standard on which the worldwide system of civil time is based.[1] It
synchronizes the actions of people located all over the world and, when it
takes the form of punctuality, is one of the most valuable qualities an
airline can possess.

To know what airport time means in daily practice, we cannot reduce it
to clock time. Instead, we have to examine how dispersed events and
processes are synchronized. All these different times come together in the
moment an aircraft becomes airborne. To arrive in Boston seven hours after
leaving Amsterdam, a heterogeneous order must be created. Aircraft, passengers, crew, baggage, fuel and catering facilities have to be at the right
place at the right time, and this can only be achieved by carefully synchronizing a complex chain of actions. This synchronization is achieved in part
before take off. For example, an airline's flight plans order both the maintenance schedules of the aircraft in its fleet and the bookings of its passengers
by travel agencies and through their websites. Whether the planned order
will become the real order of events, however, can only be known when an
aircraft becomes airborne. Passengers may arrive late at the gate; congestion
in the airways can make a different and longer route necessary; or the
baggage can be loaded onto the aircraft too late. Disruptions in the planned
order can have a variety of causes and usually end in delays.

Gleick (1999) has pointed out a 'paradox of efficiency' that characterizes contemporary commercial aviation. In a web of carefully timed move-

ments, many interrelated events have to be synchronized in order to use an airline's resources as efficiently as possible. Only then is it possible to survive in the increasingly competitive industry. But, as he shows, the more complex the order, the more vulnerable it is to the impact of small disruptions. 'In the most extreme case, everything depends on everything else. Vibrations anywhere can be felt everywhere' (Gleick 1999: 223–224). In an analysis of what he called 'normal accidents', Perrow (1986) analysed the nature of this paradox. In his understanding, risk originates from the probability of breakdowns at the system level, caused by the domino effect triggered from a sudden unexpected event. When systems are characterized both by interactive complexity (that is, not linear or sequential, but complex) and are tightly coupled, in the sense of having immediate, often unpredictable effects, they are difficult to control when errors occur. The daily operations of commercial airlines are both interactively complex and tightly coupled in the sense that the effects of contingencies are felt almost instantly at other places in the system.

If an airline like KLM wants to fly punctually, planned orders have to be repaired continuously by countering contingencies that may cause disruptions in the flight schedule (La Porte 1988). How can KLM prevent gridlock from arising in its system? As in previous chapters, an actor's perspective must be taken in answering this question. This chapter creates this perspective by looking 'in' the passage of a commercial airline flight and studying how disruptions are repaired in the moment that they occur. An airport has many locations where people work under time pressure to repair flight schedules, and where a continuous synchronization between the shopfloor and flight controllers is underway. To examine how the passages of daily flights are shaped and repaired in real-time, I carried out fieldwork in two locations at Schiphol Airport in Amsterdam, KLM's Departure Hall and the KLM Operations Control Centre, where the daily operations of its global network of connections are monitored. The research material consists of field observations and interviews with KLM employees in these places. After describing their daily work, I will analyse it from a theoretical perspective as situated action and improvisation. It will then become clear that repairing the heterogeneous order of the flight passage is a practical achievement that assumes the ability of a coin 'exchange', as one of the KLM employees said. Exchange is what keeps the operation going. It comes in several currencies and mediates between the rigid reality of plans, clocks and protocols, and a continuous flow of contingencies and everyday problems.

In the Departure Hall

To study the temporal complexity in the passages that commercial airlines sell to their customers, we can literally enter a passage by following passengers through the Departure Hall to their assigned seat on a plane.[2] At

Amsterdam's Schiphol Airport, car drivers park their cars in the long-term parking lot, designated P3, take an unmanned vehicle to a bus stop, where a bus picks them up and takes them to the Departure Hall. Those who come to Schiphol Airport by train travel from the train station's underground platforms to Schiphol Plaza, a covered square with dimmed lights. Adjacent to Schiphol Plaza is a lit throughway leading to the Departure Hall, a passage created from the knowledge that people have an intuitive tendency to walk in the direction of greater illumination. Screens hanging from the ceiling display flight arrival and departure times, while yellow, green and blue signs lead a traveller to the Departure Hall which, as in most airports, is situated directly above the Arrival Hall to separate departing from arriving passengers.

Schiphol Airport's Departure Hall 2 is designated mainly for KLM. It is the domain of the Passenger Services staff, who organizationally fall under the Division of Ground Services. Passenger Services is split into three subdivisions which mirror the three 'sides' of any flight: Departures, known as Landside by staff, which is the stage before a passenger reaches passport control, and includes passenger and baggage check-in and security checks; Airside, which begins after passport control and includes the last check-in procedures at the gate before entering the plane; and Arrivals, which begins with the arrival of passengers and continues through to baggage collection. The Departure Hall houses KLM's Special Services, Passenger Handling and the Ticket Office. Special Services provides additional services to passengers, such as transport to the gates for disabled passengers, escort services for VIPs or the Dutch Royal family. Special Services is responsible for maintaining the lounges for business-class passengers, holders of frequent flyer cards, like the Silver Wing and the Royal Wing Card, and other KLM passengers designated to receive special treatment. Passenger Handling is responsible for looking after ordinary passengers. Its main task is checking in passengers and baggage. At the Ticket Office, passengers can buy tickets or change reservations. The Ticket Office has several different locations throughout the airport, but the largest is in the KLM Departure Hall.

The governor of South Dakota: Special Services

Like any airport, Schiphol Airport Departure Hall is characterized by one-way traffic. Departing passengers report in at the check-in desk, get a boarding pass, pass through passport control, spend some time in the customs area, proceed to the gate, hand over their boarding pass and enter the aircraft. Along this trajectory there are several one-way checkpoints that every passenger must pass in order to ensure they complete it. Each passenger is identified, checked and, finally, upon going through customs, separated from the outside world. When a passenger is greeted by a crew member upon entering the aircraft, it is not only a sign of friendliness, but of caution as well. Anyone leaving a departing plane after having entered it creates a major safety risk. Passengers who reverse their trajectory after boarding an aircraft are considered potentially high security risks because such conduct suggests that dangerous objects may have been left behind in the cabin. Only in highly exceptional cases can the direction of the trajectory of the passenger through the Departure Hall be reversed.

The governor of South Dakota and his staff are en route from Vienna to South Dakota and have a several-hour layover at Schiphol Airport. During their layover they stay in the Royal Wing lounge.[3] The staff would like to visit Amsterdam. The governor himself chooses to stay in the lounge to rest. He has a kidney disease requiring special medical equipment which renders him less mobile. However, if the staff leave the airport, they must check out with their baggage and check back in for their flight to South Dakota. This process would normally not leave enough time for the staff to visit the city. But because KLM views the governor and his staff as special passengers, Special Services/Protocol decides to bypass standard procedures. An employee calls immigration and customs officers to tell them when and where she will pass with the group on their way out. The Americans follow the KLM employee on a route through the airport that is known only to insiders. They pass the row of customs offices in the opposite direction, and a security officer who checks their special Schiphol Airport passes. The customs and security employees know the KLM employee, and her earlier phone call made no further explanations necessary. On the way out, a guide who will accompany the group into Amsterdam awaits them. He will take them on a guided tour and then return them at an agreed time at the airport's entrance, where the same Special Services employee will be waiting for them to guide them back through the airport to the gate.

Back in her office, the employee finds a fax sent from the governor's office in South Dakota. It states that the governor does not want special attention to be given to his medical equipment at the gate by security officers. The fax requests KLM to handle the situation discreetly. Using diplomatic phrasing, the fax explains that 'The governor will be travelling with personal medical equipment which "could" (but should not) cause a problem when he checks in.' The KLM employee calls the security officer, who she knows by name, to give him the governor's name and boarding gate. The fax and the subsequent actions mean that the governor's medical equipment, like his staff, will pass through security without any hitches.

Pilgrims with a number: Passenger Handling

The destination of KLM flight KL734 is Jeddah, Saudi Arabia. This flight has been booked almost exclusively by Dutch pilgrims on their way to the yearly Haj in Mecca. To the KLM ground personnel a Haj flight is special. In part this is because the farewells which take place at the threshold of the check-in desk are unusually emotional. Some of the older pilgrims might not return from their journey, because they could fall in the huge crowd that surrounds the Kaaba. But the flight is also special because the pilgrims must have a special Haj visa. Saudi authorities want to ensure that the millions of pilgrims who enter their country every year for the Haj also leave it when it is over. The special visa enables immigration officers to separate them from other passengers upon their arrival. Because the Saudi authorities hold the airlines responsible for the validity of the passengers' visas, KLM invests considerable time, money and attention in checking Haj visas. After check-in, an Arab-speaking KLM employee carefully checks the text on each passenger's visa.

Normally when checking in passengers in the Departure Hall, KLM staff use the AXIS system, which allows passports and thus all of the relevant information to be scanned electronically. This not only saves time, but reduces the potential for errors and thus keeps the flow of passengers moving. But the AXIS system cannot be used for this Jeddah flight. Instead, every checked-in pilgrim receives a special code (a number), which is entered into the system that makes their special status known worldwide. This code can only be entered into an older, slower, command-oriented check-in system, which increases the time spent on each passenger and the risk of introducing errors. Ground stewardesses are all too aware of the consequences. If the code is not correct, KLM can be charged a steep fine. As one Passenger Handling employee explained:

> The system asks for nationality. Normally this would be written as 'NL', but in this case we have to put down 'Dutch'. Otherwise it will not be accepted by the Saudis. That is something you really have to know from experience, or problems will occur. The lady I just checked in did not have a surname, but the system has to have a surname, otherwise it will not issue a boarding pass. I heard somebody calling her 'Uki', so I put Uki in the system as a surname.
>
> (Interview with employee, Passenger Handling)

From the check-in counter the Dutch pilgrims must go to gate F05, where the flight to Jeddah is handled. Here the passengers are allowed to choose their seats, another feature of the flight that is not standard. The boarding passes are read by an electronic card reader, which confirms that a passenger has shown up at the gate, but the seat numbers indicated on the boarding passes are invalid. Once on the plane, they are allowed to choose their seats. The women go to the back of the plane, while the men stay in front so they do not have to sit together during their in-flight prayers.

Changing a reservation: the Ticket Office

The semicircular counter at the rear of the Departure Hall is the KLM Ticket Office. Here hurried passengers can buy a last-minute ticket for almost any KLM flight. The price of these tickets are, of course, much more than those booked within the normal window of time. Passengers whose flight was cancelled because of bad weather or who must change their tickets for other reasons also use this KLM Ticket Office. When booking a flight, the Ticket Office staff use integrated worldwide booking and reservation systems in which the flight information of most major airlines is shared. A Ticket Office employee described the old system as follows:

> In 1969, we started to work with an automated reservation system. Before that, a travel agency would call to ask if there were seats on a specific flight. You looked at a list for that flight. If there was a seat, you took a card, half of which went to the telex room and the other half you put in a wooden box. KLM used the telex to send the reservation to all KLM offices. If some flight was requested but not issued, it had a red tab. Now there are no airlines anymore where a reservation is made by hand; all booking systems are mutually connected, which enables you to see for every passenger what their journeys look like, what their destination is, the departure and arrival times, special conditions, like if they want a vegetarian meal.
>
> (Interview with employee, Ticket Office)

Tickets vary depending on the conditions under which they can be changed. The cheaper the ticket, the less the opportunity to deviate from the given conditions. A Volvo employee with a business-class ticket wanted to change his flight, but the conditions did not allow it. The Ticket Office employee knew from experience that KLM had a special deal with Volvo which allowed these tickets to be changed once, an exception that was not electronically available in the system. A man wanted to catch an earlier flight to Memphis, but it was overbooked. Just like other commercial carriers, KLM routinely overbooks its flights, which means that more tickets are sold than the number of seats. The rationale behind overbooking is that experience has shown that, for every flight, a certain number of passengers do not show up. The risk that the seats will go unsold is greater than any consequences resulting from customer dissatisfaction, because customers can always be rescheduled on another flight, or offered other forms of recompense. In this case, the employee knew from experience that, despite the overbooking, there would be a seat on this flight and booked the passenger through.

Observations in the Departure Hall

In the Departure Hall passengers follows a trajectory from the check-in counter to their seats on the aircraft. This trajectory is achieved through discipline: the passenger is transformed in steps – at the check-in counter, while passing through customs, at the gate, while boarding the plane – into an entity that 'fits' in the planned passage. From the passenger's perspective, the need for disciplining is sometimes hard to understand. Why do passengers have to report to the check-in counter two hours before departure time, and then have to wait in the customs area and again at the gate? Why is it so expensive to reschedule a flight? Why are people only allowed to take hand luggage into the cabin?

To move as quickly as possible from one waiting period to another, passengers must find their way through the airport's vast premises.[4] To walk from the check-in counter to the most remote gate on the G-pier takes between 15 and 20 minutes, something not every passenger realizes. For this reason, ground stewardesses hand out folders to passengers containing a map of the airport and the walking distances to gates in minutes. Passenger Handling employees view passengers who experience this disciplining as a lack of freedom as the least predictable factor in the complex chain of activities and events that precedes an aircraft's departure. Passengers who get lost or show up too late at the gate, who do not have the right documents, who take too much hand luggage with them, which must be collected at the gate, are the most difficult to control for KLM staff. Passengers who checked in, but do not show up at the gate are called in airport jargon '–LMCs' (Minus Last Minute Change).[5] These passengers create trouble because, for security reasons, passengers and their baggage must always be on the same plane. Unaccompanied baggage must be taken off an aircraft, which can cause significant delays. The sooner KLM employees know when a passenger is missing, the quicker they can react. For this reason KLM moved up the time a passenger has to report at the gate to within 10 minutes of boarding time. The additional time provides more space to act while remaining within the flight schedule. However, building in such buffer time has led to the extension of the duration of the total air journey.

KLM designates codes to a series of events that may cause a delay. A passenger who does not show up at the gate is given delay code 03. It is one of the 99 international IATA codes that are printed on a card which all KLM employees have close at hand. Other codes include one for carrying too much hand luggage at the gate (code 10), a defective aircraft (code 41) and a shortage of crew (64). Only a small number of delay codes are relevant to the actions of KLM staff in the Departure Hall. KLM staff have no influence on whether an arriving plane is delayed, at which gate it will arrive or whether or not it is overbooked. Their action space is thus limited. They are authorized to change only a subset of the information they see on their screens.

The work of the KLM employees in the Departure Hall is characterized by a tension. They have to comply to protocols, rules and conditions, but they also need space within the rules to solve the problems of individual travellers while at the same smoothing out any disruptions these may cause the operation as a whole. The governor's staff wishing to reverse the trajectory through the Departure Hall; the Haj-bound pilgrims who receive a different code in the system from other passengers and are allowed free seating; and the Volvo passenger trying to change the conditions of his flight – all represent exceptions that could potentially disrupt the passage. Working with Special Services, Passenger Handling and the Ticket Office assumes the ability to apply the rules and use the systems, but staff's actions also presuppose the experience that enables them to know where and how deviations can be created. The Departure Hall is just one of the many places that make a flight passage. Other places are the maintenance hangars, the baggage-handling spaces, the air traffic control tower, the kitchens of airport catering. As airports are linked in a network of global connections, these 'duty areas' are spatially distributed, not only in the airport itself, but all over the world. The intriguing question then becomes, how is it possible to coordinate the actions of countless individuals in as many places? How is it possible to create an overview of these dispersed personnel? How can we make sure that adjustments in the heterogeneous order of the passage in one place do not lead to disruptions in another? To answer these questions, I move the site of my fieldwork from the Departure Hall to the Operations Control Centre of KLM.

Creating an overview

The building in which the KLM Operations Control Centre (OCC) resides opened in September 1999, and is situated in Schiphol Airport-East, which runs along the Haarlemmer Canal, where the original airport was constructed in the 1920s. It is now a business district housing airline-related companies. The OCC has, next to the so-called Back Office, a Front Office where processes at the network level are monitored in real time. The Front Office of the control centre is a spacious, climate-controlled hall. At the front end is a massive video screen which spans the width of the hall. It was intended to show all the present flights in real time, but is currently not in use due to cost-cutting measures. Below the video wall is a row of digital clocks which display in green the current time in different cities around the world. In the middle is a clock showing in red the Coordinated Universal Time. The massive hall contains two rows of desks, each of which has two or three computer screens, other communications equipment and paper. Not all the desks are occupied, however. People are walking, talking and using their telephones. At the front of the hall, there are two televisions screens relaying a live CNN broadcast and Teletext. The Front Office is on duty 24 hours a day. People work in three shifts. Every morning the new day of operations starts with the so-called 'morning prayer' at 8 am, a short meeting to evaluate the previous day and prepare for the upcoming one.

All the KLM divisions relevant to the daily operations of the network

De besturing heeft als doel om het verschil tussen de gewenste en geleverde kwaliteit zo klein mogelijk te laten zijn

Plan
- Dienstregeling
- Resources
- Reserves
- Verbeterstromen

Gewenste kwaliteit
- Punctualiteit
- Connections & Irrate
- Verstoringskosten
- Completion factor

Werkelijkheid
- Weer
- Slots
- Capaciteit
- Techniek
- Resources
- etc.

Besturing

Maatregelen
- Annuleren
- Vertragen
- Omboeken
- Wisselen kist/crew
- Uitwijken
- Invluv
- aanpassen vliegplan

Geleverde kwaliteit
- Punctualiteit
- Connections & Irrate
- Verstoringskosten
- Completion factor

Evaluatie:
- aanpassing plan

Evaluatie:
- performance monitor

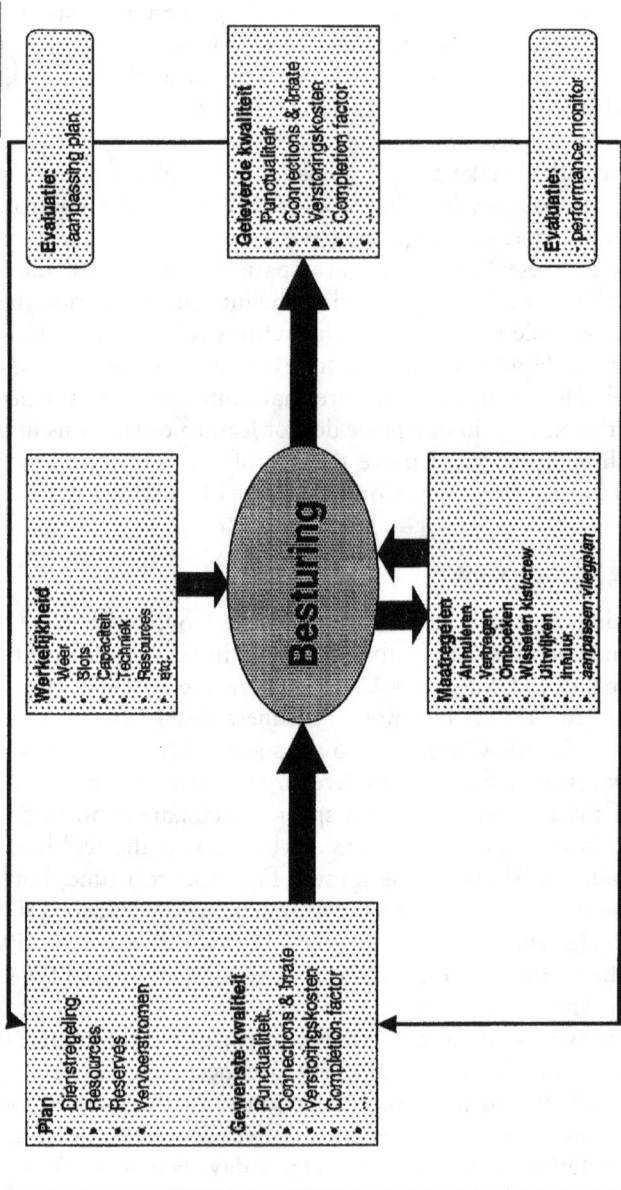

A = de wijze waarop de dienstregeling volgens oorspronkelijk plan moet worden uitgevoerd en de punctualiteit, connecties, verstoringskosten, Irrate en aantal vluchten die vluchten die hetplan op zouden moeten leveren

B = de operationele omstandigheden die „het plan' (kunnen) verstoren

C = het kiezen uit een van de maatregelen om de gevolgen van een verstoring te beperken

D = de gekozen maatregel

E = de waargemaakte punctualiteit, (no-)connecties, bagage Irrate, verstoringskosten, aantal vluchten, etc.

are represented in the Front Office. The most important employees in the Front Office are the Duty Manager Operations (DMO) and three Operations Controllers (OCs), one of whom is the Senior Operations Controller. The DMO stands at the head of a hierarchical line of staff, but is not involved in daily decisions. These are made by the OCs, who are responsible for the daily performance of the flight schedule at the network level. One Operations Controller oversees the flights of Cityhopper (the F50 and F70 fleet used for local flights); one is responsible for European flights (the Boeing 737 fleet); and a senior controller oversees intercontinental flights (the wide-body fleet). The controllers are supported by representatives from each of the divisions relevant to the daily operations of the network. Before the opening of the OCC building in 1999, which cost 55 million euros, the Operations Controllers were housed in separate buildings at the airport complex. But KLM believed that face-to-face interactions among employees would improve its ability to respond to contingencies and disruptions in its airline network, and is confident that the costly investment will pay off.

The control protocol contains instructions on how the Operations Control Centre 'controls the operation' (see Figure 5.1). The protocol describes lines of communication, decision-making procedures, rules and corporate culture. It states that the central goal of the operation is to 'minimize the difference between projected and realized quality in the performance of the flight schedule'. Control through the OCC covers the entire process, from the acceptance of the plan and the stated level of quality, to responses to surrounding factors, pro-active measures and their communication to the relevant members of the organization.

Figure 5.1 is taken from a booklet that is on every desk in the Front Office. It illustrates how the OCC defines its own steering strategy. Its point of departure is the organizational plan, which includes not only flight schedules but also the availability of planes, planes in reserve, crew and the expected number of passengers. A desired level of quality is prescribed, which incorporates an acceptable deviation from the flight schedule. In defining the desired and realized levels of quality, punctuality, delay costs, cancellations and missed connecting flights are taken as the chief

---

Figure 5.1 A chart of the flow of operations in KLM's Operations Control Centre. The organization is designed to achieve its main goal of minimizing the difference between the projected and realized quality in the performance of the flight schedule. At the heart of the organization is Control [*Besturing*], located in the middle of the chart. On its left is the plan defined according to the desired level of quality [*Gewenste kwaliteit*], and on the right, the realized level of quality [*Geleverde kwaliteit*]. Above and below the Operations Control are Reality [*Werkelijkheid*] and Measures [*Maatregelen*] which must be taken, respectively (source: internal KLM OCC brochure).

indicators.[6] There are all kinds of factors that enter into the realization of the plan, which the OCC manual describes as the ability to 'put a spoke in the wheel': weather, flight slots, technical failures, shortage of capacity on runways and shortage of personnel. If the desired level of quality is threatened, 'pro-active measures' must be taken to prevent further disruptions. A plane or crew can be changed; an aircraft can be flown to an alternative airport; extra capacity can be rented; a plane's internal configuration can be changed; or a flight can be delayed or cancelled.

Decisions about these measures are made at three different levels of control. At the flight level (level 3), decisions only have consequences for a single flight and are made by the corporate divisions involved. The OCC is involved in a decision when the disturbance has consequences for the network as a whole (level 2). These include flight delays or cancellations; a change of aircraft; a longer than expected block time (the time between the moment a plane leaves the gate (off blocks) and the moment it comes to a stop at the arrival gate (on blocks)); or when extra costs must be incurred; a deviation from the control rules is required; or the consequences of a disturbance on the network level are not yet known. The highest level, level 1, is called the escalation level and includes extraordinary incidents like accidents or hijackings. Level 1 operations are supervised by the Duty Manager Operations, who is always present in case decisions have to be made on the highest level.

Although the Front Office of the control centre is brand new, the principles that underlie it are not. The idea of housing a control centre in one room which monitors and controls a transport network in real time goes back to the nineteenth century. Beniger (1986) describes an innovation that Daniel McCallum worked out for managing the Erie Railroad in 1853. To control the network of railroads, McCallum understood the importance of collecting information about the actual situation on the tracks. He favoured hierarchical communication, feedback of information to the processes in operation and the detection of disruptions and failures in the process. In his office, McCallum had a large map on which the information about the current situation in the network at any moment was updated. To do this, the people in the organization had to send reports to the central office, every hour, every day and every month (Beniger 1986: 229). According to Beniger, McCallum's approach became a success because of the integration of three elements: the telegraph for real-time communication, the system of reporting and the organizational plan that allocated the responsibilities of workers. Thus, the superintendent knew at every moment of the day the exact location of every train and the function they had in the execution of the schedules.

In establishing McCallum's control room, three interlinked innovations proved to be crucial: the ability to differentiate between the physical speed of moving trains and speed of information;, the ability to create a means of overview over the system in real time; and a reorganization of responsibilities in such a way that the power to act shifted from local situations to the central control room. First, it was the telegraph that enabled control of complex train schedules over large distances. The telegraph marked a decisive separation of 'transportation' and 'communication' (Carey 1992: 213). At the time of the first railway lines, so-called signalmen kept watch to see if a piece of track was empty. They communicated its status to an approaching train by waving a white or red flag. The telegraph made it possible to divide the railways into blocks with signalmen transmitting a train's arrival by telegraph to the signalman at the next block.[7] This co-evolution of physical transportation and information networks is a central theme in Beniger's book, but it has been described by other authors as well.[8] Second, a system of reports and checks was set up through which upper management could evaluate all aspects of the operations. McCallum established a new routine in which subordinates had to send monthly, weekly, daily and even hourly reports to the management. To be successful and efficient, McCallum believed, 'a system of operations ... should be such as to give to the principal and responsible head of the running department a complete daily history of details in all their minutiae' (Yates 1989: 7). Finally, McCallum's 'control room' led to a shift of responsibilities. No longer was the person 'on the spot' best equipped to evaluate a specific situation and thus be held accountable for making the right decisions. Rather, the people in the control room had the best view over many different events at different times and places. The power to decide what should be done to solve a problem shifted from the local conductors to the control room.

The principles that can be taken from the historic accounts of Beniger can help to conceptualize the work that is done in the Front Office of KLM's Operations Control Centre. The Front Office made possible an overview of activities that are both spatially and temporally distributed. Suchman (1993) has pointed out that control centres, as 'centres of coordination', are designed to maintain a contradictory state of affairs. In order to function as a centre, they have to occupy a stable site to which distributed agents can connect, but they must also be able to access all other relevant situations that are distant in space and time (Suchman 1993: 115). We can now define the type of control that is enacted in KLM's Front Office as the practical achievement of both creating an overview over distributed situations and changing them in relation to each other. This achievement in turn rests on a) real-time coordination of cooperative work that is both spatially and temporally distributed; and b) a redistribution of accountabilities and responsibilities in such a way that the power to act in distributed situations is limited to a small number of employees.

In the Operations Control Centre

In this section, I will present two cases based on my fieldwork in KLM's Front Office. The first demonstrates how an overview is created through the coordination of real-time cooperative work that is distributed in space and time. In the second, I examine the (re)distribution of accountabilities and responsibilities in spatially distributed situations.

Breakdown in Barcelona

On the computer screen, which sits in front of the Operations Controller Europe, all KLM's flights for the day are displayed as coloured horizontal bars. Running across the screen are vertical lines which represent the 24 hours of a day. A dotted vertical line slowly shifts across the screen from left to right, marking the passage of UTC time (see Figure 5.2).

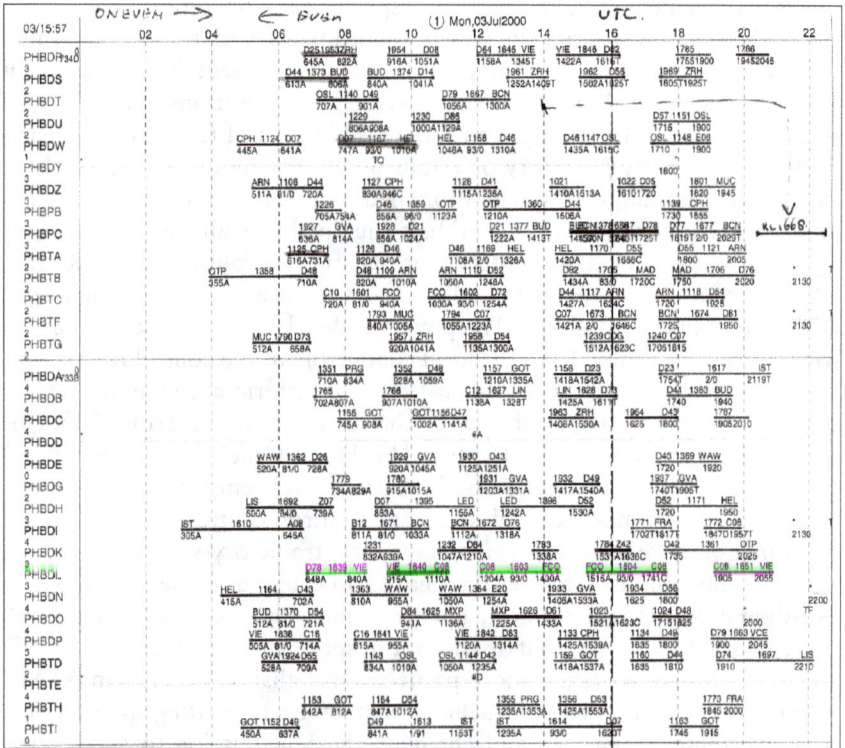

Figure 5.2 A printout of the screen image the Operations Controller Europe saw on 3 July 2000 at UTC 15.57. In the left column are the registration codes of all the planes in the European fleet. The horizontal bars indicate the flights these planes will make on this day. The longer the bars, the longer the flight. By clicking on a bar, the Operations Controller can get all the information on a specific flight. The dotted vertical line moves slowly from left to right on the screen. It represents the 'now', the actual UTC. The plane that was damaged in Barcelona, designated by the registration code PHBDT ('Bravo Delta Tango') is the third from above.

In the left column are all the planes in the European fleet. The horizontal bars represent the flight of each aircraft in the fleet. They can be shorter or longer, depending on the amount of time an aircraft is 'off blocks', the time between its departure from the gate of origin and its arrival at the gate of its destination. Departing flights, indicated by yellow bars on the Operations Controller's screen, have odd numbers; arriving planes, shown in green, even numbers. Under the bars are the block times. If a flight is delayed, part of the bar will become red. Above the bars are the departure or arrival gates and, for departing flights, the destination designated by international abbreviations. By clicking on a bar on the computer screen, the Operations Controller can get all the information he needs on any flight: the gate number at Schiphol Airport, the registration code, the names of the crew members, the plane's recent maintenance history, etc. He can move a bar to the left to indicate a delay, or to the right, for flights travelling ahead of schedule. He can also move the bar upwards or downwards to indicate a change of plane. With simple mouse clicks, the controller can adjust the flight schedule, but he knows his decisions may have a great impact in many places in the airport:

> A change of gate has to be communicated to the passengers, their baggage has to be moved to another location, catering, fueling, everything has to be adapted and re-synchronized. They are often not very happy, but there is nothing I can do about it. Here we have the overview, [out there] they only see their own processes.
>
> (Interview with Operations Controller Europe)

When a telephone rings, the OC Europe turns the speaker phones on so everyone can hear the conversation. The pilot of a 737 at the Barcelona airport reports that there is a hole in the body of his plane. A luggage tractor has taken a turn too sharply and damaged the aircraft's aluminium skin. The Operations Controller organizes a telephone conference to discuss the problem. By pushing on a display in front of him, he is able to talk simultaneously to the pilot, the engineers and the Service Manager in Barcelona and the KLM maintenance division who are sitting behind him in the Front Office:

BARCELONA MANAGER: *'We have the Bravo Delta Tango here, and it has a very deep scratch with a hole in it. We would like to have maintenance here.*

OPERATIONS CONTROLLER EUROPE: Clear, I think I have the captain on the other line. I will put you on hold for a second and then come back to you. Hold the line please. Bravo Delta Tango – is on departure from Barcelona. I now have the engineer and the captain on the other line.

PILOT: *Hello.*

OPERATIONS CONTROLLER: I will switch to the engineer in a moment, I have him on the other line. Hold on please.

MAINTENANCE ENGINEER IN THE OCC: This is Ben speaking.

OPERATIONS CONTROLLER: Jan here. I'm going to switch now: Bravo Delta Tango in Barcelona with a scratch and a hole. Everyone is switched on now, captain, engineer and maintenance.

BARCELONA ENGINEER: *There is a deep scratch of about 30 centimetres long, and in the middle of this there is a hole through the body.*

OPERATIONS CONTROLLER: Maintenance?

MAINTENANCE ENGINEER IN THE OCC: We can seal the scratches with high speed tape and then fly back to Amsterdam unpressurized.

(Recording of the actual sequence of events)

The damage to the Barcelona plane is serious enough to delay its return to Amsterdam indefinitely. This creates a number of problems which the OC Europe must resolve. Even if the plane can be repaired, safety regulations require that damaged planes must be taken out of commercial service. This means that it must be flown back to Amsterdam empty. All passengers will have to be re-routed on other flights to Amsterdam, and another aircraft must also be found for those who were booked through to Hamburg, the flight's final destination. The flight and cabin crew must be changed because it is probable that the delay will mean that they will exceed the number of hours they are legally permitted to work. Since they were also scheduled for a subsequent flight from Amsterdam, another crew will have to be found to replace them on that flight as well. The Operations Controller looks at the computer screen for a plane that will be used for the flight to Hamburg. A 737 is available, but is scheduled for maintenance. He must find out if its maintenance check can be postponed. He contacts the Duty Maintenance Manager who confirms that it can be. But he must also check whether this 737 has enough seats and freight capacity for the Hamburg flight.

In the meantime, the OCC maintenance engineers are discussing the technical details of the damage with the engineers on the ground in Barcelona. A proposal to send two engineers on the next flight to Barcelona is turned down. They will take a later flight, make temporary repairs to the damaged aluminium skin, and fly back to Amsterdam. But the Operations Controller Europe had delayed the next flight to Barcelona in case the decision was made to send the OCC engineers on it. He must now call the Duty Area Manager at the gate at Schiphol Airport to tell him that the aircraft should no longer be held for the engineers. The OC Europe moves the yellow bars on his screen. The problems the damaged Barcelona plane has caused have been solved. The adjustments are put on telex and sent to all relevant divisions. All electronic systems, from the computers in travel agencies to the public displays at Schiphol Airport, immediately register the new reality that the OC Europe has negotiated.

We improvise according to fixed rules. We stand as conductors in front of an orchestra. Every day, we start the same tune, according to a planned rhythm. Just for a moment, someone is allowed to play a different melody, but if we turn the page, there are the same notes for all sixty musicians.

(Interview with Operations Controller Europe)

Ecuadorian eruptions

One day during my fieldwork in the Front Office, there was some wind and a lot of fog. The central control tower declared 'limited view operations'. Airport capacity was reduced from 68 incoming flights per hour to 18. The reason was that the people in the tower have to be able to see the area on the runway where the aircraft makes contact, called the 'touch down area'. If they cannot see the touch down area, the distance between incoming planes, called the 'separation', must be increased. The reduced capacity of the runways had far-reaching consequences for KLM's flight schedule. Less than 10 per cent of all European flights were able to leave within five minutes of the planned departure time. The Duty Manager Operations was not very happy.

> Proclaiming a measure is easy, but recalling it is often troublesome. Before a plane departs from Schiphol Airport, twelve different processes connected to that one flight have to be synchronized, ranging from catering and cleaning to fuelling and baggage handling. If we delay an airplane, something changes for everyone and that may lead to mistakes. Everyone relies on that nice image we call 'flight schedule', but in daily practice things do not always go our way.
>
> (interview with Duty Manager Operations)

At the department of Air Traffic Management (ATM) in the Front Office, a large map of Europe is lying on a map table showing hundreds of 'airways', the fixed routes which aircraft follow through European air space. Every pilot must strictly follow the airways in the flight plan which is assembled shortly before an aircraft departs. At some places in the network, there are complex nodes of airways; at others there are 'ramps' in the air, points in air space which every plane must pass in order to be able to follow other airways. Unlike freeways, airways are constructed in layers. Every airway has several altitudes which can be used, provided the legally required separation is met. Air space is divided into sectors, each of which is controlled by regional and national Air Traffic Control (ATC) centres. When a pilot enters a new sector, it must be communicated to the relevant ATC. Sometimes a sector is so crowded that the ATC must issue what is called a slot time, which designates the specific time an aircraft can enter a sector. In practice, slot times determine the departure schedules of aircraft. The Flow Control staff in the Front Office have to request slot times for some of the departing KLM aircraft. Sometimes the demand on slot times causes delays that can only be prevented by changing the route and adjusting the flight plan. Flow Controllers have little say in the matter:

> We don't have much influence on the slot times; they are determined by Air Traffic Control at Schiphol Airport which receives them from the Central Flow Management Unit in Brussels.[9] Sometimes I can try to get an earlier slot time, but usually I simply have to wait. It is very important to keep your slot time. If we depart too late you run the risk of being put at the end of the line by Brussels, which can take hours. Flights with slot times are even more time-critical than 'normal' flights. Nothing should go wrong.
>
> (Interview with employee, Flow Control)

Flow Control is also responsible for making flight plans. This day, one of the flight planners is making a plan for a flight to Quito, Ecuador, a daily destination. This route is problematic because all three of the approach airways to the Mariscal Sucre International Airport in Quito fall within the sphere of influence of the Guagua Pichincha, an active volcano that is part of the Andes, located just 10 nautical miles west of the airport. The volcano has had four minor eruptions between 1981 and 1998. Airborne volcanic ash can damage an aircraft's engines seriously enough to cause it to crash, so skilful planning is required. The flight planner must regularly check a website maintained by the American Geological Society which registers the volcano's activity.

> Crucial in the choice for an approach route is the direction of the wind. If I have determined a certain route, I start computing. Every plane has to be within 180 minutes of an airport in case an emergency landing is necessary. This is called the ETOPS rule. This rule limits the choice of your trajectory. Apart from ETOPS, I have to pay attention to the amount of fuel. When I choose to fly a longer route, I have to take more fuel weight on board, which means fewer passengers and less freight, which is important for the reservations on that plane. Everything depends on everything else here.
>
> (Interview with flight planner)

Whereas the responsibilities and the power to act are clearly designated in the Front Office, there are other parties which can overrule the decisions made there. Examples in this case are the central control tower at Schiphol Airport and the Central Flow Management Unit in Brussels. As such, KLM's Front Office is part of a hierarchy of control centres, together creating an overview of European air space. This case also shows that not all situations are the same. Meteorological circumstances at Schiphol Airport may cause delays because of reduced airport capacity, while an active volcano in Ecuador may be less of a problem because a different routing can be found.

Work in real-time

These two cases show how an overview is created in the Front Office in order to control disruptions that occur somewhere in the planned order of an aircraft's passage. Real-time operations require that problems be solved when they occur. KLM cannot stop its operations in order to design a solution.[10] Changing a slot time for a departing flight cannot wait until tomorrow. How then are real-time decisions made? We can answer this question by examining the control protocol in Figure 5.1, in which there is a clear distinction between an a priori state of operations (the plan, the desired level of quality), a reality that can be influenced by taking measures and a *post hoc* evaluation, when the quality of the decisions is measured. Although the chart reflects the way the Front Office staff conceptualize their work, it does not make it clear how KLM employees actually repair the planned order of the passage in the moment a contingency occurs. What concrete steps do employees have at their disposal? Who decides when to deviate from the protocol?

The Front Office protocol represents possible situations in which action is required (bad weather, lack of slot times, lack of runway capacity, technical failures, etc.). But it cannot anticipate disruptive events before they occur. According to Suchman (1987), plans do not anticipate action, but rather plans and interactions are interwoven. She demonstrates this in her comparison of the way a European and Trukese captain navigate a ship. The first planned his course according to general navigation principles and then had to adjust his course continually to suit the actual situation at sea. In contrast, the Trukese captain determined the destination and then reacted in an *ad hoc* fashion while underway, reacting to the circumstances as they occurred along the journey. He used the wind, the tide and currents, the fauna and the stars, and the clouds and the sound of the water to navigate (Suchman 1987: ix). According to Suchman, all actions contain elements of both approaches. Every action is situated in the sense that, no matter how thoroughly planned it is, it will be subject to contingencies. The circumstances of our actions can never be fully anticipated and thus undergo continual change: 'By situated actions I mean simply actions taken in the context of particular, concrete circumstances' (Ibid.). Suchman does not criticize the commonsense idea that actions can be planned, but claims that they are never planned in the strong sense that cognitive science would have it. Rather, she views plans as

> a weak resource for what is primarily an *ad hoc* activity. It is only when we are pressed to account for the rationality of our actions, given the biases of European culture, that we invoke the guidance of a plan. Stated in advance, plans are necessarily vague, insofar as they must accommodate the unforeseeable contingencies of particular situations. Reconstructed in retrospect, plans systematically filter out the

particularity of detail that characterizes situated actions, in favour of those aspects of the actions that can be seen to accord with the plan.

(Ibid.: ix)

In the Front Office this means that the relation between the protocol and how things play out on the ground cannot be predetermined. Instead, considerations and judgments must continually be made in view of changing circumstances. The Front Office staff rely on protocols and procedures but, because every disruption introduces a complex of contingencies, they will always need 'rule space' to be able to react. The results of their decisions will not be an exact performance of a previously formulated protocol, but will always deviate more or less from it. The flow charts of the control protocol are thus part of ongoing situations, rather than programmes preceding them.[11]

As we have seen from following the Front Office staff around, problems have to be solved as they emerge, and operations cannot be stopped in order to design solutions. Any measure taken to remedy a disturbance will have an immediate effect on all other connected processes. Situated action can only partially account for this kind of complexity. The concept of 'improvisation' is useful here because it adds to the situatedness of actions a more explicit temporality.[12] Improvisation occurs when the moment of creation and performance coincide. An example is jazz musicians who improvise on the edge of the known and the unknown. Barrett (1998) cites the jazz saxophonist Steve Lacy:

> There is a freshness, a certain quality, which can only be obtained by improvisation, something you cannot possibly get from writing. It is something to do with the 'edge'. Always being on the brink of the unknown and being prepared for the leap. And when you go out there you have all your years of preparation and all your sensibilities and your prepared means but it is a leap into the unknown.
>
> (Barrett 1998: 606)

Improvisation, however, is not limited to the performing arts. Moorman and Miner (1998) distinguish between 42 definitions within domains as different as organizations, musical performance practice, theatre, therapeutic and didactic practices, and others. These definitions all share two meanings. A first meaning is related to the temporal character of improvising, in which making the plan and performing it coincide. As Ciborra has pointed out, the moment of improvisation suggests the immediacy, idiosyncrasy, as well as situated character of acquiring access to and deploying resources in any given situation (Ciborra 1999: 84; Ciborra 2000). A second meaning of improvisation captures the creative character of these situations. The new emerges as elements within an existing order which are given a different function or meaning in the course of time. Ciborra (1999) refers to this process as an 'ecology of improvisation' in which, for example, the instruments and artefacts in a situation are 'annotated, if not "re-invented"'.[13] To use music as an example, improvising assumes a deep knowledge of harmony, the ability to modulate through different keys, technical mastery of one's instrument and experience with many different musical idioms. The new is the result of a conscious, wanted deviation or transformation of the known. The more a musician controls the existing order, the more creatively this order can be reworked into something new. Translated to KLM's Front Office, this means that an employee must be able to oversee an emerging situation *and* to take from it the resources to solve a problem, even if they may or may not have been intended for the particular use to which they are put.

Concepts like situated action and improvisation help explain how Front Office staff can solve emerging problems and repair a passage in real time. They account for the 'coupling' of plan and action, while emphasizing the temporal and creative character of these processes. These two concepts can be used to analyse work in the Front Office, in which observer-based A-series time and linear B-series time have to be reconciled. B-series time underwrites plans and protocols, infinitely precise Universal Time and prepared sequences in which events are to follow in a strict temporal order. It is B-series time, without which a complex operation like adhering to a daily flight schedule would not be possible. But A-series time is manifested in operations that consist of emerging and evolving situations. People rely on their past experiences to predict what the future might look like. New problems are anticipated, but can never really be known until they materialize in the present. To understand the work in the Front Office, we need an analytical concept that addresses the question of how these two notions of time are brought together in daily practice.

The concept of 'situated action' accounts for the contingent character of situations and the need to constantly re-evaluate a situation on the basis of plans that are themselves undergoing change in the action. But it restricts action to the cognitive skills of pattern recognition, experience and tacit knowledge. And it is not clear how new actions are possible. In contrast, improvisation takes the emergence of new actions as a product of creativity. The new emerges when new meanings, uses or functions are given to elements in the existing order. However, improvisation assumes an actor's autonomy: to improvise one has to be *allowed* to restructure the order. The question of who is allowed to improvise and who is not remains unanswered. Conceptualizing airport time as the result of repairing flight passages makes it possible to ask *how*, in the Departure Hall and the Operations Control Centre, temporal orders are produced and related to one another, and what consequences this has for the distribution of the power of decision.

Conducting an orchestra

How can A-series and B-series time be reconciled in everyday practice? Before I return to the thread of my fieldwork, I want to elaborate on this question with an excursion into the practice of a musical performance. For an orchestra playing a score, the challenge is to give a good performance. The musical voices have to be in tune and in time, that is, they have to be coupled to each other. How can these objectives be achieved? From the perspective of B-series time, one could use a metronome. If the musicians follow the metronome's measured beats, the temporal relations between the notes they play will be fixed in time in an earlier–later order. In this way a metronome-led orchestra is able to coordinate the musicians' movements to perform a musical composition. But a good orchestral performance requires more 'lively' playing than is possible within the rigid structure of the metronomic beat. From the perspective of the A-series observer-based concept of time, each musician would play the individual voice of their instrument at their own tempo. But because there is no shared temporal frame in this approach, each musician would be unable to synchronize his or her individual performance with the other members of the orchestra, rendering the orchestra as a whole unable to produce a coherent musical performance at all.

In real musical practice, solving the problem of temporal coordination and the quality of performance is traditionally achieved by a conductor. Especially in larger ensembles, like a symphony orchestra, a conductor is indispensable. A good conductor is able, not only to act as a metronome and ensure each musician plays at the right tempo, but also to listen to the music and deviate from the prescribed relations between the notes on the page in order to create something new out of a printed score. Because accelerations and decelerations are *relational* – that is, the temporal meaning of the individual voices in a score are in relation to each other, not just with respect to the metronomic beat or the felt tempo of individual musicians – a conductor must be able to view the ensemble's performance as a whole and to be part of it at the same time. The challenge, then, of performing a musical score is achieved by listening to an orchestra as a whole, centralizing the beat and giving the conductor the authority to overrule the individual musicians.

The work that Front Office staff do to maintain the quality of KLM's flights is like that of a conductor. The planned order of the protocols and flight plans is the score. To ensure a good quality performance, more is needed than rigid Universal Time or the creative time of improvising individuals. The comparison one of the Operations Controllers made between his role and that of a conductor of an orchestra mentioned above bears analytical significance. 'Every day, we start the same tune, according to a planned rhythm. Just for a moment, someone is allowed to play a different melody, but if we turn the page there are the same notes for all sixty musi-

cians' (Interview with an OC). The performance of a complex flight schedule is like an orchestra playing a symphony because matters of tempo, creativity, oversight, authority and quality are constantly at stake. However,
for the Operations Controllers, there is one important difference between
their task and that of a conductor: the 'musicians' are not on the stage in
front of him, but dispersed all over the world. Their spatial distribution
makes it even more intriguing how the quality of the performance of the
flight plan can be upheld. How do people in the Front Office succeed in
combining A-series and B-series time and repair the temporal and spatial
orders of flight passages by connecting and disconnecting events that are
distributed in space?

Coining exchange

Sitting behind his computer display (see Figure 5.2) the Operations Controller for Europe can delay flights by shifting the green horizontal bars to
the right or change planes by moving the red vertical bars up or down. The
screen image represents the complexity of daily flight operations. It not
only provides an overview, but also the possibility to act in geographically
dispersed situations. As such, it comprises both B-series time and A-series
time. It provides a B-series map of sequential events that are in an
earlier–later relation to each other, which is manifested in the fixed temporal order of the plan. At the same time, the moving dotted UTC-line indicates the past–present–future perspective of A-series time.

The OC Europe solved the loss of the damaged Barcelona plane by
using a 737 that had been scheduled for maintenance. But he could only
achieve this by consulting the maintenance division to determine if the
plane could be taken off its maintenance schedule.

> This requires great precision. You cannot just use a plane that is
> scheduled for maintenance. Postponing maintenance may lead to
> problems in a few days, because the maintenance has to be done
> anyway. But in this case, I could reschedule the maintenance schedule
> in such a way that we will not have a problem later in the week. This
> plane was my exchange for today. I have now used it. If another plane
> is damaged, my problem will be harder to solve.
>
> (Interview with Operations Controller Europe)

I take the OC Europe's use of the term 'exchange' as a point of departure
in my analysis. By postponing the 737's scheduled maintenance, he made
sure that it could be incorporated into the planned flight schedule when
the problem in Barcelona occurred. He repaired the temporal order of
Flight KL1668 by changing the temporal order elsewhere (in the maintenance division). If it had been one day earlier or later, it might not have
been as easy to make this plane available. In the same sense, the work of

the air traffic control staff can be viewed as coining exchange by balancing the different temporal orders that constitute the flight plan on any given day. The situation at a destination airport is much like that of the active volcano near Quito International Airport. The volcano must be monitored so that the chosen approach route can be synchronized to fuelling requirements and passenger and freight capacities. It is precisely because 'everything is related to everything else', as the Flow Controller put it, that an exchange is constantly needed and coined during the day of operations.

In overseeing KLM's fleet, the parameters of the actions the Front Office staff can take are defined by a combination of protocols, codes and routines. KLM staff operate within these parameters, but they also are constantly renegotiating them. Solving problems like a broken-down plane can only be achieved by having a certain amount of exchange at one's disposal. In general terms, this means that exchange is necessary to make changes in the spatio-temporal order of related processes *in real time*. To put it another way, in repairing this order, it is the character of exchange rather than the amount of clock time that is decisive. In situations where there is little time, a disruption can be remedied when there is either enough exchange at hand or it can be coined.

In the case studies I have presented, several different forms of exchange can be identified. KLM staff in the Departure Hall and Front Office are confronted with a number of situations in which they must have exchange available or be able to coin it on site at the moment a disruption arises. Exchange comes in different currencies. First, an exchange can be taken in its literal sense of *money*. In daily operations, money is an important form of exchange. One Operations Manager pointed to KLM's longstanding aim of getting passengers to their destinations no matter what. But solving a problem can be very costly to an airline. If an aircraft cannot depart because the crew has no working hours left, and the passengers who cannot be booked on other flights that day must be put up in a hotel, the costs of solving a problem can escalate quickly. But there are also situations in which offering a hotel to passengers can help to prevent even costlier disruptions from occurring. However, as competition rises, the value of money as 'exchange' decreases. Recent competition among air carriers, created especially by low-budget carriers such as Easyjet, Southwest or Germanwings, have shrunk profit margins and increased the importance of 'commercial thinking', as the Operations Manager put it. KLM staff have become more convinced of the need to make 'commercial' judgments, even when these could harm the passengers' interests. Competition thus reduces the play area that Front Office staff have at hand to solve problems. However, KLM does not operate in a vacuum. For passengers, money is exchange as well. The more expensive the ticket, the more options one can change just before take off. The reverse is also true, as cheap flights usually leave no room for last-minute changes.

Second, *capacity*, in all its varieties (seats, crew, planes, slots, runways), is seen by KLM staff as an important form of exchange. For example, KLM has reserve crews who can be at Schiphol Airport within an hour. This might be necessary when other crews cannot get back to the airport in time, as in the case of the Barcelona breakdown. But if these reserve crews are spent in resolving a disruption and another one occurs, then a crew must be found among those who are not on standby. Such a change means a compensation in the planned schedule, which itself can create new disruptions elsewhere in the crew schedule. Apart from crews, runways represent an important capacity. As we saw in the example of operations during bad weather, the reduced runway capacity is distributed by the airport authorities. In this case, the Front Office staff has to look for other kinds of exchange. Sometimes runway capacity is more negotiable, which can be illustrated with flying during 'noise ban' hours. To reduce complaints about noise levels around Schiphol Airport, a noise ban was implemented which penalizes airlines if they take off and land between 11 pm and 6 am. The penalties are higher early in the morning than late at night. For this reason, transatlantic flights which arrive in Amsterdam shortly before 6 am are put 'on hold', and must circle overhead until the ban is lifted and they can begin their descent.

Third, *anticipation, knowledge, experience* and *information* are forms of exchange in non-material capacities. Front Office staff emphasized the importance of what they called 'pro-active work', meaning the anticipation of delays and disruptions which can create more room for acting. The Ecuadorian volcano illustrates how important it is for the Front Office to know in advance what the situation is at any given destination. Experience is also an important form of exchange. By looking at weather reports or CNN, Operations Controllers learn where to expect certain kinds of problems. In the Departure Hall, the Ticket Office staff only have to look out of the window to know how busy their day will be. They can tell from the weather outside what types of problems their customers will have. When there is fog, many people will want to change their reservations. The Passenger Handling staff can tell from the length of the queues at the check-in counters how long it will take to check in passengers, and whether it is necessary to open another ticket counter. The Operations Controller Europe knows from experience that using an aircraft scheduled for maintenance as a substitute for a damaged one can lead to subsequent disruptions. Cancelling several flights is sometimes necessary in order to prevent the effects of delays from snowballing into subsequent days. A software program called 'Traffic Flow Management Decision Support Tool' can predict the consequences of any given decision by computing from booking information the real or estimated costs of delaying an aircraft. One of the Operations Controllers said he used the tool to see what the possible consequences of a decision might be, but more than once knew from experience that the outcome would actually be different. Here we see two types of exchange in competition with each other. The support tool creates a quick indication of a decision's consequences. But since the tool works with fixed inputs, a controller's experience is also necessary.

> The program may indicate that we need 50 minutes to turn around the plane, that is the time it takes to prepare the plane for taking off again after we have landed in one of our destination airports. But I know the people who work there, and know that they can do it in 30 minutes.
>
> (Interview with Operations Controller)

Fourth, what sort of information KLM staff have at their disposal in making decisions depends in part on the *information and communication technologies* they use. The OCs in the Front Office simultaneously use conference telephoning, Internet and satellite telephoning, which enable them to reach a pilot anywhere in the world, as well as older means of communication like walkie-talkies and telex. By using these means of communication, the controllers are able to relate actions and events that are spatially distributed, thereby creating a 'virtual situation' on which they are able to act by connecting and disconnecting distanced actions and events. Virtual situations not only provide an overview, they also provide a means of acting in all parts of them. Knowing that a plane which is scheduled for maintenance can be used as a reserve increases the number of possible actions that can be taken in case of further contingencies. Another example can be given. A stone on the runway of the Guarulhos International Airport in São Paulo pierced the 'reverser door' of a Boeing 747's engine.[14] Neither the pilot nor the São Paulo engineers were optimistic about the chances of repairing the damage quickly. Both believed it would take several days. This, however, meant that the plane could not be used for its scheduled return flight, which created a major disruption at the network level. However, technical specialists in the Front Office saw the problem differently. Their information and communication network enabled them, as one put it, to 'look inside the engine' and assess the seriousness of the damage. By comparing what they found via the computer network with the standards for this plane, they invented a repair strategy that made a return flight possible, thereby reducing disruption at the network level.

A fifth currency of exchange is *risk*. My field interviews made clear again and again that taking risks should never be considered as exchange. The euphemism for risk in aviation jargon is to put 'flight safety' in danger. Disruptions were never solved by putting 'flight safety' in danger. According to the KLM staff, the safety of passengers and crew is not negotiable, a claim which is crucial for ensuring the trust of passengers. However, even within these strict margins of practice, risks were calculated into decisions. In the case of the damaged São Paulo aircraft, for example, the pilot judged safety risks differently from the Front Office technicians, thus resulting in two opposing proposals for resolving the problem. In this case, the technicians were able to make a risk assessment that was based on more solid evidence than the pilot could access, even though they worked from the other half of the world. So whereas risk is not a type of exchange which KLM staff claim they will ever use consciously, in reality it is an implicit form of exchange that is used occasionally, for example in relation to the maintenance schedules of airlines. Defects in an airplane that are considered to be a safety risk are given code A and have to be repaired within 24 hours. Other repairs can wait longer and are given codes B or C.

A final example of exchange is *authority*. Whether an employee or division can solve a disruption depends on whether they have the authority to make the decisions required to resolve any given disruption. KLM staff in the Departure Hall Ticket Office can change reservations if passengers meet the stipulated criteria, but they are not free to make exceptions. Sometimes the authority and power of a passenger can create an exchange. KLM viewed the governor of South Dakota and his staff important enough to reverse the direction of flow inside the Departure Hall. In the Front Office, authority is organized in a strictly hierarchical manner. The Duty Manager Operations stands at the top of the pyramid. But only in extraordinary situations, such as accidents or hijackings is this amount of centralization of authority needed. In KLM's daily operations, the OCs make the final decisions on delaying or cancelling flights. A Duty Area Manager working at one of the piers was angry because he was not told about a sudden gate change which could have disrupted the handling of two aircraft. The OC agreed that 'it would have been better for everyone if we would have changed the gate before landing. But we have the overview. If priorities are to be given, it is us who do it' (interview with Operations Controller). Sometimes the use of authority involves possessing *sympathy* for others working in difficult situations. One Senior Operations Controller said he realized what it meant for people on the shopfloor when plans and schedules were changed at the last minute. 'The way we approach them, the tone of voice we use is important to get the job done. When you give them a call afterwards to tell them everything worked out well, they will be prepared to go the extra mile again next time' (interview with Senior Operations Controller).

Maintaining the daily operation of KLM's flight schedule requires the ability to anticipate and react to a changing, emerging reality. If we want to understand how KLM staff solve problems, we cannot rely on the linear B-series conceptions of time that are present in KLM's plans and protocols, or the observer-based A-series time of experience and anticipation. Rather, the production and repair of many temporal orders in daily practice – working hours of cabin and flight crews, maintenance schedules of aircraft, waiting times for passengers at the gate – are related to each other like the voices in a musical score. Because KLM operations must be repaired in real time, it is crucial that the opportunity exists to change the temporal relations between distributed events and activities. In order to do this, exchange is needed.

Conclusion

The previous two chapters have argued that every journey or transit presupposes that passages have been created, heterogeneous orders made up of material and immaterial elements. The case of maintaining KLM's daily flight operations makes it clear that a passage is not only created, but is also repaired in the moment of travelling itself. Controlling complex aviation networks requires the ability to cope with the ongoing tension between plan and reality, between predictability and contingency. As Beniger (1986) and Yates (1989) have shown, from the nineteenth century, this tension has required innovations that changed the way control could be enacted. In the case of railroad networks, the control room McCallum made for the Erie Railroad in 1853 aimed at three things: making sure that the information about moving vehicles could 'travel' faster than the vehicles themselves, creating a real-time overview of the network as a whole, and redistributing accountabilities and responsibilities in such a way that the power to act on the network level became increasingly centralized at the expense of local employees. Today, information and communication technologies, shown in the countless screens that can be seen at airports, are used extensively to anticipate contingencies, to create an overview of many more or less distanced events, and to act at a distance by merging local and central knowledge and experience.

Through his computer screen, the Operations Controller Europe in the Front Office of the Operations Control Centre has an overview of KLM's European network as a virtual situation: he knows where the planes are at any time; he knows the names of the cockpit and cabin crew and how long they are allowed to work; he knows which planes are in maintenance and he knows how long for; and which flights have short turnaround times (the time needed to prepare a plane for departure after it has arrived at an airport). He will try to anticipate as many disruptions as he can, because the extent to which they can be anticipated shapes the reactions possible. Together with the Duty Manager Operations and the Operations Controllers for the national network and intercontinental flights, the OC Europe is the only employee at KLM who is allowed to shift the yellow and green bars on his computer screen, thereby effecting real-time changes in the flight schedule on the day of operations. In the Front Office, it is possible to oversee even more processes from one point at any given time. In summary, my fieldwork in the Front Office shows that performing the flight schedules is only possible by anticipating and reacting to changing and emerging situations that have been combined into a virtual situation.

If we follow Perrow, we could view the KLM network as a system that is both interactively complex and tightly coupled. Emerging problems will have rapid and unexpected effects, and this in turn accounts for the fact that problems are normally solved under time pressure. My fieldwork suggests a different conceptual framework. Time pressure is not just a shortage of time as a scarce resource, as would be the case in the rather mechanical view on tight coupling that Perrow describes. Here, when events follow each other quickly, the time to act runs out. My fieldwork shows that, in the Front Office of the OCC, virtual situations are created in which activities and events are connected and disconnected in real time. Here, coupling is not a mechanistic process, which is at risk of going out of control but, on the contrary, coupling is both a situated and a creative process of problem solving that has less to do with 'having enough time' than with 'having enough exchange'.

To understand how the KLM employees in the Front Office solve problems, we can conceptualize their work as shaping temporal orders. To change these orders, and thereby, to change the relations between spatially distanced events that make a 'virtual situation', exchange is needed. My fieldwork suggests that there are several different currencies of 'exchange': money, capacity, risk, knowledge and experience, information and communication technology, and authority. The concept of 'exchange' adds a dimension to the theoretical concepts of 'situated action' and 'improvisation' in providing a contextualized account of human action in distributed situations. Exchange is relational. If there is little time, then money, capacity, experience, information and communication technologies, taking risks, authority and sympathy all become more important. This explains, for example, why planning weeks and months ahead saves an airline money and why, under conditions of time pressure, exchanging money may be the only way to solve a problem.

As virtual situations are created in control centres like KLM's OCC, complexity can be both a source of problems and of solutions. It is precisely because the Operations Controller Europe connects two events that would not otherwise be related (a damaged plane in Barcelona and a plane scheduled for maintenance) that a problem can be solved, which in turn is only possible if no new problems emerge by doing so. The relational character of exchange explains why complexity in aviation does not just lead to a 'paradox of efficiency' in increasingly intricate webs of interrelated events that are more and more vulnerable to small disturbances. On the contrary, the innovative KLM OCC shows how virtual situations can only be controlled if they are complex enough to generate the exchange that is needed to solve emerging problems. In the next chapter, I will argue that this principle does not only apply to commercial airlines, but can be generalized and used to study the political and normative aspects of traffic control in cities and towns.

6   Sharing the road

Introduction

In Schiermonnikoog the cyclist reigns. Because visitors are prohibited from driving their cars on this small island off the northwestern coast of the Netherlands, its street scene is dominated by rented bicycles. Schiermonnikoog, designated a national park in 1989, is different from other Dutch villages in other respects. The traffic signs, parking lots, dividing lines, bicycle lanes, speed ramps, traffic lights, roundabouts, safety islands and pedestrian crossings that constitute the traffic landscape elsewhere are absent. Even sidewalks are a rarity. Cyclists, local buses, taxis, pedestrians and the occasional car of one of the island's inhabitants share the streets without any problems. Paying a little attention does the trick.

In terms of the distribution of speed among traffic participants, Schiermonnikoog can be conceived of as a model of an egalitarian society. All its 'members' have more or less the same speed at their disposal. On the Dutch mainland, the differences between fast and slow traffic are much greater. There, cars intersect the paths of other road users, such as cyclists and pedestrians, which has led to traffic safety problems. Until 1973, the annual number of road deaths in the Netherlands had increased to 3,300, most of which occurred in town and city centres. Since then, it has dropped to less than 900, in 2004. This development is all the more striking as the number of cars increased during this period from two million to more than seven million. One of the reasons for this development is the nearly complete redesign of the Dutch traffic landscape over the last 40 years. In this chapter, I will examine the redesign of the Dutch traffic landscape by focusing on bicycling, a practice that is more common in the Netherlands than in any other Western country. In 1960, cars, or 'personal transportation' as some people in the Netherlands used to call them, were still perceived as a luxury. Most people used their bikes for daily transport. Since then, the traffic landscape has had to accommodate higher traffic speeds as the number of cars increased. Space became scarce and problems with traffic flow arose in town and city centres that had been built for other types of traffic. How were these problems solved? Ideas about urban planning have played a leading role in designing solutions. In the 1960s, new, large-scale city streets were built where slow traffic was banned or segregated from motorized traffic.[1] Using both old and new techniques to regulate traffic, traffic space has been redistributed.[2]

In the 1970s, the hegemony of the car was increasingly debated, and slow traffic participants began to receive more attention from local and national governments. It was no longer self-evident that streets should be redesigned into traffic arteries. As car traffic increased, streets became contested spaces where battles raged between traffic participants and between traffic participants and local residents. These conflicting claims to space are usually discussed as a necessary and inevitable effect of increased car use. Traffic engineers worked from the imperative that car traffic should 'flow', and politicians favoured efficient and 'smart' technical solutions for reconciling the conflicting interests of different road users. The difference between resolving traffic problems and controlling air traffic at KLM's Operations Control Centre, is that a bird's eye view of the street is not available. The question of how the countless traffic participants in a big city such as Amsterdam reach their destinations on time is not answered in a control centre, instead it is at stake in negotiations in the town hall and on the street.[3] In contrast to the case of KLM, there is no central authority that has the final power of decision when time and space are contested. Where road users cross each other's paths, priority is given and taken, accelerations and decelerations are made. The question of why one road user must allow another to drive faster cannot be answered simply in terms of flow and efficiency, because the question also implies the need to justify claims and weigh interests of various traffic participants against each other. How can we discuss the political-normative character of daily traffic?

In order to answer this question, in this chapter I examine the redesign of the Dutch traffic landscape by studying *how* passages which allow traffic flowing at different speeds were made to intersect each other. Designing such 'crossings' is achieved through the use of different design styles, in which politics plays as important a role as roads, intersections and traffic signals. First, I give an account of the different ways interchanges can be designed. In a historical perspective, one can distinguish between what I call, a modern/regulative and an organic/deliberative design style. I then argue that interchanges do not merely distribute speeds that are an inherent characteristic of motor vehicles and bicycles. Instead, interchanges are constitutive of differences in speed. It is by designing traffic landscapes in specific styles that cars or bicycles can drive at high speeds in city traffic. Because passages are relational in the sense that space, time and risk must be exchanged between traffic participants, interchanges can also be understood as ensembles of passages. I use the term 'ensembles of passages' in the study of a Dutch policy aimed at increasing bicycle use implemented in the 1990s. The design manual, *Sign up for the bike*, issued in 1993, can be taken as a starting point for an analysis of the politics of passages.

Design, traffic rules and the interchange

Traffic safety became a political issue with the advent of the car.[4] But even before its arrival, people had been killed or injured in traffic accidents. Berman (1983) refers to the French poet Charles Baudelaire and his description of the chaotic nineteenth-century streets as a quintessential modern scene. Baudelaire alluded to the impotence of the pedestrian in busy city traffic in the mid nineteenth century. 'I was crossing the boulevard, in a great hurry, in the midst of a moving chaos with death galloping at me from every side' (cited in Berman 1983: 159). The archetypal modern man is a pedestrian thrown into the maelstrom of modern city traffic, a lone man contending against an agglomeration of mass and energy that is heavy, fast and lethal (Ibid.). The first victim of a car accident in the United States was a man who stepped unsuspectingly out of a trolley in 1899 and was run over by an electric taxi that was passing at 50 km/h, thereby 'illustrating all the problems of introducing autos into crowded city streets' (McShane 1994: 173). Whereas the driver thought of the street as an artery for travel, the trolley passenger conceived of it as a walkway (Ibid.) Since about 1900, measures were taken to improve traffic safety both in the United States and Europe, including the introduction of compulsory driving licences, licence plates and speed limits. Many of the innovations in traffic safety and traffic regulation were introduced by William Phelps Eno. Eno, born in New York in 1858, underlined the necessity of the management and supervision of traffic rules. His *Rules of the Road* (1903) was signed into law in New York City in 1906 (McShane 1994; Eno 1939). Eno was responsible for innovations such as stop signs, the rule that slow traffic must keep to the right, one-way streets, taxi stands, pedestrian islands and roundabouts.[5]

When cars were introduced in the early twentieth century, the rights to use public space as transit areas changed. Until then, pedestrians, cyclists, trolleys, buses and cars were all driving together on the street without the need for elaborate traffic rules. By the mid 1920s, streets had become the scene of a 'war' between pedestrians and cars, 'and the car was emerging victorious' (Belasco 1979: 116). In 1925, 25,000 people were killed in the United States from accidents involving cars. Almost 70 per cent were pedestrians, and one-third of these was less than 15 years old. The drivers of cars involved in accidents were not ordinarily made responsible for them: 'It was easier to call for stronger parental authority than to build safer cars, and easier to ban city children from neighbourhood streets than to restrict traffic' (Ibid.).

It is tempting to attribute the changes in the use of streets to the diffusion of the car. The street shifted from a multi-dimensional space used for a variety of functions to a mono-functional space where transit dominated. In this shift from a residential to a transit space, tensions caused by differences in speed emerged that had to be solved by innovations such as those introduced by Eno. This interpretation, however, is driven by technical determinism. The car, as a form of transportation technology, was not the single cause of the changing character of street space. Baldwin (1999) argues that the development of the traffic system in Hartford, Connecticut was part of a broader cultural trend towards segregating social activities in cities. At the end of the nineteenth century, there was a strong reformist movement in Hartford, as in other places on the east coast of the United States, that pleaded for cleaner and safer streets. Hygienist and moral arguments played an important role in this development. The segregation of functions in public spaces, according to Baldwin, preceded the diffusion of the car. Automobile organizations did, however, use the arguments of the Progressive Movement for the benefit of car drivers (Ibid.).

As the Hartford example shows, the growing use of cars at the beginning of the twentieth century was not the only cause of changes in public space. Other social and cultural developments helped make streets into contested spaces as well. The regulation of traffic in cities and towns has never has been a purely technical affair. Instead, the amount of space allotted to cars has always been justified with political, cultural and sometimes ethical arguments. These arguments are revealed in the way that traffic regulation and public space were debated. In these debates, there were two main issues at stake: the *design* of the traffic landscape and the application of *traffic rules* instructing road users how to proceed through a traffic landscape. I will first analyse in more detail how we can distinguish between what I call modern and organic styles of traffic landscape design. I will then show how, in the application of traffic rules in a traffic landscape, there is a distinction between what I call, a regulative and deliberative style.

Designing the traffic landscape

In designing a traffic landscape, the creation of the material conditions for the intersection of traffic at different speeds is achieved by adjusting several elements that determine any given traffic scenario, such as infrastructure, urban layout and geography. Traffic designers work on a continuum of styles, the ends of which, I suggest, are formed by two ideal types: modern and organic.

In the modern style, the problem of intersecting speeds is dealt with by *preventing* their intersection. Opposing claims to space are solved by providing each kind of traffic participant with its 'own street'. This approach to traffic design is modern because it is based on the ideas of modernist architects like Le Corbusier and Frank Lloyd Wright. They and other architects of the *Congrès internationaux d'architecture moderne* looked for solutions to growing urbanization. Central to their designs was the idea of zoning, in which different urban functions, such as working, living, recreating and being in transit were segregated. Le Corbusier's design of an urban neighbourhood, consisting of three 'systems of circulation' constructed on three levels, exemplifies the concept of zoning (Le Corbusier 1924: 220).[6] For Frank Lloyd Wright, transportation was the leading principle. Wright believed that the modern city was simultaneously 'everywhere and nowhere', and he expressed this idea in systems of divided highways. Broadacre City was Frank Lloyd Wright's vision of the ideal suburbia, with multiple centres, low building densities and one completely geared to the car. The architect introduced his solution for the problem of congested cities in 1932 in 'The disappearing city', and worked on it until his death in 1959. He made a wooden scale model showing a network of freeways connected to a grid of regional roads. On the main nodes stood 'markets', precursors of the American malls, as well as other centres of religious and cultural life (Wright 1958; De Long 1998).

However, the idea of divided traffic flow was expressed most clearly in the divided highway, built first in Germany and later in other European countries and in the United States. In the US, the divided highway emerged out of parkways, such as the Mount Vernon Memorial Highway in Washington, DC (Stommer and Philipp 1982; Carr 1987; Provoost 1996; Davis 1997). The main idea behind the divided highway, also called 'limited access highway', was that it should be accessible only to motorized traffic, have two lanes in each direction to enable easy passing and possess road junctions on a different level. Although the idea of a freeway in the city was not new, it was not until the 1960s that urban freeways were constructed in American cities (Lewis 1997).

In combining traffic flow and zoning, the modern design style not only segregated traffic from other social functions, but also kept different sorts of road users apart. By segregating traffic in these two ways, designers believed they could achieve two goals. First, traffic could flow unhindered; and second, the 'human measure' could be restored to urban life because slow traffic participants did not have to intersect with fast traffic participants. Culturally, this approach was linked to the idea of a makable society: architects, urban planners and traffic experts furnished an answer to the problems of urbanization by building good cities and roads.

The organic design style is both older and newer than the modern. Whereas the modern style attempted to solve the problem of intersecting speeds by preventing them from meeting in the first place, the organic design style seeks to *integrate* traffic participants. In this approach, the traffic landscape had to be designed in such a way that differences in speed were minimized. In practice, this means that fast road users had to adapt to slow users. This approach is old in the sense that it entails a return to the kind of traffic landscape that existed before the introduction of motorized traffic. But it is new in its opposition to the modern style, and is meant to solve some of the problems related to that style. The principle underlying the organic design of intersections is self-organization. The design does not aim at furnishing a priori patterns between traffic participants, but strives to create an arena in which these patterns emerge as a matter of course. Culturally, this design philosophy is associated with a discourse in which coercive, government-enforced rules are seen as less successful than the self-organizing power of the market.

Van den Boomen (2001) describes how 'a quiet revolution in urban design and traffic engineering is taking place in the Netherlands' (van den Boomen 2001: 1). The Dutch traffic landscape during the last three decades saw the arrival of traffic humps (the first was built in 1970 in Delft), residential areas built for slow traffic ('home zones'), urban zones with a maximum speed of 30 km/h and roundabouts. All these measures aimed at integrating slow and fast traffic participants. There was no longer room for signs, traffic lights and pedestrian crossings, or for the overpass junctions and separate bicycle lanes that characterized modernist traffic design. According to the advocates of organic design, the safest intersection is an empty square. In an empty square, a car driver becomes puzzled, slows down and tries to establish eye contact with other road users. In the town centre of the Frisian village, Oosterwolde, this 'legible street', as Van den Boomen calls it, is radicalized. Until 1998, the central square (called 'The Brink') was designed according to Dutch guidelines for road design, with pre-sorting, zebra crossings and yield signs. But in 1998 The Brink was reconstructed.

> It has become a square paved with red cobble stones, nothing more, nothing less. No signs, no side walks, no bicycle lanes, nothing, not even decorative railway sleepers. Only when you look more closely, you see the design elements that steer the gaze, such as green balustrades. An old man trudges diagonally across the square, a mother parks her car, gets out and changes her kid's trousers, a truck gives priority to a group of cyclists coming from the right.
>
> (Ibid.: 3)

Despite continual violations of traffic rules and the apparent chaos, there have been no casualties since the town square was redesigned, even though 4,500 cars pass through it each day. Before the reconstruction, there were three accidents each year. The designers succeeded in making the square safer and quieter, while improving traffic flow and the village's accessibility. This design style has not been restricted to towns and villages. Amsterdam's Dam Square, located in one of the busiest parts of the city's centre, was reconstructed in 2000 according to organic design principles. Whereas before each traffic mode, which included cars, bicycles, trolleys, buses, trucks and pedestrians, possessed a specified position on the street, now a sophisticated redesign creates the impression of a big square that is crisscrossed by everyone and everything.[7]

The application of traffic rules

Taking part in traffic is demanding. Traffic participants are expected to act in continuously changing circumstances that entail any number of moments in which a choice between one act and another is involved (Otte 1993: 43). Determining how to act in a traffic landscape presupposes having rules at one's disposal. These rules can be juridical or social, depending on whether they relate to questions of responsibility and accountability or are necessary to interpret the actions of other road users. Like traffic design, the rules used to guide traffic flow can be viewed as a continuum of two ideal types of styles in regulating actions, which I call regulative and deliberative. The regulative style of applying rules assumes that to guide traffic, clear rules and guidelines are necessary to both establish and maintain the boundaries of road users' conduct in the flow of traffic. In this approach, the application of traffic rules is the same everywhere and legally binding. If violated, a traffic participant is given a warning, fine or heavier penalty. Traffic rules thus serve the juridical function of establishing accountability and attributing culpability when broken. In principle, road users are responsible for their own actions. In the Netherlands, traffic rules are deduced from a general condition of danger that has been formulated in the Dutch Traffic Rules and Regulations as follows: 'It is forbidden to behave in such a manner that can cause danger on the road, or that the traffic on the road is or can be obstructed.' The specific rules that apply to different sorts of traffic participants can all be derived from this general condition.

Rules and material design cannot be separated in practice. To make clear which traffic rules apply to a specific situation, a variety of material provisions have to be made.[8] White lines on the pavement segregate traffic participants. Signs indicate maximum speeds. Traffic lights regulate traffic at an intersection by segregating it in time when it is not possible to segregate it in space. To take part in daily traffic, road users must be able to interpret these codes in such a way that they display the right actions. Taking part in traffic not only means that someone must be able to drive a vehicle or ride a bicycle, but also to 'read' the traffic landscape. In other words, they must be able to interpret an actual situation against the backdrop of official traffic rules. It is important to note that in a regulative style, as we find in the ideas of Eno for example, the problem of integrating different speeds is solved by a priori distribution rights and duties in traffic. Fast traffic always has priority over slow traffic, regardless of the specific circumstances, and entering a one-way street from the wrong side will always result in a penalty, as long as a police officer is present to note the offence. The success of a regulative style thus depends on education, the internalization of rules and the ability to sanction offenders.

Traffic rules prescribe how road users should act in specific traffic situations, but legislators must acknowledge that it is impossible to regulate every traffic incident. In some cases it necessary to break a traffic rule in order to respond to potentially dangerous situations. Whereas at one end of the continuum the application of rules focuses on formulating precisely how to distribute rights and duties a priori in generalized traffic situations, at the other end we find an approach which departs from the idea that traffic participants should be able to judge a situation as it emerges in the moment. This approach I have called deliberative, because traffic participants must deliberate on how to interpret a situation. This means that traffic rules play a different role in the deliberative approach than in the regulative approach.

One particularly good illustration of the deliberative approach is the four-way stop used in the United States. A four-way stop is an intersection in which drivers must make a complete stop and then decide who has the right of way. This rule, the violation of which can result in a steep fine, can be thought of as a second order or meta rule, because it aims at creating a situation in which road users can determine how the first-order traffic rule, namely 'the first to arrive at the intersection has the right of way' 'fits' into each situation. The principle behind this approach can be described in Habermasian terms as providing the conditions for understanding ('Verständigung'), in which the fact that traffic participants are able to deliberate is possible because there are a priori no differences in speed.[9] Equalizing speeds among traffic participants renders situations in which the communication can be power-free ('machtsfreie Kommunikation'). Whereas strict compliance with traffic rules, at least on paper, leads to a clear a priori distribution of responsibilities and accountability, responsibility in a deliberative approach is something that can only be determined in concrete situations.

To answer the question of how to integrate different speeds into the same space, innovative answers have been given in both design and the application of rules. Innovations can be described according to their position on the continuum between modern and organic, or regulative and deliberative. The Los Angeles freeways are a modern solution to traffic, enabling car traffic to flow at a constant speed because it is kept segregated from other traffic participants. The Dam Square in Amsterdam is an organic solution, in which differences between speeds are not taken as a starting point. In his *Rules of the Road* (1903), Eno formulated traffic rules which precede concrete situations. His ideas have become common knowledge all over the world, but they have been the issue of recent debate, and in some cases, have been overridden for approaches in which second-order rules are used to help traffic participants judge situations at hand.

Ensembles of passages

Thus far, I have understood speed as an inherent quality of a mode of transportation or even of a traffic participant. Viewed from this perspective, it is necessary to design a traffic landscape and to apply traffic rules because there *are* differences in speed. The Dutch judicial expert Otte formulated this position as follows: 'The traffic issue seems to have come into existence in 1885 and 1886, when Benz and Daimler put three and four wheeled vehicles that were driven by gas motors on the road' (Otte 1993: 7). In Otte's portrayal of the process, a car appears in the traffic landscape all by itself, as a traffic participant with a maximum speed that is 10 times higher than that of slower road users, such as pedestrians, and five times higher than cyclists. In previous chapters, I have argued that speed is not an inherent quality of vehicles, but the outcome of the ability to create fast passages. Taken as the effect of passages, the speed of cars and pedestrians can be conceived of as the product of a heterogeneous ordering that entails both material and immaterial elements of a traffic landscape: both traffic lights and the rules that dictate travel on roads. The ability to drive fast by car in a city depends upon a passage that has been made. This same is true if one wants to ride fast on a bicycle. The only difference is that it requires creating a different passage.

Those who consider speed as an inherent quality of a car usually take a spectator's perspective. The concept of passages enables analysts to construct an actor's perspective. From the actor's perspective, the innovations which have been discussed in this section, both in material design and the application of rules, are not a *reaction* to a series of already existing speed distributions. On the contrary, these innovations are *constitutive* of such differences. This change in perspective requires another elaboration in the concept of passage, which focuses on the 'coexistence' of many speeds in what I call *ensembles* of passages. The first step in the elaboration of passages is to find a way to describe differences in speed in other words than kilometres per hour.

The relationality of time, space and risk

A motorist driving at high speed in a city has little time to react to unexpected events, such as a pedestrian who is suddenly crossing the street. This means certain skills and experience are needed to drive a car in urban traffic landscapes. Car drivers are asked to prove they possess such knowledge and skills by a carrying a driver's licence. If the threat of a collision arises, a car driver (or in the Netherlands, a cyclist) can brake to reduce their speed. In doing so, the car will need a certain amount of distance before coming to a complete stop. The braking path is related to the speed the vehicle was going: the faster the car, the more metres necessary to stop it. A car driving at 30 km/h has a braking distance of 10 metres. A car going 50 km/h needs 30 metres. Braking distance can be calculated by taking the sum of the time an individual needs to react and the time a vehicle of a specific mass, moving at a certain speed, needs to come to a stop. This means that a car not only needs the road right in front of it, but that an even larger distance must be free in order to prevent collisions. The ability to estimate correctly the relation between speed, reaction time and braking distance is one of the most important skills any car driver must possess.

Even the most skilled driver would lose control of the steering wheel when driving at too high a speed or cause a collision if there were no facilities, such as shoulder space, to compensate for the inability to react quickly enough. The speed of a car thus depends on the design of the road and the rules governing specific situations. Every road has a *design speed*, defined as the speed which is normative for the road and its design elements, in such a way that car drivers can drive at a certain speed without being hindered by other road users (Kuipers 1998). The concept of design speed clarifies why a freeway, on which cars can drive at 120 km/h, has to be much wider than a two-lane road, designed for a safe maximum speed of 80 km/h. Travel at higher speeds requires more space both next to and in front of a car in order for drivers to be able to react to unexpected situations and events. In addition to the width of the road, the design speed is determined by the degree of curve in a road. The higher the degree of arc, the less a car driver has to brake to control the car. Like the Operations Controllers in KLM's Front Office, a driver has to be able to anticipate in order to have enough time to react in emerging situations. To do this, traffic designers must create an adequate amount of distance for 'stopping sight' for example. Only when a car driver (or a cyclist) can look ahead to see if an intersection is free, and thus if there is enough space to brake when necessary, is a high speed possible. Thus, speed is not only a quality of a vehicle, but always presupposes a combination of skills, technical characteristics of a car, and an ordering of the traffic landscape in terms of design and the application of rules.[10]

Speed as distribution of time, space and risk

To be able to drive fast in a car, time and space are needed to react to unexpected situations. When different traffic participants encounter each other, an exchange of time, space and risk takes place, as was clear in the example above of the pedestrian crossing the street before an oncoming car. A pedestrian who walks calmly to the other side needs a certain amount of time. If a car is approaching, a pedestrian usually knows from experience if the speed of the car and the braking distance that goes with it will leave her or him enough time to reach the other side. In this example, the *space* of the street is thus contested by the two traffic participants: the street constitutes part of the passage of the pedestrian and that of the car driver. In the movements of both the pedestrian and the car driver, a continuous exchange of time-space is taking place. The pedestrian must give space to the car driver by either standing still or walking faster, and the car driver must give way to the pedestrian by braking. The higher the speed of the car, the more space is needed to 'look ahead', to have enough time to react to unexpected situations. Conversely, the pedestrian has a very short braking distance, but needs time to cross the street. Street space is thus relational: it is part of the movement of both the pedestrian and the car driver. A street's curves also illustrate the relationality of traffic space. When a street has wide curves, a car driver can take a quick turn left or right, but a pedestrian needs more time to cross the street.

But speed not only requires a certain distribution of space, but also of *time*. A high driving speed requires space, but also changes the temporal order among traffic participants. An example is the distribution of reaction time. Among each other, pedestrians have plenty of time to react to unforeseen circumstances. For cyclists, the time is shorter. Someone who is driving in a car at 50 km/h has an even shorter reaction time. A car driver not only 'asks for' reaction time from himself, but also from other road users. After all, they have to react more quickly to changes in traffic situations. Like the redistribution of space, this shortening of reaction time on the street has consequences, particularly for vulnerable road users such as children, the elderly and the disabled. Whitelegg (1997) uses the example of the adjustment of traffic lights for pedestrians. In some places, pedestrians can only reach the other side of the road within the given period of time by starting to run. 'All traffic engineering and infrastructure planning embodies the theft of time in some shape or form and its redistribution to wealthier groups' (Whitelegg 1997: 133). The fact that cars in city traffic take time away from others is evident in another example. In busy streets, parents, usually mothers, have to keep an eye on their playing children, which Whitelegg (1993) calls a form of 'time theft' or 'time lock'.

A final sort of distribution among road users is *risk*. A traffic participant who takes risks, for example, by driving faster than is allowed, also enlarges the risk of an accident for other road users. Between motorized and non-motorized forms of transit, there are predictable asymmetries in the chances of being in a fatal road accident. Hillman, Adams and Whitelegg (1990) studied the disappearance of the independent mobility of children and young people. The title of their book, *One false move...*, refers to a traffic safety campaign in Great Britain in the 1980s. The campaign poster shows a child on the verge of crossing a street, with the phrase 'One false move and you're dead' underneath. Although as in other countries, in Great Britain, the number of traffic fatalities of children has declined since the 1970s, the claim that traffic has become safer is arguable. In 1971, 80 per cent of children of seven or eight years old were allowed to go to school without parental supervision, a percentage which dropped to only 9 per cent in 1990. As Hillman, Adams and Whitelegg claim, the number of accidents involving children, however, has not dropped because traffic has become safer, but because children are no longer allowed to go out onto the streets alone. Studies from Great Britain and Germany show that parents, out of fear of an accident, allow their children to move independently in their living environment less and less. In addition, parents spend an increasing amount of time escorting their children in traffic.

Exchanging space, time and risk

In Chapter 3 I defined the construction of passages as the ordering of heterogeneous entities in such a way that a situated relation between time and space is produced. This definition entails a relational view of space and time that enables me to study the way passages are related in everyday traffic. Accounts on the relationality of space and time argue that they are not independent from events, but constitute relations between states of affairs. Leibniz claimed that space and time constituted 'a structure of relations of a specific kind':

> space is the order of coexistence – that is, the order among mutually contemporaneous states of things; while time is the order of succession – that is, the order among the various different mutually coexisting states of things which because they are (mutually) coexisting – must, of course, have some 'spatial' structure.
>
> (Harvey 1996: 252)[11]

According to this line of reasoning, the passages of cars and bicycles are part of each other. The heterogeneous order of a passage is partly laid down in the design of traffic landscapes, for example, by segregating bicycles and cars, which makes greater differences in speed possible without putting cyclists at risk. Conversely, by integrating cars and bicycles, car drivers must adapt to the slower pace of cyclists. In both cases, the spatio-temporal ordering is expressed by rules embedded in the traffic design itself. In the former, the spatio-temporal order is fixed through a priori traffic rules. In the latter, through second-order rules which are negotiated by traffic participants in real time. Passages have speed as an outcome. For this outcome to be achieved, other passages become relevant. It follows that the designed landscape and the rules which regulate actions in it do not have intrinsic qualities as a time-space relation that *is*, and that the characteristics of a section of road or an intersection are relational. Widths and curves are fixed, but what they *do* depends on the passages they are a part of.[12] Thus, a car driver passes a different intersection than a bicycle. A car is not a priori faster than a bicycle, but only in a mutual relation with it which is determined by more than just the vehicles' qualities. Thus, the crossing of passages produces and distributes speed.

Previous chapters argued that passages are both constructed in advance, as well as in the actual moment of travel. Like the Operations Controllers in KLM's Control Centre, car drivers, cyclists and pedestrians must have an overview of a situation in order to act appropriately to it. I argued that the controllers have to have an amount of 'exchange' in order to repair disruptions in a passage arising from unforeseen circumstances. Examples of exchange in daily traffic include having enough space to manoeuvre and swerve, the time to react to unexpected events, and the skills to judge a specific situation. An exchange is partly distributed in advance, for example, in the width of a bicycle lane or curves of a street. But it is also embedded in the application of rules or the freedom to deviate from them and act on one's own insight. Because passages are related to each other, space, time and risk are exchanged continually in the act of driving, cycling or walking. A car that passes a bicycle at a high speed reduces the cyclist's space for manoeuvring, and thus the possibility for him or her to react to unforeseen circumstances. Space as exchange is moved from the cyclist to the car driver, but so is the risk of an accident. Conversely, a car driving behind a cyclist in a narrow street will 'hand in' time because the cyclist needs exchange in the form of space for manoeuvring.

Answering the question at the beginning of this chapter – how do passages cross? – assumes that we construct an actor's perspective. In this chapter, I construct this perspective by looking at the work designers do in designing passages. As has become clear, the relational character of passages is expressed both in the design of roads and the application of rules. Whereas this can be done in different styles, as has been outlined above, these styles generate specific distributions of exchange. Traffic designers do not just design a modern or an organic intersection, or apply rules based on regulative or deliberative principles. They create *ensembles* of passages in which exchange is distributed in a specific way. Thus, the various design styles discussed in the previous section imply different strategies in order for passages to 'coexist' and for exchange to be distributed among them. But if the speeds of roads users are related, who decides if and why a certain speed is more important than another? Why would a car have to wait for a bicycle or vice versa? The making of fast passages, thus, entails a political dimension. One way to analyse this is to study how traffic experts and urban planners have tried to design higher speeds for the bicycle. Should cyclists have their own bicycle lanes, or is integrating them with other traffic a better solution? Are special 'bicycle rules' necessary, or are cyclists better off if they are free to follow their own rules?

Dutch designs for the bicycle

Never has there been so much cycling in the Netherlands than there was in 1960.[13] Cycling developed from an activity for the sports-loving elite at the end of the nineteenth century to a transit practice for the masses in the early twentieth century. Even in the 1950s, the streets of Amsterdam were always a-jingle with the sound of cycle bells as people went to and from work. Since 1960, however, the bicycle lost ground, first to the scooter, and a decade later to the car. The bicycle's share in the total number of kilometres travelled sharply decreased in the 1960s before stabilizing in the

1970s (Adri de la Bruhèze and Veraart 1999: 11; Ministry of Transport 1997: 41).[14] The main reasons for the growth in motorized traffic were increasing prosperity and government policies (van den Heuvel and Peters 1998). In the 1960s, Dutch transport policies aimed at facilitating car use by improving roads in cities and the countryside. As a result, a struggle ensued between slow and fast traffic users over space and priority, which was initially lost by the bicycle. When the number of cars on the road increased without concomitant adaptations in infrastructure, the number of accidents involving slower traffic participants rose disturbingly. The national government attempted to solve the problem by building bicycle lanes and making intersections safer, but the focus remained on accommodating car use.

After 1970, however, the political response to the mobility debate in the Netherlands shifted from facilitating motorized traffic to seeking ways to reduce its contribution to air pollution, increased oil consumption, and the overall degradation of the urban and rural environments. The bicycle was rediscovered as a solution to the negative effects of the growing reliance on the automobile. Unlike the car, the bicycle was healthy, clean, silent, energy-efficient and flexible, as the Dutch Cyclists' Union claimed. In addition to reducing the vulnerability of cyclists in traffic, policy makers now found a second reason to build and improve the bicycle infrastructure: to promote a shift from 'the acceleration pedal to the bicycle pedal' (Lammers 1995: 7). In cities like The Hague and Tilburg, special cycle routes were built. But in 1981, it became evident that, although Dutch residents judged the new cycle lanes positively, they did not produce an increase of the number of kilometres covered on the bike. New bicycle lanes did not seem to be enough of a reason for people to travel shorter distances by bike (Ibid.).

Researchers and policy makers concluded that not only should they build long-distance bicycle routes, but also a dense network of cycle lanes for local transport in which each cycle path could not be more than 500 metres from another. The network should consist of uninterrupted lanes that were free of obstacles. It would have to follow the existing pattern of roads, and provide access to the main services and facilities in a town, such as public buildings, offices, recreation facilities and shopping centres. These were the goals behind the Bicycle Network in Delft, built between 1982 and 1987. At an early stage, this new cycle infrastructure did lead to an increase in bicycle use, but the increase did not continue. It did however improve traffic safety, the second aim of the policy goal. The number of traffic accidents involving cyclists in Delft decreased and remained at a lower level (Hartman 1997).

An influential white paper from the national government published in 1990, the Second Transport Structure Plan (SVV II), mentioned in Chapter 1, presented the bicycle as an important means of countering the problems caused by the increase in car use. It emphasized what in policy terms is called a 'modal shift', a shift from one mode of transport to another, for example, from using the car to using public transport for longer distances and the bicycle for shorter trips. The national government saw it as its duty to promote bicycle use, and it expressed its leading role in the *Bicycle Masterplan*, published in 1991. The policy had two main aims: more and safer cycling. Between 1986, the base year against which change would be measured, and 2010, the number of cycle kilometres should increase by 30 per cent. Improvements in coordinating bicycle and public transport schedules were supposed to lead to an increase in the number of kilometres travelled in the latter. It proposed ambitious goals for reducing road accidents involving cyclists and reducing the number of cycle thefts. From 1995 on, actions to promote the use of bicycles had to be part of all traffic policy plans at the national, provincial and municipal government levels. If there ever had been a concerted policy which gave priority to the bicycle, this was it. How was this carried out?

Cycle-friendly infrastructures

The policies outlined in the *Bicycle Masterplan*, which took effect in 1991, considered a well-functioning cycle infrastructure as the key to a sustainable and safe mobility system (Michels 1993).[15] Just how this infrastructure should look was described in *Sign up for the bike: Design manual for a cycle-friendly infrastructure* (Ploeger *et al.* 1993), which became one of the most important documents during the Bicycle Masterplan period. This handbook was drawn up by a working group comprised of a range of cycling experts and lobbyists, including the Dutch Centre for Research and Contract Standardization in Civil and Traffic Engineering and the Dutch Cyclists' Union. *Sign up for the bike* is still viewed by most Dutch municipalities as the standard by which to judge the quality of cycling facilities.

The manual begins by asking what cycling actually is. 'The designer of a cycle-friendly infrastructure should be familiar with the technical possibilities and limitations of cyclist and bicycle. The cyclist is driver, equilibrist and power-plant all at the same time (Ploeger *et al.* 1993: 13).[16] In contrast to traditional technical handbooks, which tend to begin with ways of integrating the needs of cyclists with those of faster road users, and often lead to compromises, *Sign up for the bike* focused on the needs of cyclists as users of the infrastructure. Because bicycles are powered by muscles, in cycle-friendly road design, 'energy losses are kept to a minimum' (Ibid.: 14). The design manual also took into account that bicycles can be unstable:

> Being held up by only two wheels, the cyclist is constantly busy avoiding falls. Side winds, the slipstream of goods vehicles, unevenness in the road surface and being forced down to low speeds, all help to determine stability and with that the necessary room for

manoeuvre.... The vulnerability of the cyclist is obvious from the accident statistics. The highway authority can however exert great influence here. It can give the cyclist a 'spatial crumple-zone' which acts as a space for emergency manoeuvring. Indeed, a cyclist can balance on a strip 20 cm wide, but the need for acrobatics certainly should not be a starting-point for design. When a car door is flung open the extra space on a cycle-lane could prove lifesaving. Their vulnerability also means that cyclists should not be mixed with fast moving cars and intensive heavy goods traffic.

(Ibid.)

The design manual continues to explain the disadvantages of bicycles with respect to faster road users. They have very little suspension and 'a smooth road surface is a minimum condition in meeting the requirements for bicycle-friendliness' (Ploeger *et al.* 1993). That cyclists ride in the open air has advantages and disadvantages. The shelter from wind and rain which cars offer take away some of the disadvantages, but the advantages of cycling should be maintained. Because cyclists are social beings, they should be able to ride two abreast. This also gives parents the opportunity to safely supervise their children. Finally,

a human being is not a machine (neither is a cyclist). There are certain limits to the number and complexity of tasks which can be carried out by the cyclist. A designer should respect these limitations, while taking account of less experienced and less able bodied road-users.

(Ibid.: 15)

The design manual lists five main requirements based on this design philosophy, which can be taken as criteria for good cycle-friendly design. They are coherence ('the cycling-infrastructure forms a coherent unit and links with all departure points and destinations of cyclists'), directness ('the cycling-infrastructure continually offers the cyclist as direct a route as possible so detours are kept to a minimum'), attractiveness ('the cycling-infrastructure is designed and fitted in the surroundings in such a way that cycling is attractive'), safety ('the cycling-infrastructure guarantees the road safety of cyclists and other road-users') and comfort ('the cycling-infrastructure enables a quick and comfortable flow of bicycle-traffic') (Ibid.: 24).

The authors of the design manual took the design of the cycling infrastructure as a balance between form, function and use. Infrastructure has a *form*, such as intersections, road sections or storage facilities. The desired *function* of these forms of infrastructure follows from a programme of requirements, for example, the condition that the number of accidents involving cyclists must be reduced. The expected *use* of the designed infrastructure is determined on the basis of model calculations or observations at specific locations. The equilibrium among these elements is achieved by

Table 6.1 The relation between shape, function and use in designing cycling infrastructures as imagined by the authors of the design manual. Each
element is presented in terms of its consequences in the cycle network,
cycle routes and cycle facilities

Shape	(Intended) function	(Expected) use
network • junctions • links	make direct and safe transport by bicycle possible within a coherent system	matrix of departure points and destinations (observed or calculated)
route • district • local • neighbourhood level	quality resulting from the level of route in the network • connecting • distributor • access	volume (observed or calculated)
facility • intersection • road section • crossing • storage facility	quality resulting from the level of the route • negotiating encounters • traffic • linking of facilities • offering storage space	behaviour and manoeuvres of road users (observed or calculated)

Source: Ploeger *et al.* 1993: 35.

'repeated adjustment of these three "linchpins" before the design is
"level"' (Ibid.: 34). Sometimes it may be necessary to readjust objectives
by deviating from the ideal design, for example, because cyclists' interests
have to compete with other interests, such as land use, priority of motorized traffic, or the coordination of traffic lights. Form, function and use
can be found on three levels: the network (junctions and links), the route
(district, local and neighbourhood) and the facility (intersection, road
section, crossing and storage facility) (see Table 6.1).

In terms of the vocabulary of passages that has been developed in the previous chapters, the design manual expresses an actor's perspective. It
describes the work that has to be done in order to construct faster passages
for the bike. As became clear from the section on the relationality of passages, one of the problems that then must be addressed is the 'coexistence' of
cyclists with traffic participants in what I called 'ensembles'. *Sign up for the
bike*'s suggestions for the design of road sections and intersections illustrate
how these ensembles should be designed for the bicycle to make it a faster,
safer and a more comfortable means of travelling in cities and towns.

Segregation or integration?

The authors of *Sign up for the bike* argued that the most important issue
to be dealt with when designing infrastructure is whether motorized traffic

should be segregated from cycling traffic. They contended that segregating cars from bicycles, whether physically (e.g. by building cycle lanes) or visually (e.g. by painting lines on the street or using coloured asphalt), had both advantages and disadvantages. In sections in which there are high car speeds and congestion, physical separation should usually be advocated. The advantages are that cyclists are better protected than with visual separations or mixed road profiles. Riding a bicycle is more comfortable when the bike path is separated from the road by a barrier when the car traffic is fast and intensive. Such barriers also enable car drivers to pass cyclists more easily. The disadvantages are that segregating traffic participants reduces the space cyclists have for manoeuvring, the speeds of travel are higher and the attentiveness of the car drivers decreases. In addition, Godefrooij (1997) points out that segregation often seems to aim at the free flow of motorized traffic. Cyclists are banished to the side of the road – and in some European countries – even to the sidewalk (Godefrooij 1997: 232). Visual segregation, for example by using red asphalt for bicycle lanes, offers cyclists more room to manoeuvre, but it has the effect of assuring car drivers that they can pass cyclists more easily (which often translates into faster) thus increasing a cyclist's discomfort and risk. When a physical separation is not used, car drivers sometimes use the bicycle lane to park temporarily, which can cause cyclists to swerve into the main road, another element which increases the risk this kind of segregation poses for cyclists. Finally, in a mixed profile, all traffic participants use the same space. For cyclists, a mixed profile has the advantage of allowing them more space for manoeuvring, and it usually requires less space. Moreover, as Godefrooij argues, 'Integration underlines the equality of all road users, as all have the same freedom of movement' (Ibid.: 231). The disadvantages are that mixed profile road sections are not as safe, and if there is a lot of unauthorized parking in the bike paths, then cyclists are forced to enter the traffic lanes, which can lead to cyclists feeling as if they are 'living speed limiters' (Ibid.).

According to the design manual, whether it is necessary to combine different speeds in the same space depends upon the speed and intensity of motorized traffic. The faster and denser the traffic, the greater the need to separate bicycle traffic from it. Separation in space, then, is necessary to offer all road users the exchange to react to unforeseen situations: eye contact, stopping view, anticipation and reaction, and space for manoeuvring. Conversely, the slower and less dense the traffic, the less space is needed for cycle safely. Figure 6.1, taken from the design manual, illustrates the use of space as exchange. It shows a deterrent strip, a spatial buffer which provides cyclists the exchange to swerve without hitting parked cars.

Cyclists not only encounter other traffic on road sections, but also at road junctions. According to *Sign up for the bike*, junctions are the most problematic in terms of safety and comfort. Half of all cyclist road casualties

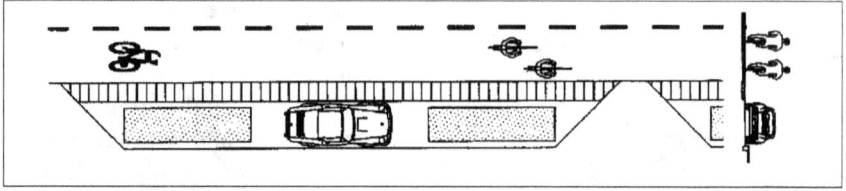

Figure 6.1 A drawing of the deterrent strip which separates parking spaces from cycle paths (source: Ploeger *et al.* 1993: 76).

occur at junctions. Junctions are problematic because roads with different functions meet there. Integrating the interests of various road users can be challenging, and those of cyclists are usually not considered the most important. As the design manual claims, 'In general the interests of motorized traffic are given more than enough consideration.' However, it strongly urges that 'the interests of bicycle-traffic are also given fair consideration. And it is particularly at junctions where bicycle traffic can gain (or rather: lose) a lot of time' (Ploeger *et al.* 1993: 149).

The design manual distinguishes between several different kinds of junctions: for example, those with and without right-of-ways or traffic lights, roundabouts or split-levels. These junctions can be analysed using the terms introduced in the discussion of *styles* earlier in this chapter, both in terms of design style and the style of rule application they possess. An example is a junction using traffic lights. It uses a regulative style of rule application (the rule to stop for red is given a priori), and it is a modern solution because traffic is separated, not in space but in time.[17] The design manual offers various measures which can be taken to make traffic lights more cycle-friendly. The green phase can be extended for cyclists who are parallel to other traffic, or allowing right-turning cyclists to ignore red lights, having more than one green phase for cyclists during each cycle and offering cycle detection at a distance using electro-magnetic devices in the pavement. In Dutch traffic design practice, these cycle- and pedestrian-friendly adjustments of traffic lights are rare, however, because they lead to greater congestion among motorized traffic, which would not be accepted politically (Wilson and Middelham 2000).

If junctions with traffic lights can be analysed as an expression of both a regulative and a modern design strategy, roundabouts are an expression of an organic design style and a deliberative style of rule giving. The right of way for any driver is determined by the second-order rule that traffic on the roundabout has priority. Roundabouts are safer than traffic-light-regulated junctions because the relatively tight dimensions of the circle reduce the speed of motorized traffic, affording road users more time to judge who has priority as well as to respond to an unexpected event. There

Figure 6.2 An ensemble of passages. Practical example, taken from the design manual for a cycle-friendly infrastructure, of a roundabout with separate-lying cycle-track and cyclists having right of way. Roundabouts like these can nowadays be found in many places in the Netherlands (source: Ploeger *et al.* 1993: 189).

are many types of roundabouts in Dutch design practice. The issue at stake in their design is whether the traffic flow is better separated or mixed. As the design manual shows, they can be designed with a mixed traffic flow, where cyclists enjoy the right-of-way status of traffic on the interchange. They can also be made with separate cycle lanes, on which cyclists may or may not be given the right of way.

The successes and failures of the Bicycle Masterplan

In 1998, the Bicycle Masterplan was evaluated against the goals of more and safer cycling formulated in 1991. Approximately 30 million guilders had been spent on studies and projects. The results were not unambiguous. The number of bicycle kilometres in the Netherlands had increased by 5 per cent in 1996 compared to the level in 1986, but it then stabilized. The number of cycle thefts remained constant, totally between 600,000 and 700,000 each year. Road safety had improved. The number of fatalities involving cyclists had decreased by 14 per cent compared to 1986, just 1 per cent shy of the goal set by the Bicycle Masterplan (Ministry of

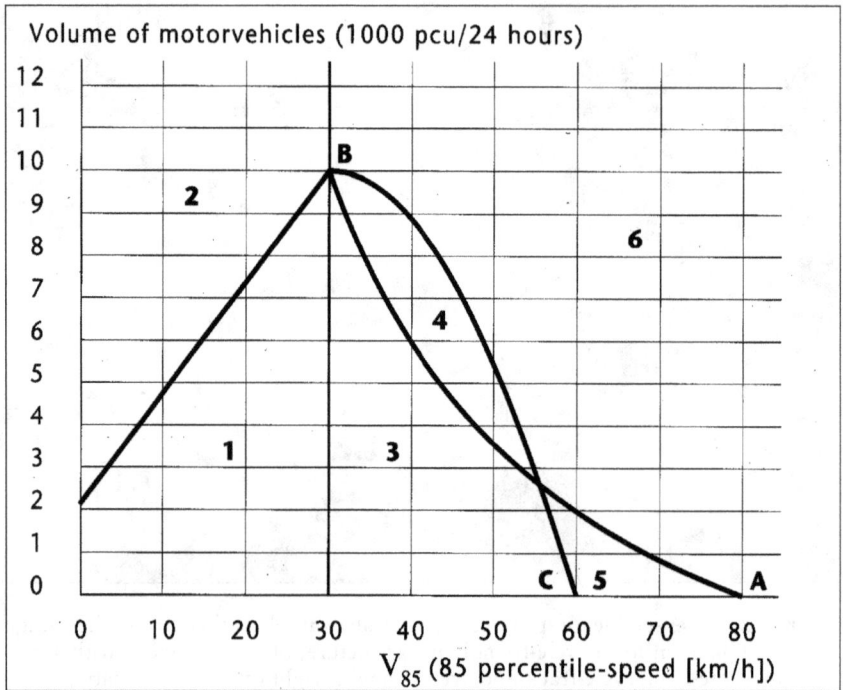

Figure 6.3 A graphic illustration taken from the design manual showing the kind of separation needed between cyclists and motor vehicles for different kinds of traffic flow. The vertical axis represents traffic volume and the horizontal axis actual speeds. 1 thus represents a road section in which there is low volume and low speed; 5, low volume and high speed, etc. (source: Ploeger *et al.* 1993: 80).

Transport 1997). But despite construction of much new cycle-friendly infrastructure, people were not cycling substantially more than before. Cycling had become safer, but not more attractive to those who travelled by car. If we are to explain the partial failure of the Bicycle Masterplan, we can do so by examining it in light of the notion of passages. So far we have seen that the traffic landscape can be designed according to certain styles. The interchanges between different road users can be understood as ensembles of passages that render specific ways in which space, time and risk are exchanged. The design manual for cycle-friendly infrastructure provided different design solutions to the problem of integrating or segregating motorized traffic and bicycles. I will now use the concepts of ensembles of passages and exchange to explain the partial failure of the Bicycle Masterplan.

The partial failures of the design philosophy are evident in a crucial graph from *Sign up for the bike*. It shows the kind of segregation between motorized and non-motorized traffic that is thought necessary, given the average speed of motorized traffic and the number of vehicles present (Ploeger *et al.* 1993: 80). The graph, shown in Figure 6.3, compares the volume of motor vehicles (vertical axis) with the actual speeds of motorized traffic (horizontal axis). The numbers in the graph signify different combinations of speed and traffic volume. In area 1, the speed of motorized traffic is less than 30 km/h and a mixed profile is recommended. In area 3, motorized traffic reaches 60 km/h, in which case a road without cycle lanes is still acceptable, although they may be desirable. In area 4, the traffic density is higher, but the speed is relatively low, so the design manual considers a cycle lane 'desirable' (Ibid.: 81). In area 5, the opposite is true. Cars drive at high speeds but, because the volume of traffic is very low, a mixed profile is considered acceptable and cycle lanes are not recommended. Cycle lanes are however recommended for area 6, in which motorized traffic flows at high speeds and high volumes.

The cause of the failure of the design philosophy outlined in the design manual to effect a shift from car to bicycle use is that it did not acknowledge the implicit political character of this graph. The graph is a perfect example of the decontextualized comparative perspective discussed in Chapters 2 and 3. The disappeared context here has a political character, as it addresses the question of who can drive fast and who cannot. The authors treat the speed and volume of motorized traffic as the most important factors in determining which kind of separation should be used in each situation (Ibid.: 79). These parameters are viewed as givens. But the speed and volume of traffic are not inherent. Viewed from an actor's perspective of creating a passage, to possess any speed at all requires a great deal of work. And in this particular case, the work has a political character. As argued earlier, speed is relational and, in order to drive fast, space, time and risk must continually be exchanged among traffic participants. This is evident in the graph. If the horizontal axis had shown the speed of bicycles instead of cars, the maximum speed would have been 30 km/h, and the areas right of the vertical line would not exist. Therefore the question of separating or integrating traffic would not even arise. It is not surprising that the authors of the design manual have difficulty imagining a world in which the maximum speed of cars would be derived from that of bicycles. Their approach to the problem shows their sense of realism. But by taking the speed of motorized vehicles as the point of departure for the design of cycle-friendly infrastructure, they make it impossible to consider the justification of this speed as a political question, and thus as a *choice*.

In the technocratic vocabulary of the design manual, scarcity and speed are givens and the task of the designer is to look for an equilibrium between form, function and use by repeatedly adjusting these three 'linchpins' in order to 'level' the design (Ibid.: 34). In practice this approach yields a great number of possible choices. If we want to explicate the political character of passages, it would be better to make the politics of passages part of the design philosophy.

The politics of passages

To speak of the politics of passages, I need to clarify how I understand politics. Passages have politics in two respects (Woerdman 1999). In the first, the making of passages is political because any given passage engenders a specific distribution of space, time and risk. In a second definition, politics refers to matters in which government is involved. These matters become policy issues and are therefore in the public domain. Here the making of passages is political because the government is involved. In the following section, I will examine the politics of passages in both respects and add a third means by which passages can be political.

The politics of passages as distribution

Passages are relational and generate distributions of space, time and risk. But an approach that considers the politics of passages as a matter of distribution has to look not only at *what* is distributed but also among *whom*. Until now, I have discussed passages as relational time-space orderings, in which exchange is distributed among cyclists, car drivers and pedestrians. For designers of cycle-friendly infrastructure, these are univocal categories. In practice, however, there are big differences among them. Children, the disabled and the elderly need more reaction time, stopping sight and manoeuvring space than an adult between 20 and 40 years of age. Whereas one cyclist can ride safely on a small cycle lane between a road and a parking space, for another a 'deterrent strip' is barely large enough. Asmussen (1996) has argued that in the design of traffic facilities the individual is taken as the most important criterion. Such an approach suggests that there is an 'average man' to be taken as the norm in traffic design. Asmussen has shown that in practice this design is often based on an individual between 20 and 55 years of age and in good health. This follows from the walking speeds, reaction times and observation distances that are implicit in the design. Because heterogeneity is the norm, Asmussen proposed a design strategy in which a 'new norm man' is taken as a starting point. Norms for traffic design should be based on the skills of what is called the 'weak' traffic participants: children, the elderly and disabled (see also Imrie 2000). Baeten, Spithoven and Albrechts (1997) also define the political character of mobility in terms of distribution, but analyse the politics of mobility as the inclusion and exclusion of specific social groups. They argue that people have unequal access to mobility, depending on the social group to which they belong (man/woman, employer/worker, child/adult, rich/poor, etc.) (Kramarae 1988). Certain groups in society have the power to arrange the mobility system in such a way that their mobility needs, their problems and their solutions are better taken care of. Other groups do not have such power at their disposal and therefore can only watch, as passive citizens, how their mobility needs, problem definitions and solutions are not or hardly taken into account (Baeten, Spithoven and Albrechts 1997: 144; see also Hine and Mitchell 2001).

The mechanisms behind the inclusion and exclusion of people, places and activities can be understood in terms of the design styles. Modern design strategies which are regulative in approach require a clear distinction between various traffic types or 'traffic identities'. As an example, on a freeway there is no room for cyclists and pedestrians. In order to guarantee the flow of car traffic, these road users must be excluded. Exclusion here means giving preferential treatment to a specific group, namely car drivers. A junction which is regulated with traffic lights accentuates the differences between traffic participants as well. In the Netherlands, there can be 'normal' traffic lights, but also dedicated lights for buses and trams, for bicycles and pedestrians. Because traffic identities are not neutral constructions, but more or less correspond to social identities, design strategies, whether modern or regulative, always have an implicit effect for the mobility of certain groups of people (Bullard and Johnson 1997). Inclusion and exclusion is produced both between traffic identities and thus between people, as well as between places and activities. A good example are the rules governing children playing in the street. When cars are given right of way, there is usually little room for children to use the streets. The activity of playing here is excluded to prioritize the benefit of driving in a car. To put it more generally, modern and regulatory design styles tend to be exclusive because they need to differentiate a priori between traffic identities.

Following design strategies that are on the organic and deliberative side of the spectrum, the goal is to minimize a priori differences among traffic identities. On the Brink in Oosterwolde or the Dam Square in Amsterdam, there are different traffic participants. But their differences are not the point of departure in the design of the traffic landscape. In these cases, inclusion is a necessary precondition for the functioning of the traffic landscape, which is organized around traffic participants negotiating their right of way in the course of traffic flow. In a village without signs, nobody is sorted out on the basis of their means of transport. Residential areas designed to slow traffic down exemplify a design philosophy which does not give priority to one activity over another, but aims at the 'coexistence' of various activities in one space. In opposition to the mono-functional traffic artery, a new type of space is created in which residential and transit space exist at the same time.

Passages as the politics of governance

As part of the public domain, the politics of passages are worked out on the level of policy making (Kesselring 2001; Vigar 2002). During the Bicycle Masterplan period, there were many policy goals which won the broad support of the Dutch parliament, such as an increase in traffic safety and a shift from car to bicycle use, all justifying the construction of friendly infrastructure. Yet this support by almost all political parties in parliament did not automatically mean that the Bicycle Masterplan designs were able to 'translate' policies to the street level. If one wants to make fast passages, such as was tried for the bicycle, it becomes necessary to ensure that the required policies have political support. Yet having political support is no guarantee for success in redesigning passages.

It is important to note that, in the politics of passages, governments act at different levels – national, regional and local – and the interest of these levels can be opposed to one another. The politics of Dutch mobility is an illustrative example. In most European countries bicycles coming from the right (or, in Great Britain, from the left) have the right of way. But this was not the case in Holland.[18] In 2001, this traffic rule was changed so that cyclists now have priority over motorized traffic when coming from the right. Traffic experts and policy makers at the national level expected that traffic safety would increase, because the new rule was less ambiguous (all traffic from the right would have right of way). The new measure would also help to slow motorized traffic, because car drivers would have to pay more attention at certain junctions. Many local road-managing authorities extended the number of junctions where car traffic would be given priority over non-motorized traffic, arguing that the new traffic rule would make intersections less safe. This modern design approach (segregating traffic, thereby giving preferential treatment to motorized traffic) went against the intentions of policy makers and politicians in The Hague, the seat of the national Dutch government, because it meant that in busy traffic areas, cyclists lost their right of way. This case illustrates that policy goals stated at the level of national government always have to be translated into local design solutions. In the translation process, the original goals may even be inverted. As the example of the new traffic rule shows, in many mobility problems there is a tension between the 'micro politics' of the street, where distributions of space, time and risk are at stake, and the 'macro politics' of governments.

Politics as a choice between ensembles of passages

Despite the broad support in the Dutch parliament for the bicycle during the first half of the 1990s, in concrete situations, cars usually have an undisputed right of way. I argue that this tension between stated policy objectives and the way they are realized at street level can be overcome. To do so, we will have to add a third definition of the politics of passages to the two that have been discussed above, which are in short politics as distribution and politics as government involvement. This third definition situates the politics of passages in the concrete ways that ensembles of passages are designed. Designing infrastructure not only means making a choice between 'the car' and 'the bicycle', or between groups of traffic participants or between different levels of government. The notion of ensembles of passages assumes that a design lays down *how* speeds can 'coexist'. Because speeds are relational, designing a passage for the bicycle must also always mean designing a passage for the car.

To clarify what is actually at stake in the design of ensembles of passages, I will make a short excursion to an argument that was made by the philosopher of technology, Langdon Winner (1986). In one of his essays, he describes how 'two men [are] travelling in the same direction along a street on a peaceful, sunny day, one of them afoot and the other driving an automobile' (Winner 1986: 8). Imagine, Winner writes, a situation in which two persons are next-door neighbours:

> The man in the automobile observes his friend strolling along the street and wishes to say hello. He slows down, honks his horn, rolls down the window, sticks out his head, and shouts across the street. More likely than not the pedestrian will be startled or annoyed by the sound of the horn. He looks around to see what's the matter and tries to recognize who can be yelling at him across the way. 'Can you come to dinner Saturday night?' the driver calls out over the street noise. 'What?' the pedestrian replies, straining to understand. At that moment another car to the rear begins honking to break up the temporary traffic jam. Unable to say anything more, the driver moves on.
>
> (Ibid.)

What we see here, Winner explains, is a collision between an automobile and a pedestrian in which no one gets hurt.

> It is a collision between the *world* of the driver and that of the pedestrian. The attempt to extend a greeting and invitation, ordinarily a simple gesture, is complicated by the presence of a technological device and its standard operating conditions. The communication between the two men is shaped by an incompatibility of the form of locomotion known as walking and a much newer one, automobile driving.
>
> (Ibid.)

Winner's example shows that forms of locomotion assume 'a world'. Building on his argument, I contend that it is not just 'forms of locomotion' that assume a world, but passages. Constructing passages can be thought of as making a 'world'. It follows, then, that designing ensembles of passages can be viewed as analogous to designing *the different ways in which these worlds are related to each other*.

If we return to the design styles with which I began this chapter, we can now say that a modern/regulative style of designing the crossing of passages renders a different 'world' from the organic/deliberative style. Whereas Frank Lloyd Wright's ideal suburb sporting multiple centres, low building densities and the ubiquitous car, exemplifies the modern style, the unsignposted island village of Schiermonnikoog and Amsterdam's desegregated Dam Square exemplify the organic/deliberative. Both design styles are comprised of ensembles of passages, but they are different from each other.

The traffic landscape in the Makkinga, a Frysian town located in a rural area in northern Holland, offers a good example of the way in which the intersection of different speeds can be treated as the creation of an ensemble of passages. In the centre of the town, all the traffic signs and priority rules have been taken away. Through streets have been visually narrowed by building shallow ditches next to the roads. The red asphalt of the bicycle lanes has been removed. When a journalist for *The New York Times Magazine* visited Makkinga for a story about its novel redesign in January 2005, Hans Monderman, the traffic safety consultant who designed the town's new traffic landscape, demonstrated the philosophy behind his design by taking her to one of the town's busy intersections. For the journalist, the journey proved surprising.

> Like a naturalist conducting a tour of the jungle, he led the way to a busy intersection in the centre of town, where several odd things immediately became clear. Not only was it virtually naked, stripped of all lights, signs and road markings, but there was no division between road and sidewalk. It was basically a bare brick square. But in spite of the apparently anarchical layout, the traffic, a steady stream of trucks, cars, buses, motorcycles, bicycles and pedestrians, moved along fluidly and easily, as if directed by an invisible conductor. When Monderman, a traffic engineer and the intersection's proud designer, deliberately failed to check for oncoming traffic before crossing the street, the drivers slowed for him. No one honked or shouted rude words out of the window.
>
> (Lyall 2005)

In contrast to the OCs in KLM's Operations Control Centre, the conductor at work in Makkinga is 'invisible'. In the 'shared space' that Monderman designed, people are able to synchronize their movements with those of other traffic participants themselves. Paying attention to the emerging situation has not been delegated to a wide variety of objects and rules, as in the modern design style, but instead has been reattributed to individual traffic participants. Variations of Hans Monderman's 'shared space' designs are currently being tried in Spain, Denmark, Austria, Sweden and Britain.[19]

Monderman argues that the standard technocratic approach to traffic design has limited itself to numbers and measures, the technocratic organization of traffic flows. In doing so, he believes that humans were pushed to the background. All norms are based on cars only: braking distances, road widths, lengths, curves. The result has been that villages like Makkinga have been turned into transit spaces. In order to allow streets to do more than just give way to the car, the traffic designers have to stop coding the village as just a traffic world where only the rules of the road count. For Monderman, designers have to forget about the traffic world and let the village be a village again. In redesigning the village, the cultural identity should play a role in the design and spatial layout.

Does making a village instead of a transit space out of Makkinga work? Partly. Most inhabitants are happy because the redesign of the village centre did not begin with the 'infrastructure' or even 'priority to slow traffic'. Instead a lot of attention was paid to the coexistence of different worlds in its redesign. But the new design has also been criticized. Some parents still feel that they have to escort their children because of the heavy traffic, and they miss the old-fashioned pedestrian crossings, even if traffic experts like Monderman claim that they are no longer necessary. Why is the design of Makkinga better than it used to be? It is better because it shows that there can be more than one answer to the question of how multiple speeds can exist together. This question has more than one answer, and none of these will satisfy everyone at the same time. In Makkinga, politics can literally be situated on the street. The intersection has been designed in such a way that no a priori differences between traffic participants and the 'rights of the fastest' have been taken as a frame of reference in the design.

Conclusion

To be able to drive a car or ride a bicycle, passages have to be made which have to be maintained in real time by the use of exchange. In city and town centres, passages have to be linked. In doing so, space, time and risk are exchanged which means that passages have a relational character. If a car and a bicycle cross each other, the car passage becomes part of the bicycle passage and vice versa. This relational character has political consequences for the design of passages. Traditional approaches to politics underline the inclusion or exclusion of people, places and activities or sometimes the contradictory role of government in justifying the differences that exist at street level. These approaches to politics cannot explain why in Dutch mobility politics of the 1990s, there remained a tension between the micro politics of the street and the macro politics of the policy goals of the various governments involved. By analysing the case for a cycle-friendly infrastructure, made in the first half of the 1990s, I have argued that this tension existed because implicitly the right of the fastest traveller is used as a frame for design solutions. As a consequence, the political character of the design is obscured from sight.

How then do we discuss the politics of passages? By considering it as the argued choice between different designs of ensembles of passages, rather than as between an endless amount of possible solutions as the 'adjustment of linchpins' of form, function and use as the design manual,

Sign up for the bike, suggests. In my definition of the politics of passages, a good traffic design schematizes this 'coexistence' of multiple passages as a problem that entails choices – that is, as a political problem. It makes visible the fact that choices about the design of the traffic landscape should not be made by traffic experts, but by the citizens themselves. They should be able to choose between two or three worked-out design proposals which can be compared in the stylistic dimensions of design and the application of rules. Only if we consider the intersection of multiple speeds *in the design itself* as the interface between various worlds, will there be room for citizens to judge designs and innovations in a context, not just as solutions to the technical problem of how to accommodate different pre-existing speeds.

In this chapter I have examined the crossing of passages at the micro level of road sections and junctions. But the coexistence of passages can also be studied at higher spatial-geographical levels. There too, we can understand the connecting of passages as the need to link different worlds into ensembles of passages, and there too should we envision the politics of passages as the ability to choose between a limited number of worked-out design solutions. The 'coexistence' of multiple speeds can be an issue at the level of commuter traffic in a city or even a whole agglomeration like the Randstad. Here too, styles are an issue. An ensemble that gives priority to the 'linking' of worlds (e.g. combining car traffic and bicycle traffic by designing places of transfer, or by combining public transport with walking) renders a different spatial and temporal ordering of the Randstad than an ensemble aimed at keeping speeds separated as much as possible (e.g. by following the ideals of Le Corbusier and Frank Lloyd Wright of a world that is derived from car travel).

A good traffic design 'excavates' the inherent political dimension that is present in the coexistence of passages, both at interchanges and in a region like the Randstad. As such, it makes these choices *explicit* rather than just making them.[20] Traffic designers, such as the authors of the design manual or Hans Monderman, can point out the various consequences of a specific design solution. But traffic participants are not only travellers but also citizens, thus they should make the choice rather than the designers. And again, their choices will not be for or against a specific means of transport, but between stylistically different designs. This urgently poses the question of how this process of choosing should be accommodated. Here again, the metaphor of the invisible conductor in Makkinga is illustrative. In order to negotiate the right of way among each other, instead of following a priori road signs and rules, the design of the square had to create the conditions to do so. How can we design ensembles of passages in such a way that the design accommodates the choice of citizens rather than that of transport experts? This question is the subject of the following chapter, where I will take up the thread of Dutch mobility politics as it has evolved since 1997.

7 Smart travel

Introduction

In the spring of 2004, the automobile manufacturer Daimler Chrysler ran an advertising campaign in the national newspapers to promote its latest design feature, computerized information systems. The ad featured a computer-animated urban centre with high-rise buildings and streets with pedestrian crossings covering their entire length. A little girl is shown on the curb of one of these streets, about to cross it on her way to school. Superimposed on this image is a photo of her mother at home, looking on reassured. The caption reads 'Because you cannot be everywhere at the same time'. Since all of the streets in this imaginary city have been turned into pedestrian crossings, the image implies that children will always be safe from the threat posed by any oncoming car. The message that Daimler Chrysler wants to convey is that their new, state-of-the-art onboard information system can assist car drivers in reacting properly to unexpected situations, such as when a child suddenly walks out into traffic, thereby rendering city streets safer (Beckmann 2004). In this example, the problem of crossing passages, discussed in the previous chapter, is not solved in the material design of infrastructure, or in the rules of the road, but by making the car itself more 'intelligent'. In Daimler Chrysler's vision of an 'accident-free driving' world, built-in information systems and sensors are able to help drivers get through bumper-to-bumper traffic, warn them of impending traffic jams 'well before the long chain of brake lights becomes visible' and even predict when a car will change lanes to pass another.[1] These information and communication technologies enable drivers to look ahead in time, thereby increasing their reaction times and enabling them to anticipate contingencies in a new way. If we are to believe car manufacturers such as Daimler Chrysler, the future in automobile design belongs to smart cars as well as intelligent infrastructures.[2]

Sixty-five years after General Motors' Highways and Horizons exhibit was shown at the World's Fair in New York, visions of the future of mobility still feature 'smart' technologies claiming to possess the ability to solve the problems of the car traveller and rendering journeys frictionless and safe. Yet there is a striking difference between smart technologies from the 1930s and those on offer today. In contrast to the technological futures proposed in 1939, today's futures lack the control towers and gantries along the roads whereby the traffic in such future scenarios could be directed. Now control has been distributed. The technologies that help to reconcile the needs of car drivers and schoolchildren crossing the street alike have become ubiquitous. These transport informatics, as they are called, encompass a broad range of wireless and wire-line, communications-based information and electronics technologies which are integrated into a vehicle or transport system's infrastructure (Juhlin 1997). Examples range from dynamic electronic road pricing, which aims at controlling road usage in real time, to commercial route navigation systems which help car drivers to locate themselves geographically or determine the shortest routes to their destination.

Such 'intelligent' electronic traffic information systems are increasingly linked to new generations of telecommunications systems and locating technologies used to track the physical locations and movement of people and goods. While the image of a future world in which every single object is accessible electronically and can be traced may sound dystopian and far-fetched, locating technologies are indeed rapidly changing the way we travel (Schwarz 2004). The central question in this chapter is how we can use the vocabulary of passages developed in the previous chapters to analyse innovations based on transport information systems, such as electronic road pricing. To answer this question, this chapter returns to Dutch mobility politics as discussed in Chapter 1. There, the traffic manager inside the Traffic Information Centre (TIC) in Utrecht was able to oversee traffic in the large conurbation in the central western region of the Netherlands called the Randstad. He could see traffic jams emerge on the screen of the two-metre wide video wall in the TIC's main hall, but he could do nothing about them. The power to act remained at the level of the car driver. But because the car driver lacks the ability to see the overall traffic situation, backups emerge. The subject of this chapter begins in 1997, when the Dutch government began to develop new road usage policies to reduce standstills, both on Dutch highways and in the public debate on mobility problems. The centrepiece in the new approach was a road pricing system based on fixed gantries that would be placed on roads in the Randstad. In 2001, a new system was proposed which used location-based technologies. On paper, the new system suggested that there could be a single, straightforward solution to a well-worn problem. Electronic road pricing, however, did not succeed. This chapter examines its failure from a number of theoretical perspectives before focusing on an explanation employing the vocabulary of passages.

Pricing the roads

In 1997, preparations began for implementing the new transport structure plan, called the National Traffic and Transport Plan (NVVP). The NVVP was envisioned as a follow up to the Second Transport Structure Plan (SVV II), the white paper published in the 1990 that had sought to halve the expected increase of car use up to 2010. In the six years following its passage, an increasing number of politicians and policy makers started to doubt the feasibility of its objective. Mobility was no longer seen as something that had to be discouraged. The definition of the problems related to mobility growth had also changed. No longer did the accent lie on the harm done to the environment. Now the main problem was the reduction in accessibility caused by congestion. The government also changed the way it approached citizens. Tactics such as moral appeals to the public, which achieved their persuasive power from images of dying forests and a warming globe, now gave way to a businesslike approach, in which the road was viewed as a 'market'. Furthermore, the national government no longer conceived of itself as the central directing actor in the implementation of policies. It was now deemed inappropriate for the national government to monopolize 'problem ownership'. Instead, the national government believed it should embark on 'interactive policy making' in which all policy measures would be negotiated with a range of social institutions representing the public. Citizens would be made more mobile, but only at a price. How was this to be achieved?

The way the government decided to solve the social dilemmas caused by increased mobility was an approach in which those who drove more, had to pay more. The government introduced a variable levy on kilometres travelled, while considering abolishing fixed automobile taxes altogether. One member of the Ministry of Transport's planning group I interviewed who had been responsible for preparing the NVVP, described the policy shift as follows:

> In the days of the Second Transport Structure Plan we conceptualized mobility as supported by an integrated traffic and transportation system, like a set of tubes with faucets and valves that could be turned on and off. There is a strong centralist element in the idea that one can steer a complicated social phenomenon as mobility in such an engineer-like fashion. The essential change in the NVVP *is the idea that mobility is the result of preferences and choices of individual people.* Instead of turning on and off faucets, we should be trying to influence the way people make choices by introducing economic principles: prices are high when demand is high or when external costs are high. Mobility is to be viewed like a market.
>
> (Interview 2000, emphasis added)

Another important characteristic of the new approach was the emphasis put on what was called the 'technology track'. 'Smart' technologies were to be used to control the flow of traffic. For example, cars could be electronically 'linked' to each other after merging on the highway with an Automatic Vehicle Guidance (AVG) system that would control the distance between vehicles. With this system in place, less space would be needed between cars, which would reduce demand for extra road capacity. The NVVP envisioned several other smart technologies to be used in conjunction with the AVG system, such as the Dynamic Route Information Panels (DRIPs), which informed drivers about upcoming traffic jams and other disruptions, Dynamic Parking Reservation Systems, and an Intelligent Speed Adapter, which automatically adjusted a car's speed to the maximum allowed (e.g. 50 km/h in city centres). The Cabinet expected the Dutch citizenry to travel 30 per cent more in 2020 than at present and to transport twice as many goods. But they would have 'the most intelligent highways in Europe' to compensate for the increased burden.

The NVVP equated innovation in mobility with technological innovation, with the latter meaning essentially 'smart' uses of state-of-the-art information and communication technologies (Ministerie van Verkeer en Waterstaat 2001: 122). If the *behaviour* of travelling people turned out to be difficult to influence – the received view after 30 years of policy making – it could perhaps be steered. Although the government viewed Dutch citizens as critically minded consumers who would never slavishly follow directions, new policy instruments would be developed to counter the unwanted effects of this freedom. The government expected that the dissonance between individual goods and collective bads could now be solved using new technologies. Shortly before 2000, the ministry described its roads of the future in a vocabulary in which market strategies and information technologies were central. The centrepiece of this approach, expressing the market philosophy in technical terms, was electronic road pricing.

In 1998, a new Cabinet was installed and a new Minister of Transport, Tineke Netelenbos, appointed. It fell to her to oversee the shift from the SVV II to the NVVP. One of the plans that the new coalition government had agreed upon was to introduce electronic road pricing before the end of the new Cabinet's term in 2002. Earlier, in March 1997, the Ministry of Transport had agreed with five industrial consortiums to evaluate technical systems for road pricing. According to the criteria the ministry had envisioned, reliable and unanimous payment should be possible without impeding the free flow of traffic. Some 70 fixed toll gantries were to be built in the Randstad that would cover its most congested road sections. When a car passed a gantry, the time of entry would be recorded and compared with the time when it passed through a second gantry upon exiting the road section.

In the summer of 1999 however, the ministry experienced a serious setback. The Dutch automobile association (ANWB) and a leading right-wing national newspaper started a protest among certain segments of the population against electronic road pricing. A survey commissioned by these organizations showed that more than 80 per cent of Dutch citizens did not believe that road pricing would lead to shorter traffic jams. The automobile association argued that the public would be charged for their road use, but would still get nowhere. It suggested constructing 'pay-lanes' to allow motorists to choose between spending money and saving time or saving money and spending time. The Ministry of Transport did not like this solution because it meant adding capacity to existing roads, which was both expensive and would activate latent demand. The minister, Tineke Netelenbos, decided to delay the introduction of road pricing in the Randstad, and run 'trials' of the new toll gantry system as a means of demonstrating to motorists that they would indeed benefit from road pricing. The trials were to last two years, from 2001 to 2003, and would then be evaluated for factors such as safety, quality of life and environmental benefits. From this point on, the electronic system would charge each motorist entering the Randstad on weekdays between 7 am and 9 am. At the same time, the government promised to work on alternative policies, including more peak-hour public transport and new forms of public transport.

The majority of parliament doubted whether road pricing using a limited number of gantries would be an effective tool for reducing congestion in the Randstad. They wanted to call off the idea and introduce a kilometre levy on a national scale. The government proposed that in 10 years the country would switch to a system based on levies imposed on the number of kilometres driven. It was believed that this system could eventually replace the present one of fixed road taxes. This plan proposed that every car would have an onboard system that registered the total number of kilometres driven when and where, enabling the government to tax individuals for driving in places that were heavily congested during certain times of the day. The new technology was ideal for meeting the government's new approach to mobility, but it would take a long time to develop and implement.

In February 2001, Roel Pieper, an Internet expert and former manager at Philips, well known as an outspoken advocate of the so-called 'new economy', was asked by the Ministry of Transport to investigate the possibilities for introducing this new approach to road pricing earlier.[3] Instead of placing poles at fixed distances along the road to enable electronic photographs to be taken of each passing car, Pieper was asked to investigate a much more flexible system based on locating technologies. These technologies would make it possible to differentiate between high and low traffic density on roads at any moment of the day. Roads would no longer be roads, accessible at any time as long as one paid a fixed tax. Instead, the cost of access to roads could be changed at any time by a central actor, according to the number of cars that were presently using them. To understand what made this such a promising technology for solving mobility dilemmas, I need to examine these locating technologies, before continuing the story of Dutch road pricing.

Locating travellers

Thrift (2004) has interpreted the proliferation of locating technologies as changing our 'knowledges of position', the simultaneously mundane and highly complex ability to know when and where people and objects will turn up. He argues that in a society which is becoming more mobile, knowledges of position take the form of a knowledge of *address*. Thrift identifies an important change in the character of addresses. Whereas traditionally an address was fixed geographically, as in the case of a postal address comprised of a street name and a house number, nowadays addresses are increasingly moving with the people and goods they are intended to locate. This, he argues, is a consequence of other innovations, such as the bar code; the .sig file used in electronic network address systems; the SIM-card used to locate and identify mobile phones; the RFID-chip, which can be used to identify and locate almost any object; and smart cards, which contain computer chips which can be used in any situation where people have to identify themselves.

That people and goods can be located *while they are moving* has radical consequences for practices of travel. When Thomas Cook travelled around the world in 1872, travellers to remote locations were hard to find for those who stayed at home. When in transit, a traveller could not be reached other than by mail, which had to be picked up in a post office along the way. Travellers were accustomed to sending letters such as the ones that Cook wrote to *The Times* and *Leicester Papers*. By the late twentieth century, all this had changed. In *Dark star safari*, the travel writer, Paul Theroux, described his journey from Cairo to Capetown as 'a revenge on mobile phones and fax machines, on telephones and the daily paper, on the creepier aspects of globalization that allow anyone who chooses to get their insinuating hand on you' (Theroux 2002: 3). For Theroux, the accessibility of everyone at all times is 'pure horror', and 'Africa is one of the last great places on earth a person can vanish into' (Theroux 2002: 4).

But even in Africa vanishing has become difficult. Internet cafés can be found in almost any small or remote village and cell phones are widespread. The globe has become almost entirely accessible because of information technologies such as the Internet and the cell phone, which make it possible to communicate almost any time and anywhere. Before the mobile phone, someone sitting on a train running behind schedule had to wait until they reached their destination before they could call to inform others why they had not shown up. It has become common not to fix a place and date before setting out on a journey, but simply to call someone and suggest a meeting place and time while underway instead. Moreover, a meeting is no longer only enacted in the moment of physical co-presence, but often extends before and after it as the participants continue to call each other, thus creating what Katz and Aakhus (2002) call 'perpetual contact'.[4] This sense of perpetual contact has become even stronger when it became possible to send emails with wireless broadband connections. Perpetual contact here takes the form of perpetual connection, which in turn leads some travellers to create their own webpages on which the ones who stay at home can follow every single move they make (Molz 2004). The crucial difference between these technologies and older ones like the wired telephone is that people can communicate regardless of where they are because the telephone, and therefore their address, has itself become mobile.[5]

In some theoretical reflections on the social embedding of information and communication technologies, it has sometimes been suggested that place would become irrelevant. In the 'space of flows' (Castells 1996) and the virtual communities on the Internet (Rheingold 2000), physical location would eventually be a thing of the past. This dislocated presence in the worldwide webs of transportation and communication would be a radicalization of what Augé (1995) has called 'non-places', places that derive their identity solely from their position as nodes in networks of transportation or commerce, such as airports or supermarkets. If one can be virtually present everywhere, location no longer makes a difference. But the latest generation of information technologies has renewed the importance of location. Eric Laurier (2001) has observed that most mobile phone conversations start by asking where the other end of the connection is located.

> Why, you wonder, do people always say where they are during mobile phone calls? Why do they need to know – can't they talk to one another about something more important? Aren't they just talking for the sake of talking? Who cares where they are at this precise moment in time?
>
> (Laurier 2001: 485)

Location matters for parents who want to know where their children are. It is in part for them that the American company uLocate Communications, Inc. markets location-based services. Because mobility is a fact of life, the company explains on its website, 'uLocate has developed a cost effective service that provides reassurance and peace of mind'.[6]

Locating systems like uLocate use underlying technologies such as the Global Positioning System (GPS) or the signal of a mobile phone. To locate a person or object, it is not enough to know its abstract coordinates in space and time. These have to be combined with geographical data in order to a create a map containing information about the actual places, such as buildings, streets or other terrain details, where a person is located. Of the many new locating technologies that are being used now, the

GPS-based route navigation systems are among the most popular. These systems render traditional road maps superfluous and talk drivers directly to their destination. Navigation systems are also now available for bicycles, portable computers and handheld devices. Public transport companies have begun using different kinds of locating technologies to provide their customers with 'seamless journeys'. Using long-range smart cards, travellers can enter and exit trains, buses and subways without having to pay or pass a conductor. The system registers their journey from beginning to end and sends a monthly bill automatically to their home address (Rietdijk and Spoelstra 2001).

Not only can people be tracked and traced in real time, but goods can as well. The possibility of combining all sorts of information on shipments with real-time tracking has enabled the American company UPS to offer customers what they call 'synchronized commerce'. Information about goods in transit is made instantly available to customers all over the world, thus helping, the company claims, to shorten supply chains and cut costs. Truck company managers are able to determine exactly where their drivers are as soon as they leave the warehouse. It is not only this tracking and tracing software that has profoundly reshaped the work of truck drivers, but also the EU-funded development of digital tachographs which will replace analogue tachographs in order to provide more exact information on driving, resting and eating times and locations.[7] The truck cabin used to be the domain of a free 'cowboy of the road' who could determine his own routes and times. Now it has become a node in synchronized logistic networks that leave hardly any room for manoeuvre for the individual driver (Aarts 2001).

Locating technologies like the ones outlined above are relevant to mobility politics because they open new possibilities of *real-time* control and regulation of travel (Levin 2000; Bennett and Regan 2004). It was precisely this promise of real-time control that Roel Pieper capitalized on when he held a press conference in March 2001. There he presented his plan called MobiMiles. He concluded that the implementation of a nationwide system of kilometre levies in the Netherlands was indeed possible within two or three years. Every car would be fitted with a 'trusted wallet', a computer chip with GPS-locating technologies enabling its movement to be traced in real time. By dividing the network of roads into a number of categories (graded from one to five depending on the degree of congestion), a car driver could be charged for road use without having to know exactly where he had been. The central actor in Pieper's scheme was supposed to be a 'Trusted Third Party', a public–private organization which would be supervised by the Ministry of Transport. For this organization to make up the bill, the payment details would not have to indicate where the user was at a particular point, but only which road category was used, so that the motorist's privacy would not be infringed upon. According to Pieper, this eliminated both an important social obstacle and political counter-argument. In a pilot programme to test the proposed system, an appliance would be installed in participating cars to calculate whether and how much motorists were required to pay. Payment was to be made by an 'electronic purse', smart card or mobile phone.

The promise of an ideal technical system available in the short term led all parties in the debate to abandon the system of fixed toll gantries. Everyone involved in the deliberation process now seemed to be in favour of the rapid introduction of a kilometre levy based on travel in specific times and places. From the perspective of policy making, this approach seemed the best way to achieve a number of goals. The road could now be seen as a market: when demand for capacity was high, the price of road use could be raised. This fits well with the neo-liberal approach to mobility politics. Pricing car use in congested areas would also help reduce demand, which meant that no new roads would have to be built. This in turn attracted the support of environmental organizations.

The consensus did not last long, however. Only days after Pieper's press conference, constituents who had shown strong public support for the kilometre levy, such as the automobile association ANWB, politicians on the right of the political spectrum, and pro-car interest groups began to protest. A kilometre levy, they argued, should not be differentiated in terms of time and place, which was necessary for making it an effective instrument against congestion, but should simply replace existing taxes. The social democrats in the coalition also agreed on this 'flat levy', even if it meant the end of pricing policy, one of the main strategies pursued by the national government in the NVVP. Pieper's MobiMiles exited the scene of Dutch mobility politics as quickly as they had appeared.[8]

A failed innovation

As an intervention in the Dutch politics of mobility, Pieper's proposal was remarkably successful in creating a consensus, even if it proved ephemeral. It had achieved two steps. It had claimed that a new kilometre levy system was close enough on the horizon to be an alternative to the system of gantries, a technological system which, although considered technically inferior, was, after many years of experimentation and trials, finally ready for implementation. Pieper's optimistic projection that 'trusted wallets' could be implemented by 2005 also asserted that the new technology could be projected far enough into the future to settle the debate just before the 2002 elections without loss of face for the parties involved. After all, the government had stated that a form of road pricing would be implemented before the end of the term. Pieper had been able to show how mobility dilemmas could be resolved simply by introducing a new technology. His report sketched out a future that was open enough to draw in many actors. It showed promise because it solved many problems at the same time. Because of its focus on technology, it left it to others to solve the many difficult social and juridical issues that would accompany the implementation of the MobiMiles regime. And it appealed to the public because it introduced into the debate a powerful rhetoric of the Internet economy. So why did it fail?

The road as a market

A first line of argument to explain MobiMiles' failure is internal to the economic discourse underlying the imposition of congestion levies (Calfee and Winston 1998). Theoretically, road pricing had been advocated by transport economists for decades as a promising policy instrument, although it had also been criticized on the same theoretical grounds that predicted its success (Van Mierlo 2001). Because the assumptions of the economic model, that is, that people will choose rationally between travelling at expensive and less expensive moments, are perceived as valid, the failure of electronic road pricing is caused by the faulty translation of these theoretical assumptions into daily practice. For example, experts were not able to convince politicians, policy makers and citizens of the validity of their scientific insights.

How was the economic theory put into practice? In 1990, when the Second Transport Structure Plan (SVV II) appeared, road pricing was seen as a means of reducing the growth of car mobility in general, and thus as a policy which met concerns about environmental impact and increasing traffic flow. However, during the 1990s, road pricing increasingly came to be seen as an instrument for reducing congestion, especially in the Randstad, instead of curbing car use in the country as a whole. Market mechanisms would be introduced in transport policies that would, it was believed, eventually produce a reduction in both environmental damage and traffic congestion. The Pieper report fitted neatly into this neo-liberal steering paradigm. The superiority of the new locating technologies over the existing fixed toll gantries was underscored by Pieper's presentation of them as an ideal means of transforming roads into markets: when demand was high, prices would rise in real time. And it gave car drivers a choice.

Despite this theoretical clarity, the MobiMiles plan can be viewed as a reduction of complex mobility dilemmas into an economic logic which presupposed new technologies as a way of implementing this logic. The scheme was presented as a means of facilitating choosing in an economic sense (people pay more when demand is high), but failed to address the political aspects of the social dilemma (people pay for the collective good). We can now explain the failure of the Pieper plan in these terms: because people saw no alternative ('public transport is simply insufficient'), or believed they would not get value for their money ('I pay, but there is still a traffic jam'), they would refuse to pay. The government asks people to pay for road use, but it does not deliver on its promises to provide better services. In the meantime, the discursive framework used to convince people of the necessity of choosing in the second sense (as a responsible citizen, aware of the negative consequences of his or her behaviour) is heavily eroded.

An electronic panopticon

Apart from an internal analysis focusing on the economic aspects of the failure, we can examine how external social and political factors also played a role. This perspective on the failure of electronic road pricing in the Netherlands draws on a body of literature on the 'surveillance society' (Lyon 1994; Levin, Frohne and Clift 2002; Lyon 2001; Lyon 2003). Here the central metaphor is not the market but the panopticon. Michel Foucault's study of the panopticon has been pivotal for understanding the 'microphysics of power' which characterize many modern forms of surveillance (Foucault 1979). Scholars have raised the question of how the microphysics of power can be applied to spaces beyond the prison (Elmer 2004: 18). As Lyon claims, it is the fleeting and mobile character of modern societies that gave rise to new forms of surveillance: 'They locate us, target us, and attempt to coordinate our activities' (Lyon 2001: 26).

While in economics-based analyses, technology is treated as a neutral facilitator of market relations, Foucauldian accounts are concerned with how technologies are used to achieve control over individuals. The array of technologies examined from this perspective include closed circuit television (CCTV) (Norris and Armstrong 1999), biometrics (Van der Ploeg 2003), intelligent transportation systems (Juhlin 1997; Graham and Wood, 2003), smart cards and online profiling (Elmer 2004). Many of these authors argue that the use of sophisticated computer systems, communication technologies and locating technologies threaten individual freedom and privacy. From a Foucauldian perspective, the Pieper plan can be interpreted as a means of enhancing government control over individuals through the surveillance of individual road users. Policies which require the processing and storage of information by a central organization are often criticized for their potential for being used to subvert the privacy of individuals. It was precisely because of this kind of objection that Pieper based his technological innovation on identifying the road categories drivers used rather than on locating their precise positions on the road. Nevertheless, some saw his proposal in the context of an attempt by the Dutch government to keep track of its citizens.

But social issues other than privacy can be identified in the debate. Technologies possessing the capability for surveillance can also be used as a means of what Lyon (2003) has called 'social sorting'. In *Splintering urbanism*, Stephen Graham and Simon Marvin argue that the 'networked metropolis', the city as it is shaped through its systems of infrastructure provision – telecommunications, highways, energy and water – has undergone a transformation. Whereas these infrastructures were designed to provide access to the largest possible number of people, they have increasingly developed into privatized, customized infrastructures. Globalization, liberalization and neo-liberal economic politics have led to a fragmentation of the urban landscape, which can be seen in 'virtual' energy markets, access-controlled streets, CCTV-surveilled urban skywalks, and personalized multimedia and communication services: 'New, highly polarized urban landscapes are emerging where "premium" infrastructure networks – high speed telecommunications, "smart" highways, global airline networks – selectively connect together the most favoured users and places, both within and between cities' (Graham and Marvin 2001: 15). Graham and Wood (2003) argue that the technical possibility of segmenting infrastructures which previously would have been equally accessible to anyone has created new social inequalities, such as premium networked infrastructures which bypass less favoured places and users.

From this perspective, the Pieper plan follows a broader sociotechnical development aimed at transforming Dutch highways. Built in the 1950s, 1960s and 1970s, on the assumption of democratic access, electronic road pricing would gradually transform Dutch highways into segmented zones separated by boundaries which are flexible in space and time. Access to road space would become a priced commodity (Graham and Marvin 2001: 5). Locating technologies are among the many new technologies that enable an even more precise zoning and 'debundling' of infrastructures, thereby enhancing a culture of control characterized by an almost automatic inclusion and exclusion of social groups. The ANWB and both right- and left-wing political parties sometimes used the argument of social exclusion in opposing road pricing, although overall it played a minor role in the debate.

Both of these perspectives indicate possible reasons why Pieper's innovation failed to be implemented. Yet, from the economic perspective, the technology itself disappears from view because it can only be understood as a neutral means of installing the economic logic that regulates demand for road capacity. As a result, the politics of the matter vanishes as well. These political dimensions reappear in the perspective of the Foucauldian panopticon and social sorting though premium networks as issues of social control and surveillance. How can a vocabulary of passages add new elements to these perspectives on the failure to implement electronic road pricing on Dutch roads? And what can we learn from this case study if we want to generalize and develop new ways of understanding the nexus of time, innovation and mobilities?

Innovating passages

The vocabulary of passages is built upon the pragmatic assumption that in order to travel, *labour* is required. This labour can be identified and reconstructed from different actors' perspectives. One of these is the travellers' perspective. Travellers do not have to invent their journey over and over again. On the contrary, the history of travel in technological cultures can be written as a series of innovations that led to faster as well as less problematic, more predictable journeys. Today travelling is an activity that goes unnoticed most of the time, precisely *because* no problems arise in the course of doing it. The work that has to be done to bring travellers from one place to another has been backstaged. The landscape of highways and bicycle lanes, road signs and road maps, stations and airports hardly captures the public's attention. Yet, if we are to know more about the innovation of mobility, we have to concentrate on the work that is rendered invisible in the ordinary practices of travel.

Viewed in terms of passages, innovation can be defined as a change in the way this work has been redistributed in the concrete practices of travel. These changes never have just one cause, however. They are complex. To give an example from Chapter 4, that the car became a success in the United States cannot be explained solely by the fact that car drivers could travel faster and more flexibly. To understand how the car rendered geographical and temporal flexibility, it is necessary to examine how the heterogeneous elements in American passages were connected, by reconstructing a context in which a chain of innovations is required: thus not just the conveyor belt, gas stations, drive-ins and motels, but also new travel myths such as those about Route 66 and ideals about the liberating effects of driving a car. The work of maintaining a car, finding a bed for the night and navigating over long distances was delegated to gas stations, motels and the Interstate Highway System.

Underlying this pragmatic approach is the pivotal importance of *context* in assessing the success and failure of innovations. The need to reconstruct contexts in analysing passages makes it possible to avoid a number of pitfalls that de Wilde (2000b) has pointed out in an article on innovation theory. First, he argues, it guards against logical errors, such as the pars pro toto present in the argument about the model T-Ford making America a mobile society and the claim that people drive in cars because they are faster than the train, analysed in Chapter 1. Moreover, the concept of passages requires a sensitivity to the historicity of innovations, thereby precluding presentist accounts in which the ideas of the present are taken as explanations of past events. Moreover, adding context avoids viewing innovations as an improvement for everyone, everywhere. The concept of passages makes us more aware of the profit-and-loss account of innovations. In this sense, a political dimension is embedded in passages in which the normative implications of innovations cannot be overlooked. Finally, a contextualist approach to travel innovations avoids technical-determinist or economic reductionism. The fact that a journey by car can be faster than by train is not just an effect of the vehicles themselves. The consequences wrought by technological innovations in transport must be understood as social and cultural effects as well. For example, in the

United States, cars represent the cultural values of freedom and self-reliance.

Heterogeneity

Using ideas from the last three chapters, I now want to elaborate on the failure of road pricing as a mobility innovation in more detail. Chapter 4 argued that the 'flow' of traffic on American highways assumed that connections between the heterogeneous elements in the passage could be made, for example, by the standardization of signage, hotels and restaurants. Once created, however, this 'flow' led to new problems for cars entering the national parks in increasing numbers, which in turn required new design solutions. Introducing a pricing mechanism aimed at changing the spatio-temporal ordering of passages, by spreading the number of cars in time to create a more evenly distributed use of the roads, rather than by building more roads and thus augmenting capacity. But as the experience in the United States suggests, this strategy would only have been successful if it had been combined with other innovations. Since many traffic jams appear at places where cars exit the highway and enter city centres, the circulation of traffic at these points can be achieved by means other than raising the price of using the road. Designing such 'intermediary landscapes', however, was not foreseen in the policy plans. The desired 'flow' on the highways in the Randstad assumed a chain of innovative design solutions: material infrastructure, such as the electronic purse and a reliable locating system, as well as immaterial elements, such as new laws that protect car drivers' privacy. Not identifying and addressing the complex design requirements that follow from the need to connect the various heterogeneous elements in new passages was one reason for the failure of the congestion charge.

By focusing on locating technology, Pieper ignored the fact that a successful innovation also means that connections have to be made to the world as it exists. This point has also been made in critical innovation theories. An example is Bruno Latour's (1996a) now classic study of the failure of Aramis, a fully automated, unmanned light-rail system in Paris. Written like a detective story, Latour asks who 'killed' Aramis: the politicians, the technicians or the public. Although Aramis was introduced as a very promising technology, it failed because it was never able to meet the demands of all the actors involved in the innovation. For Latour, the success or failure of an innovation depends on its ability to 'connect' to existing networks which provide it with the strength to remain stable for a period of time. Instead of a trajectory that can be calculated with some precision, like the ballistic trajectory of a bullet, Latour argues that innovation processes assume constant negotiations with what is already in place: technologies, values, practices, habits. Latour's argument that the trajectory that innovations will follow is unpredictable is exemplified in the case studies presented in this book.[9] The relationality of passages pre-supposes that innovations will always have unforeseen consequences. The success or failure of an innovation depends on the highly contingent ways in which the new will become part of the old. Such an approach assumes that innovators should be willing to 'test' their innovations in the context of existing networks. For Pieper and the policy makers involved, testing merely meant trying out if a technology worked under specified conditions, instead of developing it in a constant negotiation with what was already in place. As a result there was no possibility of developing the innovation in a continuous learning process.[10]

Exchange

The failure of electronic road pricing can also be analysed in terms of the concepts developed in Chapter 5. To a car driver, a traffic jam is a disruption of a projected journey. The activity of re-ordering the passage assumes that such exchange is available. As argued in Chapter 5, there can be different currencies of exchange, such as extra capacity, money, information and communication, authority. To provide the car driver with exchange, the government could build congestion lanes which are accessible only during rush hours and provide extra capacity. But there are other options for coining exchange as well, some of which have already been mentioned: automatic vehicle guidance systems to shorten the distance or separation between vehicles, and the use of onboard information and communication technologies to provide the car driver with information about alternative routes. How and for whom does electronic road pricing create exchange?

As we saw in the case of KLM's Operations Control Centre, creating an overview is crucial for coordinating real-time operations that are distributed in space. Controlling and regulating the constant flux on highways can be understood from this perspective. New locating technologies change both the ways an overview is created and its locus. Nowadays, car drivers underway on the road can use a route navigation system that not only provides real-time information about traffic congestion, but also suggests alternative routes. Considered in these terms, the MobiMiles plan had a serious drawback, in that it did not create an overview on the local level. Car drivers would know that a road section had gone up in price, but only when they were on it. Instead of making an overview of emerging situations on Dutch roads available at the local level, car drivers would still be ignorant about them in anticipating upcoming disruptions.

New locating technologies not only change the way an overview is created, but also change the locus of the authority to act in local situations. Road pricing would effectively reduce the number of exchange currencies to just one, namely money. When a traffic jam occurs, car drivers would have no other option than to spend money, and even this does not guarantee that they would be able to re-order their passage. Not only does road pricing hardly increase the ability of car drivers to re-order their passage, a central authority would determine the price of road sections in real time. This effectively transfers the authority to use a specific form of exchange to re-order a passage from the car driver, who is used to being free to determine the issue in the moment it arises, to a centralized authority which makes road use more expensive at specific places and times, and thus less accessible. For car drivers who are used to the maximum individual flexibility that driving a car affords them, this shift in the locus of authority from the local to the central level was unacceptable. The failure of the electronic congestion charge was caused therefore by what car drivers saw as a reduction in their ability to use various forms of exchange to keep control over their own journey.

Choice

Chapter 6 showed that the relational character of passages in distributing time, space and risk entails that any design solution for the crossing of passages is inherently political. For road pricing to be successful as a design for an ensemble of passages on the scale of a region the size of the Randstad, these political ramifications should be made explicit in its design in order to give people a choice. At this point it is useful to consider the work of the philosopher of science and technology, Annemarie Mol (1997), on how the act of choosing itself can be the subject of examination. Mol argues that we usually focus on the alternatives between which one can choose, but fail to acknowledge the arrangements in which choices are presented and framed. In other words, we fail to see that the process of choosing itself has to be made possible through specific arrangements. These, Mol contends, should be analysed as the outcome of situated politics.

It is interesting to use this empirically based philosophical perspective to evaluate the way choosing is staged in Dutch mobility politics around 2000. The control and command perspective implied in the Pieper plan was depoliticized when it favoured 'choosing as consumer' instead of 'choosing as a citizen'. The first type of choosing is an activity governed by notions of optimizing utility according to the economic rationale of self-interest. The fact that people want to drive cars is portrayed as a 'revealed preference' that maximizes their utility. This preference pattern can be altered when the price of car mobility rises, because driving a car has to be weighed against other opportunities. In the second type of choosing, people are more than just economic subjects; they are responsible citizens as well. If people acted only out of their own interests, the collective interest could be harmed. This distinction between choosing as an individual customer of mobility and choosing as a citizen who is aware of the social consequences of his or her actions lies at the core of the social dilemma that has dominated mobility politics since the 1970s.

The prevailing neo-liberal market approach addressed car drivers primarily as consumers of mobility. But many car drivers objected to the use of a kilometre charge, believing that it would ultimately prove ineffective in reducing the traffic congestion. As an example of realizing approaches using rational choice theory, the kilometre charge failed because the government neglected another form of choosing, namely the social dilemma created by the need to choose between individual goods and collective bads. By paying on the road, car drivers could not only follow their own interests, but could also solve the dilemma. When scarce road capacity is redistributed in time, fewer new roads are necessary. In the Pieper design for an ensemble of passages in the Randstad, the second type of choice disappeared in the arguments used to justify it, and therefore support for the plan eroded (Peters and Hajer 2001). Electronic road pricing also failed because the government did not succeed in legitimizing the political-normative order that the innovation of passages presupposes.

At least on paper, Pieper's high-tech electronic road pricing scheme was compelling in its simplicity. The daily problem of traffic jams could at least be partly solved by using a new generation of 'smart' technologies based on the principle of locating road users in space and time. Yet, when viewed from the perspective of passages, it becomes apparent that such an approach toward mobility innovation, despite years of research and deliberation between governments and social actors, ignored the complexities of the mobility practices it sought to change. As the previous chapters have shown, mobility problems always have the character of a dilemma: there is not just one best way to link the heterogeneous elements in a passage, to coin exchange in a specific situation, or to give form to ensembles of passages. Whereas Pieper's policy was meant to influence the choices of car drivers and thus make a faster journey possible, the overriding feeling among car drivers was that they had nothing to choose from at all.

Conclusion

This chapter has used the concept of passages to analyse a new road pricing scheme based on locating technologies proposed by the Dutch government in the second half of the 1990s. From 1997, the Dutch government tried to redistribute the ownership of problems caused by increasing car mobility. It now sought to address these problems by sharing the responsibility to solve them with individual car drivers. Road pricing was put back on the political agenda as a means to do so. Using a technology based on fixed toll gantries, in this road pricing scheme, car drivers were required to pay for their use of the road during rush hours. When it proved difficult to persuade constituents that the measure would be effective, Roel Pieper introduced a new technological solution, based on locating technologies, to distribute the road levy according to the actual

use of the road. Although this dynamic form of electronic road management appeared promising, it proved to be a failure.

To answer the question of how we can use the vocabulary of passages
to analyse mobility innovations, I have examined the use of dynamic electronic road pricing as an example of transport informatics that enable
'smart' travel. Within this vocabulary, the success or failure of these technologies is explained by answering how heterogeneous elements in a
passage are connected, what exchange becomes available and for whom,
and how innovations can legitimated by making explicit their inherently
political character. These questions build upon the pragmatic assumption
that in order to travel, *labour* is required. This labour can be identified and
reconstructed from different actors' perspectives as the way problems are
rephrased into design problems in order to be solved. If travelling is all
about solving problems, the central question then becomes: who is solving
what problems for whom? Is it the task of the government to solve the
problem of a traffic jam for individual car drivers? How can individual car
drivers be held responsible for solving the problems that follow from their
ways of travelling? When the government introduces a regime of electronic
road pricing to solve one problem, does it not create new problems for car
drivers?

The vocabulary of passages thus opens an 'ironic perspective' on mobility problems. As Gusfield (1981) claims, the impact of this perspective

> is then to hold up that which is taken for granted, familiar, common-
> place as something strange and problematic. If phenomena are made
> into topics of analysis the audience may be moved into a new
> perspective towards them. The cultural frameworks otherwise unrec-
> ognized now become matters of awareness. . . . Like the artist, the soci-
> ologist creates the possibility of alternative worlds. By showing the
> institutional and/or cultural frames in which actions become meaning-
> ful, he states that things could be different.
>
> (Gusfield 1981: 191)

This ironic perspective enables us to question supposed self-evidences in
the debate on mobility problems and their solutions. For example, the
claim that traffic jams have to be reduced at all costs is no longer unproblematic.

An approach based on creating and sustaining passages directs the
debate towards the specific cultural framework in which mobility problems are reconstructed as public problems. The pragmatic and ironic
perspective on the innovation of mobilities opened up by the concept of
passages reveals how any innovation can cause unexpected 'shifts', to use a
term from the vocabulary of transportation scientists. But these shifts are
not necessarily in the mode of transport, as in a modal shift. A shift may
also occur in the sort of problems that are solved or created; in the author-

ity to act; in institutional levels of control; in the way people can make a choice; and in the way social dilemmas are addressed and reformulated. As the example of road pricing in the recent history of Dutch mobility politics shows, innovations not only solve problems, but reinvent them as well. Problem and innovations continuously co-evolve. In the light of the fierce debates in the Netherlands on the use of electronic road pricing based on locating technologies like GPS, it is ironic to see that an increasing number of drivers now use route navigation systems equipped with traffic jam detection capabilities, which direct drivers through alternative routings. Congestion may ultimately be solved by smart technologies applied on the local level, without any government intervention in traffic regulation. The irony is, that in fleeing congested areas which have been 'seen' by intelligent computer systems, car drivers may end up causing new gridlocks somewhere else down the road.[11]

Conclusion
The art of travel

This book began in the control room of the Traffic Information Centre in Utrecht. Inside, traffic managers were busy supervising the flow of traffic on the dense network of roads that runs through the urban agglomeration known as the Randstad. The traffic managers were able to gather a lot of information about the flow of traffic on the roads and transmit it to car drivers, but they did not have the means to prevent traffic jams from occurring. I used their inability to prevent traffic congestion as a metaphor for the gridlock in the public debate about the problems that stem from the increase in travelled kilometres. In Chapter 1, I showed the ambiguity in these debates. On the one hand, public policies have aimed at facilitating faster car travel, while on the other, the government had the task of solving the problems of growing mobility without falling back on the alternative of slowness. In the 1970s, the reduction of car mobility became the paradigm for solving public problems such as growing congestion. Subsequent cabinets have developed a range of policy measures attempting to induce people to travel less, or at least differently and more sustainably than before. But most of these measures never got beyond the politicians' stated intentions. Despite having made some progress in increasing traffic safety and reducing harmful emissions, the Dutch government has not succeeded in resolving the mobility dilemmas it has faced.

I have argued that Dutch mobility politics since the 1970s can be viewed as a politics of time gains, which is based on two assumptions: (1) time can be gained by travelling faster, and (2) the production of travel speed does not necessarily have to lead to social problems, as these can in principle be solved. Transport scientists, however, view such assumptions as wrong. For them, travelling faster does not lead to gains in time over the long run, but only to an increase in the distance covered. But because they use a decontextualized conception of time, they have not been able to formulate an alternative for faster travel other than travelling more slowly. The prevailing discourse on mobility innovations has thus continued to view mobility from a comparative perspective, in which clock time serves as an abstract and neutral denominator and innovation can only be envisaged in one dimension, speed, which boils down to a choice between acceleration or deceleration. I have developed a situated notion of travel time, which takes into account the co-evolution of time and travel practices. As the five case studies presented in this book have shown, people produce a specific use and sense of time in the act of travelling. Time does *not* remain constant when travellers change their travel practices. Situated travel time embeds the contexts of concrete and historical travel practices, which I have examined as the construction, repair and justification of passages. After a brief summary of the book's argument, I will discuss how the concept of passages can be helpful in reformulating three agendas: the public debate on mobility problems, the debate on mobility innovations and the research on travel in technological cultures.

Passages

Travelling fast requires a lot of work along the way. This work usually remains invisible in studies of modern mobility. Just as Goncharov saw the steamer *Pallada* slice effortlessly through the ocean waves, so the acceleration of transportation and traffic is usually taken to be the cause of social change. From Goncharov's perspective as a spectator, which I argued characterizes that of theorists of modernity such as Giddens, Harvey and Bauman, the steamship and the steam train are taken as the cause of the separation of time and space, which defines modernity. By taking an actor's perspective, as exemplified by the steamship's captain, it becomes clear that speed is not so much a cause as an effect which is created in practices of travel themselves. I have examined how Thomas Cook had to solve a myriad of problems for his travellers before they could travel fast. Cook's ability to minimize the friction of the unexpected is what made speed possible in travelling around the world. Thus, by asking how the situated spatio-temporal order of a journey is achieved, an actor's perspective can be reconstructed to show what work had to be done to create passages as well as to repair and justify them. Actors' perspectives can be many, but what Thomas Cook, the public servants of the US National Park Service, the KLM employees in the Operations Control Centre at Schiphol Airport and the designers of cycle-friendly infrastructure have in common, is that they have to solve design problems. In order to travel fast and without friction, a spatio-temporal order had to be created, which in turn was achieved by solving the problems of travellers before and during their journeys. Chapter 3 concluded with the *methodological* starting point that, as an active achievement, passages can be studied by reconstructing the actors' perspectives.

Cook made passages by connecting heterogeneous elements. These included material elements, such as railroads, steamships, hotel coupons and travel guides. But they also included immaterial elements, such as teetotallers' ideals and place myths. Ordering heterogeneous elements in a passage creates a situated relation between time and space. Chapter 4 illustrated how such orderings are made by examining the spatio-temporal flexibility of car travel in the United States. Travelling with a car over large distances required the linkage of manifold innovations, which was often achieved through standardization. However, with the creation of every new passage, new problems appear as the effects of them. Thus the spatio-temporal order must undergo constant adjustment as was shown in the history of the national parks. The 'flow' of the passages to the national parks led to an increase in visitors, which created a tension between their 'use' and 'preservation' as well as between standardization and identity. There was not one optimal solution for this design dilemma. The history of national park design shows that different solutions were developed at different times. The rustic design philosophy of the 1930s, aimed at merging nature and culture, gave way to a modernist design philosophy in the 1950s and 1960s, when the aim became the circulation of cars through the parks, and the shortening of the time individuals spent in them. Viewing mobilities from the perspective of passages entails an *ontological* claim in that the unit of analysis is the situated process of ordering that creates them in the first place. This ordering is heterogeneous in that material and immaterial elements must be linked which create a specific constellation of time and space. In general, passages are dynamic and produce effects, such as an increase in the number of travellers, which in turn may lead to new design problems.

Passages not only have to be adjusted over time, but also in the moment of travelling itself. The type of design problems which arise require an extension of the vocabulary of passages. The operations in the Departure Hall at Schiphol Airport and at KLM's control centre described in Chapter 5, suggest how discrepancies between the planned and realized order of passages can be repaired. KLM employees need what they called 'exchange', such as money, capacity, knowledge, experience, information, communication or authority to restructure a disrupted passage. Planning ensured the allocation of resources before an aircraft's departure, but the closer to take off they came, the greater the need for exchange that could be coined in real time. To be able to generate exchange at any moment, an overview is needed of the actual distribution of resources in any given network. First, the better one can anticipate a disruption of a passage, the more time there will be for solving problems arising in the course of moving through it. Second, an overview means more exchange can be generated, because it enables one to know where spare parts or extra capacity can be found in the network. The authority to coin exchange on the day of operations, however, is not equally distributed within the organization: enlarging the overview of ongoing events in KLM's dispersed fleet entails minimizing the number of people who are allowed to act in any given disruption. Only the Operations Controllers possessed the authority to coin exchange in order to solve problems. The design commission that KLM faced when it built its control centre was to make sure that events at widely dispersed locations were eventually synchronized at the moment of an aircraft's departure. A tension between planning and improvisation was created in solving every disruption. This tension underlines the *real-time character* of passages. The elements of the passage are not only connected beforehand, but they must also be continuously synchronized during the actual making of the journey.

Passages are relational. Where a cyclist has to brake, a car driver must accelerate or decelerate. In Chapter 6, I looked at the consequences of the relationality of passages. Intersections and road sections, traffic lights and roundabouts are not neutral elements in the design of passages. They can be conceptualized as ensembles of passages. Ensembles of passages do more than generate specific distributions of time, space and risk. They function as a means of enabling different traffic participants to live together in the worlds created by them. This leads to a double conclusion. First, if one designs ensembles, one is effectively doing politics. And second, in allowing the politics of passages to be debated publicly, more than just one 'optimal' design solution must be offered to give citizens a choice. Historically, there have been many styles in the design of traffic landscapes and in the way that acting in them is regulated. Each style of ensemble creates a different 'world'. Thus the design of ensembles of passages always assumes effects that have an implicit or explicit *political-normative* character and that should ideally be made explicit in the design itself. Building new passages, therefore entails the work of legitimating and justifying these effects.

Table C.1 summarizes the different elements that constitute passages which have been discussed in the book.

Problems

Using the concept of passages, the problems created by the increase in mobility can be redefined as problems of design. Such a reconceptualization of the problem is not meant to disregard the utility of other approaches in addressing mobility problems, such as those coming from transport sciences. I would certainly not want to claim that changing a vocabulary brings us closer to solving the problems created by increasing

Table C.1 An actor's perspective on passages is created when we study the work that goes into creating, repairing and justifying them. This work is not straightforward, but is characterized by solving design dilemmas

Actor's perspective	Creating heterogeneous orders	Repairing disruptions in real time	Justifying a political-normative order
Design dilemmas	Standardization vs identity	Planning vs improvisation	Integration vs segregation

mobility. I do want to claim, however, that my vocabulary enables us to create new insights into their causes and thus holds the potential for improving the quality of the debates discussed at the beginning of the Conclusion.

That the mobility of people tends to increase has rarely, if ever, been contested in public debates. Public debates have focused instead on finding acceptable solutions to problems created by this growth. As Chapter 1 showed, travel time is crucial to this debate. Anyone who begins by asking why traffic jams are a problem in the first place will face a sceptical reaction. Traffic jams are an anathema because people conceive of cars as a means of saving time. But, as this book has argued, trying to save time by travelling faster only leads to a paradox. Traffic experts like Hupkes have argued that the 'law' of constant travel time demonstrates that no time can be saved by travelling faster. The irony of such an argument is that they end the debate before it has even begun. Travelling faster leads to increased demand for more speed, and the only way out is slowness. But, as the irritation caused by traffic jams shows, slowness is rarely a realistic solution.

The vocabulary related to the concept of passages provides other ways of debating mobility problems. Travelling does not only mean 'saving' time, but also the construction of situated kinds of time. The co-evolution of travel and temporal practices can be illustrated briefly by some examples taken from the case studies in this book. Through new forms of circulation and representation, the Mission 66 programme made the American national parks accessible to larger numbers of visitors. But time was not constant. The changed journey to and through the parks changed their spatio-temporal configuration. In solving the tension between park use and park preservation created by their increased accessibility, someone visiting Zion National Park in 1960 experienced a different park than someone arriving there in 1930. In KLM's Operations Control Centre, the measured and coordinated time of UTC was by no means sufficient to understand the intricate balance between planning and improvisation which characterized the Operations Controllers' work. In exchanging money, risk, capacity, information, knowledge, experience and authority, the Operations Controllers re-ordered and restructured time. And since passages are relational, the time gained in one will always be the time lost in another. Time is not constant in these examples either. Its distribution along with that of space and risk is a political process. And finally, the discussion of electronic road pricing articulated in more detail the inherently political character of distributing time and space. Who is supposed to solve which problems for which group of travellers? How are choices for specific design solutions justified? From an actor's perspective, which the concept of passages entails, the central question is no longer *how* the government should solve traffic jams, but in what ways will the proposed designs to do so change the distribution of time, space and risk?

The concept of passages enables us to reformulate mobility problems and, in doing so, the agenda of public debate as well. Once we get rid of the reduction of travel time to 'absolute' and measurable travel time, which politicians and voters tend to assume in envisioning the future, the debate can be directed to the advantages and disadvantages of passages that can make faster travel possible. The focus then becomes the different *styles* in which mobility problems can be resolved. Rigid notions of clock time as a beacon for steering give way to a debate on the different kinds of 'exchange' that are available to repair planned orders. Distributions of space, time and risk between traffic participants are subjected to debate, rather than functioning as neutral by-products of an optimal solution which in fact favours some and not others.

In the end, the choice for or against traffic jams in debates about mobility problems is not what is really at stake. Anyone wanting to travel faster or slower will be faced with design dilemmas, and innovative solutions will have to be found. It is precisely this insight which enables us to redefine innovation not as the choice between fast and slow, but between design solutions. How should we think of this new way of arranging choices? When new buildings or larger urban structures are designed, it is common to invite architects to propose a design. These design proposals are made in the form of drawings, scale-models and, recently, computer-animated visualizations, which are then subjected to a debate.

When designing traffic landscapes, however, such a process is rare if non-existent. If a process similar to architectural competitions for new buildings were adopted for designing traffic landscapes, one can imagine that a limited number of proposals could be presented to the public, and the differences between them worked out in the terms specified in Table C.1. Each proposed design could be questioned: which dominant actor's perspective is implied in each proposal? What design dilemmas are apparent? In what style should designers situate their design solutions, and what 'worlds' would result from this? Thus, assessing each proposal with the vocabulary of passages provides a conceptual and political clarity in the debate about alternative mobility futures. The perspective which is created by the concept of passages has consequences for the way we judge and choose: not just between fast and slow, but between different 'worlds'.

Innovations

One general conclusion that can be drawn from the case studies presented in this book is that innovations can be expected where and when travellers experience problems, or where the solutions to such problems lead to additional ones. When viewed pragmatically, it is possible to identify the *locus* of innovation processes, if not their outcomes. Reconstructing actors' perspectives and examining how the spatio-temporal ordering of passages are created, repaired and justified made it possible to develop a method of identifying design problems which relate to concrete mobility innovations. Design solutions were described in terms of the heterogeneous elements which must be connected within a passage, without excluding the need to bring contingent events into accord with the planned spatio-temporal order in *real time*.

Can we be more specific about the locus of innovations? The case studies suggest that design assignments which initiated innovations could always be found where *connections* had to be constructed. Many of the innovations that Cook introduced can be seen as examples of such connections. The train tickets from different railway companies to European destinations which Cook sold to his customers had literally to be connected to be sold as a coupon. Connecting train tickets was of course only one of the manifold connecting strategies that Cook used to create a seamless journey for his passengers. In the American national parks, a general connection had to be made between car passages that generated 'flow' and the wilderness that these passages rendered accessible. This was made possible by building park roads, hiking routes, vista points, parking lots and visitor centres. These 'intermediary landscapes' were designed first in a rustic and later in a modernist style. In the 1950s and 1960s, during the Mission 66 programme, connection strategies aimed at reducing the amount of time visitors spent in the parks, while still giving the impression that they had visited the wilderness. Every day, KLM must create connections between various events that make any given flight possible. Synchronizing these events is necessary in order to execute the flight plan. In this case, connections take the shape of synchronicity between events distributed in space. Planning furnishes a way of synchronizing events and processes before take off but, since there are always disruptions on any given day of operations, the planned flight schedule must be adapted in real time. Innovation can be found where events and processes have to be connected under time pressure by coining exchange in *real time*. Finally, the designers of cycle-friendly infrastructures have to connect different passages in order to accommodate different speeds, by integrating or separating traffic participants. The political-normative character of these connections is expressed in the way these 'ensembles' create a world.

The design assignments that are at stake when connections have to be made are not unambiguous, but have the character of a dilemma. Complete standardization and maximum 'flow' is difficult to combine with a unique identity. On the one hand, executing the KLM flight schedule exactly as planned is impossible because contingencies will always occur while, on the other, a wholly improvisational approach is also impossible because controlling a worldwide network of flights requires some form of central coordination and planning. Creating completely separate passages in a traffic landscape is impossible because it leads to mono-functional urban spaces that are hardly inviting to city dwellers. In short, there are no single or optimal ways of resolving design dilemmas. On the contrary,

Table C.2 The vocabulary of passages

Actor's perspective	Creating a heterogeneous order	Repairing in real time	Justifying a political-normative order
Design dilemmas	Standardization vs identity	Planning vs improvisation	Integration vs segregation
Connecting strategy	Building intermediary landscapes	Coining exchange	Designing ensembles
Design styles	Rustic vs modern	Centralized vs decentralized	Modern/regulative vs organic/ deliberative

there are different *design styles* in which innovative connections can be created. In Chapter 4, the rustic style popular in park design in the 1930s, which focused on blending a park's infrastructure into the local surroundings, thereby enhancing local identities, stood in sharp contrast to the modernist style featured in the Mission 66 programme, which sought to standardize design elements, such as visitor centres and park roads. It is possible to distinguish between a centralizing and a decentralizing style when the ability to coin exchange is concerned. To conclude, in designing cycle-friendly infrastructure, designers could design intersections and roads in either a modern, regulative style or in an organic, deliberative style (see Table C.2). If the innovation of passages always takes the form of connecting different passages, such as building intermediary landscapes, coining exchange and designing ensembles, these connections can be considered as design solutions. In choosing between design solutions, one chooses a solution in a specific style. If travel presupposes the existence of passages, and passages are constructed out of various kinds of connections, designed in specific styles, it becomes possible to discuss travel innovations as we would scientific or artistic innovations.

Mobilities

'There are no roads, only being on the road.' The Italian composer, Luigi Nono, used this sentence, taken from some graffiti on the wall of a South American monastery, as the motto for one of his musical compositions. It evokes a profoundly romantic vision of travel, which is taken as a metaphor for life itself. The early romantic walkers delighted in looking back on the path they had created travelling by foot. Their journeys had no predetermined goal. Travelling itself was the reason they got underway. The act of walking also provided them with a new means of being reflective: while walking, one would become a better thinker. When looking back on this book, one could easily come to the conclusion that modern mobilities leave little room for reflection of the kind that early nineteenth-century walkers cherished. So successfully have the problems for travellers been solved, that the act of travel has become almost automatic. Instead of looking back on where they have come from, travellers now prefer instead to look ahead and wonder when they will reach their destination. In the concluding paragraphs, I want to briefly look back on what has been argued in this book and ahead to new topics and questions that might be addressed.

In developing the concept of passages, I have not only tried to create new perspectives on travel time and the many ways travel practices have been innovated. I have also argued for a different way of reflecting on the transformation of travel in technological cultures, one that goes beyond the dualisms between measured travel time and experienced travelled time, between travel as a goal in itself and as a means of reaching a destination, and between slowness and speed. Passages provide a way of escaping these dualisms. They enable a much more precise means of examining *how* and *where* practices of travel changed. Any journey, however planned and pre-structured it may be, will entail uncertainties, and these presuppose ways of overcoming them. That is as true for the journey on foot made by Johann Gottfried Seume in 1802 as it is for the journeys KLM's transcontinental fleet of aircraft make daily today. What has changed are the means of reducing the uncertainties, the ability to construct new types of passages and to synchronize them over greater distances, and the strategies to justify and maintain them in a political-normative sense. Concepts from the vocabulary of passages, such as an actor's perspective, design dilemmas, connection strategies and design styles, create a research framework that can be used to study *how* people travel, how they solve problems on their way and how some of these problems can be solved beforehand.

By considering travel as an art that has to be learned, which can assume manifold styles, and which offers no single solution to the dilemmas raised in its course, this book hopes to open a new conceptual space for research. After all, travel practices do not only change because of innovations. These innovations embed assumptions that define which problems should be solved and for whom. Reflections on these assumptions are hard to find in current debates on mobility issues, in which the utopia of the double-click instant journey is joined by a dystopian end of travel. In contrast to the image that such rhetoric suggests, less has changed in the way we travel since the days of the *ars apodemica*, as the art of travel was called in the early modern period, than we are inclined to believe. This claim, central to this book, can also be formulated as a research objective. By studying the mobilities that constitute our daily lives, we can learn more about the world we live in. It is common knowledge that the root of the English word 'travel' is the French word 'travail', meaning work. It is precisely this work, all too often rendered invisible in debates on new roads to the future, that is the subject of the study of passages.

Notes

1 Reasoning with travel time

1 The main cities in the Randstad are Amsterdam, Rotterdam, The Hague and Utrecht.
2 Interview with Ary Koot, public relations manager of the Traffic Information Centre, 2 October 2001.
3 In an interview with the Dutch newspaper *NRC Handelsblad* in 1994, the Minister of Transport said that she did not consider traffic jams as a problem. 'I would rather see that car drivers are in a traffic jam, then they will choose public transport' (Van der Malen and Pama 1994). An editorial published a few days after the controversial interview argued that this 'cynical approach' should not be the basis of mobility politics (*NRC Handelsblad*, 25 October 1994).
4 The 'innovation fair' and the conference, 'Choosing for Innovation', both organized by the Dutch Ministry of Transport, were held on 22 May 2001 in Rotterdam.
5 The *Main Road Structure Scheme 1966* [Structuurschema Hoofdwegennet 1966], which presented a plan for the Dutch traffic system in the year 2000, predicted the construction of 5,300 kilometres of new roads up to 2000, and counted on a threefold increase in car traffic by that year. Two years later, a new government road plan confirmed the need for an interconnected network of divided highways (Ligtermoet 1990; Provoost 1996; Schot *et al.* 2002).
6 For an overview of the effects of Dutch mobility politics in cities like Amsterdam, Rotterdam and Utrecht in the postwar years, see Schuyt and Taverne (2000) and Provoost (1996).
7 The *Toekomst Projectie 2000* claimed that the number of cars in the Netherlands had risen from 522,000 to 2.5 million between 1960 and 1970. The actual number of cars in 2000 was 6.5 million, according to Statistics Netherlands, one million less than predicted.
8 For analyses of the Dutch response to the Club of Rome Report, see Hajer (1995) and Peters (1997c).
9 These are Amsterdam, Rotterdam, Utrecht and The Hague.
10 The ministry has a longstanding tradition of using titles which emphasize working together.
11 Until then, policy practices had focused on introducing a market approach into public transport by, for example, privatizing the national railways and regional and local bus companies.
12 The preference for a deliberative model, in which consensus between different social actors is strived for in a continuing process of negotiation, is not new in Dutch politics. Geul (1998) describes the old Dutch method of wheeling and dealing, a tradition that according to him goes back to the seventeenth century.

13 The Dutch government introduced car-free Sundays as part of their response to the Arab boycott on oil in 1973.

14 Recent studies have shown that the health risks due to fine dust particles and emissions of nitrogen dioxide are considerable. In the Netherlands, people living next to highway arteries and busy urban roads are expected to live on average one year less than could be expected under normal conditions.

15 The conjecture that travel time is constant is at least a century old. In 1902, H. G. Wells described the relation between increasing travel speeds and the expanding structure of cities which people travel through for two hours a day (Wells 1999: 25). *Time Budgets of Human Behaviour* by the Russian sociologist Pitirim Alexandrovitch Sorokin (Sorokin and Berger 1939), is the first study of time use which pays attention to travel time. Sorokin distinguished between 'transportation', in the sense of arriving somewhere by means of transport, and walking, either to and from the house or for pleasure. He found that people spent an average of 81.6 minutes per day on 'transportation' as opposed to an average of 55.5 minutes walking per day. He also discovered that an increase in the total distance travelled had come as a result of improvements in the transport systems.

16 This included Doxiades, Clark, Lee and Ogden, Buckminster Fuller, and Hägerstrand.

17 The hypothesis however does not unproblematically refer to a state of affairs in reality. On the contrary, the BREVER law is founded on assumptions about the character of travel behaviour; the character and size of the research population; implicit definitions of concepts like 'trips', 'travel time' and 'law'; the reliability and commensurability of data that have been acquired through different types of research (diaries, questionnaires, interviews); and expectations about the generalizability of the findings from different studies. The BREVER law can be viewed as a 'stylized fact', a construction in which a number of assumptions are present.

18 Mokhtarian and Chen (2004) conclude on the basis of more than two dozen aggregate and disaggregate studies that travel time expenditures are not constant, except at the most aggregate level. According to them, the underlying mechanisms that explain the regularity on the aggregate level are not well understood.

19 Szalai claims that humans possess 'a fundamental substrate of human imperatives where the use of time is concerned' (Szalai and Converse 1972: 11). Schafer (1998: 459) proposes that the 'ultimate reason' for a constant time budget for travel is unclear, and can probably be linked to a 'basic human instinct'. He refers to an article by Marchetti (1994), in which the 'anthropological invariants in travel behaviour' are explained from the fact that humans are territorial animals.

20 See Peters *et al.* (2001) for an analysis of these explanations of constant travel time.

21 Examples of this line of argument can be found in Schafer and Victor (1997), Schafer (1998) and Schafer and Victor (2000). They claim that constant travel time and money budgets are found in 11 different regions in the world, and also that the constant exists for a range of transport systems. Schafer uses constant travel time to support his prediction that, under conditions of growing economic prosperity, there will be a sharp increase in the number of kilometres travelled worldwide by 2050.

2 Narratives on travelled time

1 The importance of speed as a defining element in Western culture was first pointed out to me by Leo Jansen, former director of the Dutch governmental programme on Sustainable Technology Development, in an interview in 1991. On the relation between driving speed and environmental damage, see Baaijens *et al.* (1997). For an exhaustive overview of the relation between what he calls 'the speed and mobility culture' and the different kinds of societal costs that result from it, see Davis (1994).

2 However, Thrift (1996) describes various literatures related to what he calls, a 'complex of speed, light and power'. In his analysis of the changing meaning of mobility in the nineteenth and twentieth centuries, he argues that mobility, as such, cannot be understood as a by-product of modernity. There have always been many forms of mobility, and, conversely, modern mobility is only given to very few. Macnaghten and Urry (1998) describe mobilities as 'spatial practices', but do not elaborate on the specific ways speed is actually produced within these practices, or on the effects a certain travel speed may have on the perception of places and travelled time. Millar and Schwarz (1998) put together an anthology of texts and essays on speed which was published as the catalogue to the exhibition *Speed* at the Photographers Gallery and the Whitechapel Art Gallery in 2001. In their introduction, they claim that 'speed is not so much a product of our culture as our culture is a product of speed' (Millar and Schwarz 1998: 16). Kaufmann (2002) analyses what he calls the 'speed potentials' of different modes of transport.

3 In 2005 the slogan 'Prenez le temps d'aller vite' was still used by the SNCF.

4 'Wer geht, sieht am Durchschnitt anthropologisch und kosmisch mehr, als wer fährt' (Seume, Drews and Kyora 1993: 543).

5 In his reconstruction of Seume's journey, Drews (1991) shows that he actually covered more kilometres by coach and boat than by foot.

6 Wallace (1993) emphasizes the insulated character of these 'small, idiosyncratic cultural islands'. A 'culture shock' could be experienced by someone travelling even 'short' distances, and travelling meant passing through 'circle after circle of local movement and knowledge in which they, as people from more than a day's walk away, were disoriented and essentially lost' (Wallace 1993: 25).

7 The Dutch historian, Auke van der Woud, examines the formation of spatial order in the Netherlands between 1798 and 1848 in *The empty land* (1987) [*Het lege land*]. He argues that the rural imagination was linked to the material ordering of landscape. Because the ghost world had its own spatial characteristics, changes in the landscape would have consequences for the ghost that inhabited it. When encountering an old woman on the road, it was customary to make a footprint across the footprint of the woman, creating the sign of the cross. When dirt roads were paved during the first half of the nineteenth century, this custom could only disappear (van der Woud 1987: 558).

8 As in the case of the English word 'walk', the German word 'Spaziergang' is most often used to indicate a relatively short, circular walk on foot that begins and ends at the same place. However, as in the title of Seume's book, *Spaziergang nach Syrakus*, it could also be used to indicate a much longer journey on foot.

9 Bagwell (1988) and Vance (1986) make it clear that in a number of countries (England, the Netherlands and the United States) transport on water played an important role. In the Netherlands, the barge was more important than the coach until well into the nineteenth century. An extensive network of barge services connected Dutch cities and proved to be much more reliable than road transport (de Vries 1981).

10 Jarvis (1997) has criticized Wallace's main argument, that the popularity of walking can be explained by improvements in travel opportunities and changes in the landscape as a result of enclosure practices. He argues that walking became popular in the last decades of the eighteenth century, well before the developments that Wallace mentions had begun. Jarvis claims that walking arose in relation to a new generation which wanted to liberate itself from its social background (Jarvis 1997: 28).

11 For Angelika Wellmann (1991) 'the walk' is even the 'ground figure' in all of literary history. In her view, literary walks in 1800 are an extension of earlier literary walks (Wellmann 1991: 9). Claudia Albes (1999) argues that the walk can be seen as a story model. Whereas a walker can turn left and right as he or she fancies, the structure of a walker's text is discontinuous, which means that disparate themes can be handled without having to treat them with methodical thoroughness (Albes 1999: 14).

12 The ideal of a zero friction journey found its ultimate form in the virtual travel behind a computer screen, where a traveller is only a few mouse clicks away from any destination (Makimoto and Manners 1997; Knoke 1996).

13 Stagl (1995) analyses 'the art of travel' between 1500 and 1800 as a practical form of acquiring knowledge. This *ars apodemica* was seen as an art or craft that was linked to the practice of travel.

14 For the notion of technical determinism as a 'logical sequence account', see Bimber (1990).

15 Note that Bagwell (1988) also uses the term 'revolution' in his history of transportation in Great Britain, but situates its start around 1750.

16 The idea that the means of transport are literally the cause of progress is expressed in many nineteenth-century images of steamships and steam-powered trains. For example, this idea is evoked in paintings of a steam train moving from east to west on an American prairie. It 'brings with it all blessings of technology and settled life in an orderly and rapid passage across space and time' (Smith and Marx 1994: 11).

17 This argument is made in Sharp (1981), esp. Chapter Five. A classical text on time and economics is Shackle (1983). For an example of the economic approach to travel time, see Bruzelius (1979). On 'time preferences' in relation to travel demand, see Kirsch, Nijkamp and Zimmermann (1988).

18 This fragment is also cited by Wolfgang Sachs in his analysis of the car as a cultural icon to illustrate the conflict between unlimited desire and limited time. Because the number of hours in each day cannot be increased, the only way out of this conflict is to hurry or to plan better (Sachs 1992: 167).

19 In *Technics and civilization* (1934), Lewis Mumford points to this efficiency paradox when he discusses the 'mechanical routine', the temporal regularity that is characteristic of modern machine civilization. Referring to Thorstein Veblen and Bertrand Russell, he asks whether new technologies like the typewriter, the telephone and the automobile 'are not to be credited with an appreciable economic loss, because they have increased the pace and volume of correspondence and communication and travel out of all proportion to the real need'. Mumford also summarizes Russell's argument that

> each improvement in locomotion has increased the area over which people are compelled to move: so that a person who would have to spend half an hour to walk to work a century ago must still spend half an hour to reach his destination, because the contrivance that would have enabled him to save time had he remained in his original situation now – by driving him to a more distant residential area – effectually cancels out the gain.
>
> (Mumford 1963: 272)

20 Another example of this line of reasoning can be found in the Tutzing Time Ecology Project, a German initiative that focuses on the central importance of time to the understanding of human–nature relations. Modern time use, which is aimed at control and economic growth, and the project defines as the 'current socio-environmental crisis' are closely linked. Members of the project have argued for a return to natural rhythms and timescales (Adam *et al.* 1997; Held and Geissler 1995). Slowing down as a way of life is practised by so-called 'time pioneers', whose lifestyle has been studied by Hörning, Gerhard and Michailow (1995). Time pioneers strive for 'time wealth' rather than give in to the norm of speed in Western culture, which they see as bound up with material wealth. They prefer to exchange part of their income for time, but without assigning any new purpose to the time which they thus create. For an investigation into the travel behaviour of time pioneers, see Baaijens and Nijkamp (1997).

21 Virilio formulated this 'dromology' first in *Vitesse et Politique* (1977). In later books, he elaborated on the theme of 'raging still-stand' (Virilio 1984, 1993a, 1993b). For an introduction into Virilio's ideas, see Der Derian (1998) and Armitage (2000).

22 Adam (1990) and Urry (2000a) provide critical analyses of McTaggart's argument and his distinction between A-series and a B-series positions in time.

23 A reprint of McTaggart's 1908 article can be found in Poidevin and MacBeath 1993.

24 To give an example, Thrift has argued that social time in medieval Britain was not static, but changed in relation to new regimes of disciplining human actions, such as following stricter prayer schedules, the use of devices such as mechanical clocks, and texts such as the well-known hour books (Thrift 1996: 169–212).

25 Lewis Mumford (1934) noticed that the 'mechanical elements' with which we surround ourselves are also used to rearrange events in space and time.

> The refrigeration of eggs, for example, is an effort to space their distribution more uniformly than the hen herself is capable of doing: the pasteurization of milk is an attempt to counteract the effect of the time consumed in completing the chain between the cow and the remote consumer.
>
> (Mumford 1963: 271)

3 The passages of Thomas Cook

1 I have taken this information from the introduction to the Dutch translation of *The Voyage of the Frigate Pallada*, by Yolanda Bloemen and Marja Wiebes (Gontsjarov 1987: 20–21).

2 For extensive accounts of time-space geography, see Parkes and Thrift (1980) and Gell (1992).

3 In later work Hägerstrand acknowledged the existence of times that are not quantifiable. He distinguishes between symbolic and embedded time: 'embedded time in the visible and tangible reality and symbolic time, an abstract and "freestanding" entity, invented to summarize a large number of experiences and observations' (Hägerstrand 1988: 39, underlining in the original).

4 For a detailed discussion of Janelle's concept of 'time-space convergence', see Parkes and Thrift (1980). The notion of 'time-space convergence' is at the heart of so-called 'tempographic' maps that do not show distances between places in kilometres, but in clock time. The appearance of a map changes in relation to the means of transport used. Thus the elements of a time-space map are organized in

proportion to the travel times between them. If the travel times between two points are short, they are represented on the map as lying close together, if they are long they appear as more distant (Spiekermann and Wegener 1994: 654).

5 Schivelbusch (1986) points out that the topos of the annihilation of space through time was related especially to the traditional *experience* of a time-space continuum, an experience which stemmed from the fact that old transportation technologies were organically embedded in nature. 'The railroad did not appear embedded in the space of the landscape the way the coach and highway are, but seemed to strike its way through it' (Schivelbusch 1986: 37).

6 Giddens refers to Heidegger in dealing with the tension between presence and absence. Also see Gregory (1989) and Lash and Urry (1994: 23) for analyses of time-space relations in structuration theory.

7 World Standard Time (WST) was implemented in October 1884. That year, 41 delegates from 25 countries gathered in Washington DC for the International Meridian Conference at the invitation of the President of the United States. See also Kern (1983) and Blaise (2000).

8 'Time-space distanciation' presupposes mechanisms that restructure actions lifted out of concrete, face-to-face situations. Giddens takes symbolic tokens (i.e. money) and expert systems as examples of such 'disembedding mechanisms', which are part of modern social institutions. Both mechanisms are based on new forms of *trust*.

9 Objections like these against the technological determinism embedded in the metaphor of the 'shrinking world' and the 'annihilation of space through time' can also be found in Kirsch (1995) and Stein (2001). May and Thrift (2001) give a detailed account of the economic and technical determinism to which Harvey's notion of 'time-space compression' in particular can lead.

10 Thomas Cook & Son became the official name of the firm when John Mason Cook joined his father as a business partner in 1871. Lash and Urry (1994) have called Thomas Cook & Son 'probably the most impressive economic organization to emerge in nineteenth-century Britain'. For them 'twentieth-century organized capitalism is better described as "Cookism" than "Fordism"' (Lash and Urry 1994: 261).

11 Lash and Urry claim that the year 1841 was a landmark in more than one respect in the history of modern travel. It marked the beginning of modernity as a social-geographic phenomenon. In Great Britain a *national* train schedule appeared for the first time. In York, the first European hotel housed in a railway station opened. Cunard started the first transatlantic steamship service, and in the United States, the Wells Fargo Company was founded (Lash and Urry 1994: 261; Brendon 1991: 12).

12 In the nineteenth century, the number of suitcases people brought with them when they travelled was considerable, especially on longer journeys. Upper-class dress codes prescribed that travellers should be able to change clothes several times a day after reaching their destination (Gregory 1991).

13 Some have claimed that Jules Verne took the idea for *Around the World in Eighty Days* from Thomas Cook's trip around the world. According to Verne's niece and biographer, Marguerite Allote de la Fuÿe, her uncle saw a Cook's tourist leaflet on a boulevard in Paris. The brochure explained how better connections between national railroads and shipping lines made a journey around the world like an extended holiday, and could be done in only three months at most. According to Allote de la Fuÿe, 'the trains and buses and steamers of Cook's and other tours began to whirl faster in his head, describing an uninterrupted circle around the globe' (cited in Brendon 1991: 150).

14 In earlier versions of this chapter, I considered using the term 'corridor' instead of 'passage', but whereas corridor has a predominantly spatial connotation,

passages also indicates the passage of time in an A-series conception of time. The term passages more closely relates to the idea of travel as both a spatial and a temporal practice. Moser and Law (1999) define passages as parts of trajectories that cross boundaries. It has also been used by others to indicate a transition or translation. In his study on autism, Hendriks (2000) uses it as meaning a new place of action where autists and non-autists can cross over. Michel Serres (1980) has written about the 'passage to the North-West' that is taken as a metaphor for bridging the gap between the natural sciences and the humanities. In his important study of the cultural history of travel, Leed (1991) describes the sequence 'departure – passage – arrival' as the basic structure of every journey. Finally, the word 'passage' has connotations with the romantic idea that travel not only means transportation, but also transformation, as in a 'rite of passage'.

15 This argument is also made by May and Thrift (2001: 3), who in their Introduction argue that the challenge is to move away from the strict distinction between time and space in the social sciences and humanities. Instead, they argue for thinking in terms of multiple, heterogeneous and uneven TimeSpace.

16 A polder is a piece of land which has been created in place formerly covered by the sea by building a dike around it and pumping the water out. They are pieces of land that lie below sea level in which the water is continuously being pumped out by means of a complex system of canals and pumps.

17 My choice in using van der Woud's definition of order is arbitrary. The concept of 'order' and the question of social order are central to the social sciences. The corpus of work on social order is too large to list here, but those relevant for my account include Law (1994), who has researched styles of ordering, Schatzki (1996), and Schatzki, Knorr-Cetina and Von Savigny (2001), who have theorized orders as the results of practices.

18 On the relation between the precise adjustment of time and place in the operations of railways on the one hand and the rise of standard time on the other, see Landes (1983), Bartky (1989), Stephens (1989) and Blaise (2000).

4 Roadside wilderness

1 Wachs, Crawford and Wirka (1992) point out that the shape of American cities was strongly influenced by their size when cars became a more important means of transport. Older cities like Boston and New York were already large and had well-functioning systems of public transport. Newer cities like Los Angeles and Phoenix were shaped to a large extent by the ubiquity of cars, which led to much lower building densities than in the eastern US. Also see Monkkonen (1988) on the influence of cars on the development of US cities and towns between 1780 and 1980.

2 Belasco (1979) emphasizes the point that motorists viewed temporal flexibility as an advantage over train travel.

> In motoring there were no 1 A.M. departures, no rushed meals at some seedy depot lunch counter, and no rude awakenings by an anxious porter at 5:30 A.M. In a 'highway Pullman,' the driver was his own station master, engineer, and porter, with no one's time to make except his own.
>
> (Belasco 1979: 22)

3 Henry Ford himself contributed to this image. See his autobiography, *My life and works* (1922), in which he recounts how his ideal – motorizing the American nation – was cautiously planned. On Fordism, see Flink (1990).

4 Goddard (1994) describes how railroad companies kept their prices artificially high on short distances. This measure led to rising costs for small farmers who

were dependent on the railroads for transporting their goods to local markets. The car offered them an alternative means of transport and thus independence from the railroads.

5   In the early 1920s, 7 per cent of the roads in rural areas were designated as part of a national through road network, which equalled 169,000 miles in 1923 and grew to 235,000 miles by 1945 (Vance 1986: 508).

6   The same numbering strategy was followed in assigning route numbers to the first Interstate highways built in the 1950s.

7   Lewis views the Interstate Highway System as 'the largest franchise in America', which, he argues, is why the commercial enterprises that dot the freeways' edges rival each other in 'sameness' (Lewis 1997: 285).

8   At the beginning of the century it was not yet obvious that the electric-powered car would lose out to its gasoline-powered competitor (see Mom and Kirsch 2001).

9   Following McDonald's, fast food chains like Burger King and Kentucky Fried Chicken were designed around a rationalized and standardized food service.

10   'Slow, arduous, and close to nature, autocamping revived what tourists imagined to be a more leisurely pace, personal independence, simplicity, and family solidarity of preindustrial times' (Belasco 1979: 45). Lackey (1997) argues that the first generation of motorists, especially in the West, felt connected to the pioneers who had arrived decades earlier. Alone in their cars, given over to wind and weather, they could relive the popular Frontier myth – something that train travellers, bound to unwanted company, speed and fixed routes, did not experience (Lackey 1997: 4).

11   Jakle, Sculle and Rogers (1996) argue that franchising started relatively late in the motel industry – in the 1960s and 1970s – with the construction of the Interstate highways. Until then, the motel industry had been comprised of small 'mom-and-pop' businesses. Chains such as Alamo Plaza, founded in the 1940s, and Holiday Inn in the 1950s were the exceptions.

12   For an account of the symbolism of the road in Transcendentalist philosophy, see Lackey (1997), especially Chapter 3 on 'Transcendental Motoring'. See also Belasco (1979) on the ideal of self-reliance that early motorists cherished.

13   For accounts of the tension between preservation and use in the US national parks, see Nash (1982) and Hays (1987).

14   Orgeon was the first state to introduce a gasoline tax of one cent per gallon in 1919. A decade later, all the remaining US states had introduced a gasoline tax. The first federal gas tax was created on 6 June 1932.

15   The design ethics of Downing formed the philosophical point of departure for nature preservation in the US, because they helped to translate the notion of 'wilderness' into design terms (McClelland 1997: 19).

16   *Lying lightly on the land* is the title of an exhibition on building parkways and park roads held between 6 June 1997 and 1 March 1998 by the National Park Service and the Historic American Buildings Survey/Historic American Engineering Record. It was curated by Timothy Davis of the Historic American Engineering Record. The exhibition can be visited online at <http://www.cr.nps.gov/habshaer/lll/> (accessed 4 May 2005).

17   The concept of 'intermediary landscape' resonates with other concepts which attempt to capture the hybrid and constructed character of landscapes. The first is 'middle landscape' (Marx 1964), a landscape 'between' the nineteenth century pastoral ideal and the urban, technological world symbolized by the railroads. According to Marx, these 'middle landscapes' always have both a narrative and a material component. Second, Shields (1991) writes about 'places on the margin' and uses the concept of 'liminality' to underline that

these places are in more than one sense situated on a threshold, which in the case of Brighton, lay between land and sea, work and leisure, but also between different social and moral codes of conduct.

18 The National Park Service historian, Ethan Carr, characterized the national parks as democratic vacation spots.

> They are not very expensive. It's probably the least expensive option for most Americans for a vacation. In the East it's not necessarily that way because you would have to fly west, but in the West and much so in California, really the cheapest way to go on vacation was to pile the kids in the stationwagon and drive to the National Park. Gasoline is cheap, there's no tolls on the road. There are entrance fees, but they are modest. And you camp, which is inexpensive. This begins in the 1920s, when parks become tremendously popular, because they are affordable. Before the automobile, they were very expensive. People had to take trains, stay in hotels. It was an experience reserved for people with money.
>
> (Interview with Ethan Carr, June 2000)

19 Bernard De Voto wrote:

> The national park system must be temporarily reduced to a size that Congress is willing to pay. Let us, as a beginning, close Yellowstone, Yosemite, Rocky Mountain, and Grand Canyon National Parks – close and seal them, assign the Army to patrol them, and so hold them secure till they can be reopened.
>
> (De Voto 1953: 49)

20 See for example, H. Holly, 'National parks need $$$ and sense', *Woman's Home Companion*, May 1955, 13–15; A. Netboy, 'Crisis in our parks', *American Forests*, May 1955, 24–27; C. Stevenson, 'The shocking truth about our national parks', *Reader's Digest*, January 1955, 45–50.

21 Eisenhower even asked why this proposal had not been made when he took office in 1953. 'Report of the Cabinet meeting on January 27 1956', National Park Service History Collection RG 23, Preliminary Inventory, Folders: Series I – Higher Echelon.

22 'Pioneer dinner launches Mission 66', *National Parks Magazine*, April–June 1956, 59–60.

23 Wirth was personally involved in the minutest details of the promotion campaign for Mission 66. He designed the cover of the Mission 66 brochure, which featured an *all American family* – father, mother, son and daughter – superimposed onto a picture of the Liberty Bell.

24 In the 1956 annual report, Wirth claimed that park development was 'based upon the assumption' that

> when facilities are adequate in number, and properly designated and located, large numbers of visitors can be handled readily and without damage to the areas. Good development saves the landscape from ruin, protecting it for its intended recreational and inspirational values.
>
> (Sellars 1997: 181)

25 In her history of Mission 66 visitor centres, Allaback (2000) elaborates on their similarity with shopping centres, where a range of services was made available for customers arriving by car. Whereas the plan of the earlier 'park village' was more decentralized, the Mission 66 visitor centres brought together different functions in one building – museum, bookshop, park administration – which enabled more control of what was called 'visitor flow' (Allaback 2000: 24).

26 Patin (1999: 48) argues that national parks should be considered as museums,

not only because they were meant to preserve wilderness areas for later generations, but also because they applied the same techniques as museums did to
regulate and organize the visitor's gaze, including 'the design of entrances, the
display of information, the control and direction of traffic patterns, and the
regulation of the position of the visitors'. See also Grusin (1995) on representing nature at Yellowstone.

27 Urry (1990) has analysed the 'tourist gaze' in persons looking at the originals
of well-known images and pictures.

28 Speeding up the experience of nature by using new technologies of representation did not end with Mission 66. Nye (1997: 21) claims that techniques, such
as the IMAX theatre at the Grand Canyon, enable visitors to see parks in a
way they could not without taking time-consuming hikes.

29 Ansel Adams' photographs taken in the national parks come to mind (see
Spaulding 1995).

5 Airborne on time

1 Universal Coordinated Time, maintained with atomic clocks located around
the world, replaced Greenwich Mean Time in 1928. However it is sometimes
still referred to colloquially as Greenwich Mean Time (GMT).

2 This section is based on fieldwork undertaken in 2000 at the Passenger Services
Department located in the KLM Departure Hall 2. Quotations are taken from
transcriptions of recorded interviews and actual events.

3 At Schiphol Airport, KLM has European and intercontinental lounges, each of
which has two quality classes: the Royal Wing, which features the highest-
quality facilities and the Business Class lounge. Both offer a variety of services
for passengers, including free drinks, newspapers and magazines, workstations
with Internet connections, telephones, and pad and pencils, among others. The
Royal Wing lounge also contains showers, couches and a Ticket Office where
passengers can change their reservations.

4 On the one hand, an airport like Schiphol is an instrument to process passengers
as quickly as possible. But on the other, it has become increasingly important that
passengers have enough time to spend their money at the shops in the customs
area (Kloos and de Maar 1996). The contrast between efficiency and functionality
of the check-in counters and the numerous shops and commercial 'islands' in the
customs area is striking. The commercial 'labelling' of waiting time often creates
problems for passenger handling. Passengers sometimes forget their boarding time
or realize too late that they should have already been at the gate.

5 The phrase 'minus last minute change' means the total number of passengers
minus one at the last moment.

6 No absolute indication of the desired level of quality can be given, as it
depends on external circumstances like weather conditions, capacity or market
strategies.

7 Pope (2001) gives a detailed description of this system of control in his account
of 'The Clayton Tunnel disaster' in 1861, in which two trains collided in a
tunnel when communication – by telegraph – failed.

8 Thrift (1990) writes that by 1868, 21,751 miles of telegraph line had been set
up in Great Britain, transmitting over six million messages a year, from 3,381
points open to the public, often at railway stations. 'The service had proved its
worth in all manner of situations, as an aid to police work, as a means to get
news rapidly in print and, most especially, as an essential adjunct to railway
operation' (1990: 469).

9 The Central Flow Management Unit (CFMU) in Brussels is responsible for bal-

ancing air traffic demand in relation to the available air space in Europe, thereby helping to reduce congestion in European airways.

10 There are, however, critical situations that demand the operation be stopped, as became clear on 11 September 2001, when US air space was closed and no commercial flights were allowed for several days.

11 This way of doing things is not contested by OCC staff. They recognize that in daily practice there is room to deviate from the rules and protocols if the circumstances ask for it. To one of the DMOs 'rules serve as a guideline, but at the same time, we as sensible men will differ from the rules if necessary' (Interview with Duty Manager Operations). This manager also emphasized that the control rules leave room for interpretation and deviation:

> Usually we do not delay airplanes for freight if the passengers are already on board. But what if we have to transport the trained horses of Olympic champion Anky van Grunsven? These horses are accompanied by people with a business class ticket and they have a certain value for KLM, so we will delay the flight.
>
> (Interview with Duty Manager Operations)

12 Margaret Meredith pointed out to me the important work of the American sociologist Howard Becker on improvisation in what he calls 'art worlds' (Becker 1982). Many researchers have taken the act of improvising by artists as a metaphor to develop new strategies for control in organizations. Instead of minimizing what is improvised by providing as many rules, protocols and plans as possible, these authors claim that, on the contrary, improvisation can be seen as an important source of creativity and innovation (Crossan 1998).

13

> For example tools and artefacts which populate the task environment, such as workstations, pencils, desks etc. are always annotated, if not 're-invented', (De Certeau 1984) with personalized adaptions, such as 'hacks', 'macros' and a plethora of 'add-ons'. More subtly, Scribner (1984) suggests that practical thinking and improvisation take place through sophisticated processes by which the task environment and its affordances (people, artefacts, information) (Gibson 1997) are internalized into problem setting and solving. To the point that even written, formal instructions are interpreted by experienced workers not as a (pre-planned) way to solve a problem or execute an action, but as an 'input to an, as yet, unspecified problem' to be addressed.
>
> (Ciborra 1999: 84)

14 A 'reverser door' is a part of the engine that bends the thrust of the gases that come from the jet engine at the rear of the exhaust funnels, creating a braking effect.

6 Sharing the road

1 Until 1960, as many kilometres were covered on bicycles as in cars in the Netherlands. But since then, the number of car kilometres has increased tenfold, while the number of bicycle kilometres has decreased slightly (Statistics Netherlands). The influence of cars on city planning has been the subject of many urban planning and geographical studies. A classic example is Jacobs (1961). For recent American examples, see Holtz Kay (1997) and Safdie and Kohn (1998). Provoost (1996) describes debates about car mobility in Dutch cities.

2 The first traffic lights in Amsterdam were erected in the Leidsplein and used for the first time on 17 October 1932. They were controlled from the Traffic

Bureau (Bureau Verkeerswezen) located on the Overtoom (Niewold and Paarlberg 1997: 9).

3 Large Dutch cities, like Amsterdam, Rotterdam and The Hague, have traffic control rooms where all traffic lights in the city can be controlled and traffic controllers can watch busy intersections via closed circuit TV (Niewold and Paarlberg 1997).

4 The need to regulate the use of streets as a transit space has a long history. The Romans used one-way roads, pedestrian crossings, parking rules and even roundabouts. In the seventeenth century, London had rules dictating that pedestrians must walk on the pavement (Sennett 1994). In cities and towns, horses and carriages frequently caused deadly accidents. The Locomotive Act was passed in 1865 in England, setting a speed limit of 4 mph in the country and 2 mph in towns. Also known as the Red Flag Act, this law stipulated that any self-propelled vehicle, such as steam carriages, must be preceded by at least three persons, one of which had to walk 55 yards in front with a red flag to forewarn other traffic of its arrival and to reassure startled horses. The law was changed in 1878. The red flag was no longer obligatory, but someone still had to walk in front of the vehicle. It was finally repealed in 1896.

5 Noise abatement formed an important context for these measures. As Bijsterveld (2001) has argued, ordering traffic flows through silent visual signs and material obstacles ensured that it was no longer necessary for car drivers to avert the danger of a collision by honking.

6 Berman (1983) claims that Le Corbusier's ideas sprang from a personal experience in the summer of 1924 when he was driven from the street by cars during an evening walk. Shocked, he compared the streets and the city of his middle age with that of his youth, '*the road belonged to us then*' (Berman 1983: 165, italics in the original). A few weeks later, according to Berman, Le Corbusier made a daring mental leap. Instead of rejecting the ubiquity of the car because it threatens the space of the pedestrian, the pedestrian himself must drive a car. 'This "new man" needed "a new street" that would be a "traffic machine" (Ibid.).

7 The reconstruction of Dam Square created considerable debate. After a fatal accident on the square in August 2001, transport experts concluded that, despite the integration of traffic participants on the square, it had not created any extremely unsafe situation. However, some minor changes in the design were implemented (press release, City of Amsterdam, 21 January 2002).

8 These material expressions of traffic rules have a history. McShane (1994) describes how the increasingly complex traffic patterns in New York City were bound to rules. Artifacts that may seem self-evident to us were once variable, like the traffic lights introduced by Eno. Initially, these lights had an upper blue light and a lower yellow light, revealing that the subsequent choice for a red and a green light was arbitrary.

9 In his theory of communicative action, Jürgen Habermas develops the idea of communicative rationality in an attempt to identify and reconstruct universal conditions of possible understanding (*Verständigung*) (Habermas 1981).

10 Michael (1998) emphasizes the importance of the interaction between man and machine in the case of driving a car, and proposes to refer not just to cars or persons but to 'car-sons'. Dant (2004) uses the term 'driver-car' for the assemblage of car and driver. Dant sees the 'driver-car' as 'a form of social being that brings about distinctive social actions in modern society – driving, transporting, parking, consuming, polluting, killing, communicating and so on' (Dant 2004: 61). Although both Michael and Dant use ideas from actor network theory to theorize the hybridity of the 'car-son' and the 'driver-car', both fail to

take into account the role of the traffic landscape in the actions of their hybrids.

11 In his article on relative time and space, Latour (1997) describes two travelling twins, one on his way in a high-speed train through the French countryside, the other on foot through a deep jungle. In describing how we should conceptualize the two different time-spaces these modes of travel render, he refers to the Leibnizian tradition that considers space and time as expressing a relation between entities. Instead of one Space-Time, Latour argues there will be as many spaces and times as there are relations between entities. 'Thus, progressing along trails will not produce the same space-times as going smoothly along networks. It makes an enormous difference if those bodies are suffering bodies among other suffering bodies, or a relaxed air-conditioned executive in a bullet train' (Latour 1997: 172). For other theoretical observations on relational time-space elaborating on the differences between an absolute and a relative notion of time, see Earman (1989), Poidevin and MacBeath (1993) and Harvey (1996).

12 This resonates with Latour's observation that material objects in the traffic landscape can be understood as actors. In an often cited example, he analyses a speed bump. According to Latour, the act of conveying the message – reduce your speed! – has been delegated from a policeman to a traffic sign and hence to a material obstacle on the road. Roads, signs, speed bumps – in short, the traffic landscape – can thus be conceived of as a reservoir of delegated actions. According to Latour, social order is not only achieved by social arrangements, but actions are to a large extent dependent upon the non-human actors which surround us (Latour 1993).

13 Thanks to the data of the bicycle tax that the Dutch government introduced in 1889, we now know that in 1899 there were 94,370 bicycles in the Netherlands, and that one out of every 53 people owned one (Adri de la Bruhèze and Veraart 1999: 17). The number of bicycles in Holland quickly rose from 324,000 in 1906 to 1.8 million in 1924 to four million in 1940. During that year, half of the Dutch population owned a bicycle. This increase kept pace with changes in the use of the bicycle. From a sports vehicle for the well-to-do middle class, it became a means of transport for tradesmen and shopkeepers as well as for factory workers (Ibid.: 19).

14 The Netherlands still has the highest number of bicycles per capita (more than one) in the European Union, followed by Denmark and Germany respectively. The total number of bicycles in the Netherlands in 2001 was 17.8 million (source: Statistics Netherlands).

15 Cycle-friendly infrastructure has been researched for 30 years in the Netherlands and other countries. For an international comparative perspective on cycle use in European cities, see Adri de la Bruhèze and Veraart (1999). For other analyses on urban cycling, see McClintock (1992), Tolley (1997) and Dekoster *et al.* (1999).

16 According to the design manual, this combination of tasks includes a number of more or less conflicting features which give the cyclist his/her special position in traffic:

> Muscle power, for example, functions as a natural speed limiter, while at the same time a certain speed is indispensable in giving the bike stability. Also, on the one hand a bicycle is vulnerable, and on the other hand manoeuvrable and very flexible in traffic. According to the Highway Code bicycles are classed with slow-moving traffic, but in towns they are among the quickest modes of transport.
>
> (Ploeger *et al.* 1993: 13)

17 The authors of the design manual view traffic lights as 'electronic fly-overs' which embed political decisions.

> As always with the distribution of scarce resources, the distribution of scarce green time is also in the first place a political and not a technical decision. With each modern traffic-control installation, however technical and flexible it may be, subjective principles are the basis. These principles are fixed in a regulation strategy and are open to discussion.... With a regulation strategy where the cyclist gets as much priority as possible, it will more often (have to) happen that e.g. during peak-periods cars will have to make double stops while cyclists can turn left in one go. This is the consequence of politically choosing for the promotion of bicycle use.
>
> (Ploeger *et al.* 1993: 201–202)

18 The historical explanation for this exception is that, during the German occupation between 1940 and 1945, the authorities of the German army thought that the numerous bicycles formed an obstacle to the swift movement of their vehicles. They thus issued a rule stating that bicycles always had to give right of way. The rule was not withdrawn after the end of the occupation.
19 Details on the EU Shared Space project can be found on the project website, <http://www.shared-space.org/> (accessed 8 May 2005).
20 In their inquiry into forms of contemporary politics, Gomart and Hajer (2003) have examined the political role of techniques (of drawing, speaking, writing, building, showing, arguing, etc.) that are employed in design processes.

7 Smart travel

1 Details about this vision of 'accident-free driving' can be found on the website of Daimler Chrysler under the heading of Innovation. See <htpp://www.daimlerchrysler.com> (accessed 9 May 2005).
2 De Wilde (2000a) has criticized the use of the predicate 'smart' by advocates of information and communication technologies. In his view, smartness can never be a quality of a technology per se, but is rather a quality that can only be judged within a context of use.
3 The Minister of Transport, Netelenbos, was convinced that creating an effective kilometre levy system would take at least 10 years. In the meantime, 'traditional' road pricing with gantries would have to be used. Why she changed her position on the issue is not clear, but it is likely that, when confronted with the prospect of having to defend this unpopular position during the 2002 elections, she decided to create a way out.
4 Thrift refers to this as hyper- or micro-coordination, a just-in-time practice in which human encounters are continually revised.
5 For an exhaustive examination of the social theoretical consequences of this, see the articles in the special issue of Environment and Planning D (2004) on presences and absences. Green (2002) analyses the ramifications of the 'current explosion in mobile computing and telecommunications technologies' in its potential of transforming, what he calls 'everyday' time and space (Green 2002: 282).
6 This text can be found on uLocates's website, <http://www.ulocate.com> (accessed 7 May 2005).
7 The implementation of a digital tachograph in the European Union proves to be a long and arduous process. At the time of completing this book in spring 2005, the introduction of the digital tachograph was again postponed because of technical and procedural problems.
8 The website of the Ministry of Transport no longer contains any reference to

the MobiMiles report and, when asked for an interview, Roel Pieper claimed that he was too busy to give one on his shortlived intervention.

9 If the outcome of innovation processes is uncertain, they can be conceptualized as a learning process. The so-called 'Strategic Niche Management' (SNM) approach, worked out by Hoogma *et al.* (2002), aims at formulating strategies to make this learning process successful. The SNM approach opens a policy perspective on sustainable transport by organizing a series of experimental 'niches' for promising new sustainable mobility technologies. The authors describe eight experiments, such as car sharing and public bicycles, and show how their development within protected niches can help to reveal more about users' preferences, social costs and gains, and the regulation of new technologies. Strategic Niche Management approaches innovation from the idea that designers have social visions and values that, often implicitly, influence their designs. If technologies are introduced in society, their fate is dependent on the behaviour of consumers, producers, politicians and policy makers. They determine if and how a technology will be part of daily life. The authors argue that this 'co-production' of the technical and the social is insufficiently recognized in the debate on the future of mobility (Ibid.).

10 This methodology of assessing the quality of innovation trajectories was developed by the PROTEE project in 1998 and 1999 within the EU Fifth Framework Research Programme. It was developed by an international consortium of research institutes, including the Centre de la Sociologie de l'Innovation (CSI) in Paris and the Faculty of Arts and Culture at the University of Maastricht. This research programme furnished a set of indicators for assessing the quality of innovation processes in multimodal freight transport. The PROTEE Final Report can be found at the website of the EU Transport Research Knowledge Center, <http://www.europa.eu.int/comm/transport/extra/web/index.cfm?color=yellow> (accessed 7 May 2005).

11 I am indebted to Wiebe Nauta for pointing out this irony to me.

Bibliography

Aarts, L. (2001) 'De ontaarde cowboy', unpublished thesis, University of Maastricht.

Achterhuis, H. J. (1997) 'Mobiliteit en schaarste', in *K&M: Tijdschrift voor empirische filosofie*, 21(3): 240–253.

—— (1998) *De erfenis van de utopie*, Amsterdam: Ambo.

Achterhuis, H. J. and Elzen, B. (eds) (1998) *Cultuur en mobiliteit*, The Hague: SDU.

Adam, B. (1990) *Time and social theory*, Cambridge: Polity Press.

—— (1995) *Timewatch: the social analysis of time*, Cambridge: Polity Press.

—— (1998) *Timescapes of modernity: the environment and invisible hazards*, London: Routledge.

Adam, B., Geißler, K., Held, M., Kümmerer, K. and Schneider, M. (1997) 'Time for the environment: the Tutzing Time Ecology project', *Time & society*, 6(1): 73–84.

Adri de la Bruhèze, A. A. and Veraart, F. C. A. (1999) *Fietsverkeer in praktijk en beleid in de twintigste eeuw: overeenkomsten en verschillen in fiets gebruik in Amsterdam, Eindhoven, Enschede, Zuidoost-Limburg, Antwerpen, Manchester, Kopenhagen, Hannover en Basel*, The Hague: Ministerie van Verkeer en Waterstaat.

Akrich, M. (1992) 'The de-scription of technical objects', in W. E. Bijker and J. Law (eds) *Shaping technology/building society*, Cambridge, MA: MIT Press, pp. 205–224.

Albes, C. (1999) *Der Spaziergang als Erzählmodell: Studien zur Jean-Jacques Rousseau, Adalbert Stifter, Robert Walser und Thomas Bernhard*, Tübingen: Francke.

Allaback, S. (2000) *Mission 66 visitor centers: the history of a building type*, Washington, DC: National Park Service.

Allen, J. and Hamnet, C. (1995) *A shrinking world?: global unevenness and inequality*, New York: Open University.

Alting, H. and Kroef, R. van der (1998) *Thomas Cook 100 jaar in Nederland*, Groningen: Histodata.

Amato, J. A. (2004) *On foot: a history of walking*, New York: New York University Press.

Amin, A., Massey, D. and Thrift, N. (2000) *Cities for the many not the few*, Bristol: Policy Press.

Armitage, J. (ed.) (2000) *Paul Virilio: from modernism to hypermodernism and beyond*, Thousand Oaks, CA: Sage.

Asmussen, E. (1996) *De nieuwe normmens: mens ... maat der dingen: op weg naar integrale veiligheid en toegankelijkheid voor iedereen*, The Hague: POV Zuid-Holland.

Augé, M. (1995) *Non-places: introduction to an anthropology of supermodernity*, London: Verso.

Ausubel, J. H., Marchetti, C. and Meyer, P. (1998) 'Toward green mobility: the evolution of transport', *European review*, 6(2): 137–156.

Aveni, A. F. (1989) *Empires of time: calendars, clocks, and cultures*, New York: Basic Books.

Baaijens, S. and Nijkamp, P. (1997) *Time pioneers and travel behaviour: an investigation into the viability of 'slow motion'*, Amsterdam: Tinbergen Institute.

Baaijens, S., Bruinsma, F., Nijkamp, P., Peeters, P., Peters, P. and Rietveld, P. (1997) *Slow motion: een andere kijk op snelheid*, Delft: Delftse Universitaire Pers.

Baeten, G., Spithoven, A. and Albrechts, L. (1997) *Mobiliteit: landschap van macht en onmacht*, Leuven: Acco.

Bagwell, P. S. (1974; 2nd edn 1988) *The transport revolution*, London: Routledge.

Baldwin, P. C. (1999) *Domesticating the street: the reform of public space in Hartford, 1850–1930*, Columbus: Ohio State University Press.

Banister, D. and Button, K. (eds) (2000) *European transport policy and sustainable mobility*, London: Spon Press.

Barnett, J. E. (1998) *Time's pendulum: the quest to capture time, from sundials to atomic clocks*, New York: Plenum Trade.

Barrett, F. J. (1998) 'Coda – creativity and improvisation in jazz and organizations: implications for organizational learning', *Organization science: a journal of the Institute of Management Sciences*, 9(5): 605–622.

Bartky, I. R. (1989) 'The adoption of standard time', *Technology and culture*, 30(1): 25–56.

Bauman, Z. (1998) *Globalization: the human consequences*, Cambridge: Polity Press.

—— (2000) *Liquid modernity*, Cambridge: Polity Press.

Bausinger, H., Beyrer, K. and Korff, G. (eds) (1991) *Reisekultur: von der Pilgerfahrt zum modernen Tourismus*, Munich: Verlag C. H. Beck.

Beck, U., Hajer, M. A. and Kesselring, S. (ed.) (1999) *Der unscharfe ort der politik: empirische fallstudien zur theorie der reflexiven modernisierung*, Opladen: Leske & Budrich.

Becker, G. S. (1965) 'A theory of the allocation of time', *The economic journal*, 75: 493–517.

Becker, H. S. (1982) *Art Worlds*, Berkeley: University of California Press.

Beckmann, J. (2004) 'Mobility and safety', *Theory, culture & society*, 21(4): 81–100.

Behringer, W. (1990) *Thurn und Taxis: die Geschichte ihrer Post und ihrer Unternehmen*, Munich: Piper.

Belasco, W. J. (1979) *Americans on the road: from autocamp to motel, 1910–1945*, Cambridge, MA: MIT Press.

—— (1982) 'Cars versus Trains: 1980 and 1910', in G. H. Daniels and M. H. Rose (eds) *Energy and transport: historical perspectives on policy issues*, London: Sage Publications, pp. 39–53.

Beniger, J. (1986) *The control revolution: technological and economic origins of the information society*, Cambridge, MA: Harvard University Press.

Bennett, C. J. and Regan, P. M. (2004) 'Editorial: surveillance and mobilities', *Surveillance & society*, 1(4): 449–455.

Berger, M. L. (1979) *The devil wagon in god's country: the automobile and social change in rural America, 1893–1929*, Hamden: Archon Books.

—— (2001) *The automobile in American history and culture: a reference guide*, Westport, CT: Greenwood Press.

Berman, M. (1983) *All that is solid melts into air: the experience of modernity*, London: Verso.

Bertman, S. (1998) *Hyperculture: the human cost of speed*, Westport, CT: Praeger.

Bijker, W. E. and Hughes, T. P. (eds) (1987) *The social construction of technological systems: new directions in the sociology and history of technology*, Cambridge, MA: MIT Press.

Bijker, W. E. and Law, J. (1992) 'General introduction', in *Shaping technology/building society: studies in sociotechnical change*, Cambridge, MA: MIT Press, pp. 1–16.

—— (1995) *Of bicycles, bakelites, and bulbs: towards a theory of sociotechnical change*, Cambridge, MA: MIT Press.

Bijsterveld, K. (2001) 'The diabolical symphony of the mechanical age: technology and symbolism of sound in European and North American noise abatement campaigns, 1900–40', *Social studies of science*, 31(1): 37–70.

Bimber, B. (1990) 'Karl Marx and the three faces of technological determinism', *Social studies of science*, 20: 333–351.

Blaise, C. (2000) *Time lord: Sir Sandford Fleming and the creation of standard time*, London: Weidenfeld and Nicolson.

Bode, S. and Millar, J. (1997) *Airport: the most important new buildings of the twentieth century*, London/Amsterdam: Photographers Gallery/Netherlands Design Institute.

Boer, E. de (1986) *Transport sociology: social aspects of transport planning*, Oxford: Pergamon Press.

Boggelen, O. van (1995) *Fietsvriendelijke rotondes: tips voor politici, bestuurders en verkeerskundigen*, Woerden: Fietsersbond ENFB.

Boomen, T. van den (2001) 'Towards the legible street', available online <http://www.hamilton-baillie.co.uk-papers-Tijstranslation5.doc.url> (accessed 7 May 2005).

Boorstin, D. (1962) 'From traveler to tourist: the lost art of travel', *The image, or, what happened to the American dream?*, New York: Atheneum.

Borst, A. (1990) *Computus: Zeit und Zahl in der Geschichte Europas*, Berlin: Klaus Wagenbach.

Bouwens, A. M. C. M. and Dierikx, M. L. J. (1996) *Op de drempel van de lucht: tachtig jaar Schiphol*, The Hague: SDU Uitgevers.

Brendon, P. (1991) *Thomas Cook: 150 years of popular tourism*, London, Secker & Warburg.

Brilli, A. (1997) *Als Reisen eine Kunst war. Vom Beginn des modernen Tourismus: die Grand Tour*, Berlin: Verlag Klaus Wagenbach.

Brinckerhoff Jackson, J. (1984) *Discovering the vernacular landscape*, New Haven, CT: Yale University Press.

—— (1994) *A sense of place, a sense of time*, New Haven, CT: Yale University Press.

Brown, B., Green, N. and Harper, R. (2002) *Wireless world: social and interactional aspects of the mobile age*, London: Springer.

Brune, T. (1991) 'Von Nützlichkeit und Pünklichkeit der Ordinari-Post', in H. Bausinger, K. Beyrer and G. Korff (eds) *Reisekultur: von der Pilgerfahrt zum modernen Tourismus*, Munich: Verlag C. H. Beck, pp. 123–130.

Brunn, S. D. and Leinbach, T. R. (eds) (1991) *Collapsing space and time: geographic aspects of communications and information*, London: HarperCollins Academic.

Bruno, L. C. (1993) *On the move: a chronology of advances in transportation*, Detroit, MI: Gale Research.

Bruzelius, N. (1979) *The value of travel time: theory and measurement*, London: Croom Helm.

Bryman, A. (1995) *Disney and his worlds*, London: Routledge.

Buiter, H. and Volkers, K. (1996) *Oudenrijn: geschiedenis van een verkeersknooppunt*, Utrecht: Matrijs.

Bullard, R. D. and Johnson, G. S. (1997) *Just transportation: dismantling race and class barriers to mobility*, Gabriola Island: New Society Publishers.

Bunce, M. F. (1994) *The countryside ideal: Anglo-American images of landscape*, London: Routledge.

Bush, J. D. (1975) *The streamlined decade*, New York: George Braziller.

Cairncross, F. (1997) *The death of distance: how the communications revolution will change our lives*, Boston, MA: Harvard Business School Press.

Calfee, J. and Winston, C. (1998) 'The value of automobile travel time: implications for congestion policy', *J. Public Economics*, 69(1): 83–102.

Callon, M. (1986) 'The sociology of an actor-network: the case of the electric vehicle', in M. Callon, J. Law and A. Rip (eds) *The dynamics of science and technology: sociology of science in the real world*, London: MacMillan Press, pp. 19–34.

Carey, J. W. (1992) *Communication as culture: essays on media and society*, London: Routledge.

Carr, E. (1987) 'The parkway in New York City', paper presented at the Second Biennial Linear Parks Conference, Boone, NC.

—— (1998) *Wilderness by design: landscape architecture and the National Park Service*, Lincoln: University of Nebraska Press.

Castells, M. (1996) *The rise of the network society*, Oxford: Blackwell.

Ciborra, C. U. (1999) 'Notes on improvisation and time in organizations', in *Accounting, management and information technology*, 9: 77–94.

—— (ed.) (2000) *From control to drift: the dynamics of corporate information infrastructures*, Oxford: Oxford University Press.

Clark, P. and Staunton, N. (1989) *Innovation in technology and organization*. London: Routledge.

Claudon, F. (1988) *De romantische reis*, Utrecht: Kwadraat.

Clifford, J. (1997) *Routes: travel and translation in the late twentieth century*, Cambridge, MA: Harvard University Press.

Cohan, S. and Hark, I. R. (eds) (1997) *The road movie book*, London: Routledge.

Cohen, B. (1989) *Trylon and perisphere: the 1939 New York World's Fair*, New York: Abrams.

Cohn, D. L. (1944) *Combustion on wheels: an informal history of the automobile age*, Boston, MA: Houghton Mifflin Company.

Copeland, J. (1968) *Roads and their traffic 1750–1850*, Newton Abbot: David and Charles.

Crang, M. (1998) *Cultural geography*, London: Routledge.

Crang, M. and Thrift, N. (eds) (2000) *Thinking space*, London: Routledge.

Cresswell, T. (ed.) (2001) *Mobilities*, London: Lawrence and Wishart.

Cross, G. (1993) *Time and money: the making of consumer culture*, London: Routledge.

Crossan, M. M. (1998) 'Variations on a theme – improvisation in action', *Organization science: a journal of the Institute of Management Sciences*, 9(5): 593–599.

Danly, S. and Marx, L. (1988) *The railroad in American art: representations of technological change*, Cambridge, MA: MIT Press.

Dant, T. (2004) 'The driver-car', *Theory, culture & society*, 21(4): 61–79.

Davis, A. (1994) 'The speed and mobility culture: the sacrifice of health and quality of life', *Traffic engineering & control*, 35(10): 568–576.

Davis, T. M. (1997) 'Mount Vernon Memorial Highway and the evolution of the American parkway', unpublished thesis, University of Texas, Austin.

Davison, G. (1992) 'Punctuality and progress: the foundations of Australian standard time', *Australian historical studies*, 25(99): 169–199.

De Long, D. G. (ed.) (1998) *Frank Lloyd Wright and the living city*, Weil am Rhein: Vitra Design Museum.

De Voto, B. (1953) 'Let's close the national parks', *Harpers magazine*, October 1953: 49–52.

Dekoster, J., Schollaert, U., Bochu, C. and Lepelletier, M. (1999) *Cycling: the way ahead for towns and cities*, Luxembourg: Office for Official Publications of the European Communities.

Der Derian, J. (ed.) (1998) *The Virilio reader*, Oxford: Blackwell.

Dienel, H.-L. and Trischler, H. (eds) (1997) *Geschichte der Zukunft des Verkehrs – Verkehrskonzepte von der frühen Neuzeit zum 21. Jahrhundert*, Frankfurt: Camppus Verlag.

Dierikx, M. L. J. (1999) *Blauw in de lucht: koninklijke luchtvaart maatschappij 1919–1999*, The Hague: Sdu Uitgevers.

Dijst, M. J. (1995) *Het elliptisch leven – actieruimte als integrale maat voor bereik en mobiliteit – modelontwikkeling met als voorbeeld tweeverdieners met kinderen in Houten en Utrecht*, Utrecht: Koninklijk Nederlands Aardrijkskundig Genootschap.

Dijst, M. J. and Kapoen, L. L. (eds) (1998) *Op weg naar steden van morgen: perspectieven op verkeer, vervoer en inrichting van stedelijke gebieden*, Assen: Van Gorcum.

Dijst, M. J. and Vidakovic, V. (1995) 'Stabiele verhouding tussen reistijd en verblijfstijd', *Verkeerskunde*, 1995(4): 37–41.

Dohrn-Van Rossum, G. (1996) *History of the hour: clocks and modern temporal orders*, Chicago, IL: University of Chicago Press.

Draaisma, D. (1993) *Het verborgen raderwerk. over tijd, machines en bewustzijn*, Baarn: Ambo.

Drews, J. (1991) 'Wo man aufgehört hat zu handeln, fängt man gewöhnlich an zu schreiben', paper presented at Johann Gottfried Seume in seiner zeit: Vorträge des Bielefelder Seume-Colloquiums 1989 und Materialien zu Seumes Werk und Leben, Bielefeld.

Duncan, J. and Gregory, D. (eds) (1999) *Writes of passage: travel writing, place and ambiguity*, London: Routledge.

Dunn, J. A. (1998) *Driving forces: the automobile, its enemies, and the politics of mobility*, Washington, DC: Brookings Institution Press.

Earman, J. (1989) *World enough and space-time: absolute versus relational theories of space and time*, Cambridge, MA: MIT Press.

Elias, N. (1988) *Über die zeit*, Frankfurt am Main: Suhrkamp.

Elmer, G. (2004) *Profiling machines: mapping the personal information economy*, Cambridge, MA: MIT Press.

Eno, W. P. (1939) *The story of highway traffic control, 1899–1939*, Saugatuck, CT: The Eno Foundation for Highway Traffic Control, Inc.

Eyerman, R. and Löfgren, O. (1995) 'Romancing the road', *Theory, culture & society*, 12(1): 53–79.

Fabian, J. (1983) *Time and the other: how anthropology makes its object*, New York, Columbia University Press.

Feifer, M. (1985) *Going places: the ways of the tourist from imperial Rome to the present day*, London: Macmillan.

Filarski, R. (1997) 'Opkomst en verval van vervoersystemen: de ontwikkeling vanuit een historisch perspectief', *Tijdschrift voor vervoerswetenschap*, 33(2): 107–132.

Fischer, L. (1997) 'Induzierter verkehr und die these des konstanten zeitbudgets', *Internationales verkehrswesen*, 49(11): 551–556.

Flink, J. J. (1990) *The automobile age*, Cambridge, MA: MIT Press.

Ford, H. and Crowther, S. (1922) *My life and works*, New York: Garden City Publishing Co. Inc.

Forrester, J. (1983) *Bicycle transportation*, Cambridge, MA: MIT Press.

Foucault, M. (1979) *Discipline and punish: the birth of the prison*, New York: Vintage.

Fraser, J. T. (1987) *Time, the familiar stranger*, Redmond, WA: Tempus Books of Microsoft Press.

Freeman, M. (1999) *Railways and the Victorian imagination*, New Haven, CT: Yale University Press.

Friedland, R. and Boden, D. (eds) (1994) *NowHere: space, time and modernity*, Berkeley: University of California Press.

Fuchs, J. M. and Simons, W. J. (1968) *Voort, in 't zadel, kameraden: een eeuw fietsen in Nederland*, Amsterdam: De Bussy.

Galison, P. (2003) *Einstein's clocks, Poincaré's maps: empires of time*, New York: Norton.

Geels, F. W. and Smit, W. A. (2000) 'Failed technology futures: pitfalls and lessons from a historical survey', *Futures*, 32: 867–885.

Gelernter, D. (1995) *1939: the lost world of the fair*, New York: Free Press.

Gell, A. (1992) *The anthropology of time: cultural constructions of temporal maps and images*, Oxford: Berg.

Geul, A. (1998) *Beleidsconstructie, coproductie en communicatie: zes beproefde methodieken van beleidsontwikkeling*, Utrecht: Lemma.

Giddens, A. (1981) *A contemporary critique of historical materialism*, London: Macmillan.

—— (1984) *The constitution of society: outline of the theory of structuration*, Cambridge: Polity Press.

—— (1990) *The consequences of modernity*, Oxford: Polity Press.

Gieryn, T. F. (2000) 'A space for place in sociology', *Annual review of sociology*, 26: 463–496.

Gleick, J. (1999) *Faster: the acceleration of just about everything*, London: Little, Brown and Company.

Glennie, P. and Thrift, N. (1997) 'The values of temporal precision', plenary lecture, 'Time and value conference', Centre for Cultural Values, University of Lancaster, January.

Goddard, S. B. (1994) *Getting there: the epic struggle between road and rail in the American century*, New York: HarperCollins Publishers.

Godefrooij, T. (1997) 'Segregation or integration for cyclists? The Dutch approach', in R. Tolley (ed.) *The greening of urban transport: planning for walking and cycling in Western cities*, Chichester: John Wiley & Sons, pp. 229–238.

Goeverden, C. D. van and Heuvel, M. G. van den (1993) *De verplaatsingstijdfactor in relatie tot de vervoerwijzekeuze*, Delft: Technische Universiteit Delft.

Goeverden, K. van (1999) 'De betekenis van de wet van BREVER', paper presented at the Colloquim Vervoersplanologisch Speurwerk, Delft 1999.

Gomart, E. and Hajer, M. A. (2003) 'Is *that* politics?' in B. Joerges and H. Nowotny (eds) *Social studies of science and technology: looking back, ahead*, London: Kluwer Academic Publishers.

Goncharov, I. A. (1965) *The voyage of the frigate Pallada*, London: Folio Society.

Gontsjarov, I. A. (1987) *Reis om de wereld*, Amsterdam: De Arbeiderspers.

González, R. M. (1997) 'The value of time: a theoretical review', *Transport reviews*, 17(3): 245–266.

Goudsblom, J. (1997) *Het regime van de tijd*, Amsterdam: Meulenhoff.

Graham, S. and Marvin, S. (2001) *Splintering urbanism: networked infrastructures, technological mobilities and the urban condition*, London: Routledge.

Graham, S. and Wood, D. (2003) 'Digitising surveillance: categorisation, space, inequality', *Critical social policy*, 23(2): 227–248.

Green, N. (2002) 'On the move: technology, mobility, and the mediation of social time and space', *The information society*, 18: 281–292.

Gregory, A. (1991) *The golden age of travel 1889–1939*, New York: Rizzoli.

Gregory, D. (1989) 'Presences and absences: time-space relations and structuration theory', in D. Held and J. B. Thompson (eds) *Social theory of modern societies: Anthony Giddens and his critics*, Cambridge: Cambridge University Press, pp. 185–214.

—— (1994) *Geographical imaginations*, Oxford: Blackwell.

Grewal, I. (1996) *Home and harem: nation, gender, empire, and the cultures of travel*, London: Leicester University Press.

Gronemeyer, M. (1993) *Leben als letzte Gelegenheit: Sicherheitsbedurfnisse und Zeitknappheit*, Darmstadt: Wissenschaftliche Buchgesellschaft.

Grossklaus, G. (1995) *Medien-zeit, Medien-raum: zum Wandel der raumzeitlichen Wahrnehmung in der Moderne*, Frankfurt am Main: Suhrkamp.

Grusin, R. (1995) 'Representing Yellowstone: photography, loss, and fidelity', *Configurations*, 1995(3): 415–436.

Gusfield, J. R. (1981) *The culture of public problems: drinking-driving and the symbolic order*, Chicago, IL: University of Chicago Press.

Habermas, J. (1981) *Theorie des kommunikativen Handelns*, Frankfurt am Main: Suhrkamp.

Hacking, I. (1985) 'Styles of scientific reasoning', in J. Rajchman and C. West (eds) *Post-analytic philosophy*, New York: Columbia University Press, pp. 145–165.

Hägerstrand, T. (1970) 'What about people in regional science?' *Papers of the Regional Science Association*, 23: 7–21.

—— (1988) 'Time and culture', in G. Kirsch, P. Nijkamp and K. Zimmermann (eds) *The formulation of time preferences in a multidisciplinary perspective: their consequences for individual behaviour and collective decision-making*, Aldershot: Avebury, pp. 33–42.

Hajer, M. A. (1995) *The politics of environmental discourse: ecological modernization and the policy process*, Oxford: Clarendon Press.

—— (1999) 'Zero-friction society', *Urban design quarterly*, 71: 29–34.

—— (2000) *Politiek als vormgeving*, Amsterdam: Vossiuspers.

Hajer, M. A. and Halsema, F. (eds) (1997) *Land in zicht! – een cultuurpolitieke visie op de ruimtelijke inrichting*, Amsterdam: Uitgeverij Bert Bakker.

Ham, W. van (1989) *Tot gerief van de reiziger: vier eeuwen Amsterdam-Haarlem*, 's-Gravenhage: Sdu Uitgeverij.

Hamerslag, R. (1998) 'Verplaatsingstijdbesteding en mobiliteit: de beperkte bruikbaarheid van de wet van Brever', paper presented at the Colloquim Vervoersplanologisch Speurwerk 1998: Sturen met structuren, Delft, November.

Hamilton, A. (2000) 'The art of improvisation and the aesthetics of imperfection', *The British journal of aesthetics*, 40(1): 165–185.

Hamilton, J. (2005) *Thomas Cook: the holiday-maker*, Stroud: Sutton.

Hamilton-Baillie, B. (2004) 'Urban design: why don't we do it in the road? Modifying traffic behavior through legible urban design', *Journal of Urban Technology*, 11(1): 42–62.

Hanson, S. (ed.) (1995) *The geography of urban transportation*, New York: Guilford Press.

Hartman, J. (1997) 'The Delft bicycle network revisited', in R. Tolley (ed.) *The greening of urban transport: planning for walking and cycling in Western cities*, Chichester: John Wiley & Sons.

Harvey, D. (1990) *The condition of postmodernity: an enquiry into the origins of cultural change*, Oxford: Blackwell.

—— (1996) *Justice, nature and the geography of difference*, Cambridge, MA: Blackwell.

Hassard, J. (ed.) (1990) *The sociology of time*, London: MacMillan Press.

Hawthorne, N. (1851; edn 1965) *The house of the seven gables*, New York: Scholastic Book Services.

Hays, S. P. (1987) *Beauty, health, and permanence: environmental politics in the United States, 1955–1985*, Cambridge: Cambridge University Press.

Healey, P. (1997) *Collaborative planning: shaping places in fragmented societies*, Basingstoke: Macmillan.

Heath, C. and Luff, P. (2000) *Technology in action*, Cambridge: Cambridge University Press.

Heggie, I. G. (ed.) (1976) *Modal choice and the value of travel time*, Oxford: Clarendon Press.

Heimann, J. (1996) *Car hops and curb service*, San Francisco, CA: Chronicle Books.

Held, M. and Geissler, K. (eds) (1995) *Von Rythmen und Eigenzeiten: Perspektiven einer Ökologie der Zeit*, Stuttgart: Universitas.

Hellemans, F. (1998) 'Napoleon and internet: a historical and anthropological view on the culture of punctuality and instantaneity', *Telematics and informatics*, 15: 127–134.

Hendriks, F. and Tops, P. (2001) *Politiek en interactief bestuur: interacties en interpretaties rond de ontwikkeling van het Nationaal Verkeers en Vervoersplan*, 's-Gravenhage: Elsevier bedrijfsinformatie.

Hendriks, R. P. J. (2000) *Autistisch gezelschap: een empirisch-filosofisch onderzoek naar het gezamenlijk bestaan van autistische en niet-autistische personen*, Lisse: Swets & Zeitlinger.

Hetherington, K. (1997) *The badlands of modernity: heterotopia and social ordering*, London: Routledge.

Heuvel, M. van den and Peters, P. F. (1998) *De roep om snelheid en verte: een studie naar de versnelling van vervoer in historisch en maatschappelijk perspectief, 1839–1997*, Tilburg: Katholieke Universiteit Brabant.

Hillman, M. and Whalley, A. (1979) *Walking is transport*, London: PSI.

Hillman, M., Adams, J. and Whitelegg, J. (1990) *One false move...: a study of children's independent mobility*, London: PSI.

Hine, J. and Mitchell, F. (2001) 'Better for everyone? Travel experiences and transport exclusion', *Urban studies* 38(22): 319–332.

Hlavin-Schulze, K. (1998) *'Man reist ja nicht, um anzukommen': reisen als kulturelle praxis*, Frankfurt am Main: Campus Forschung.

Hofland, H. J. A. (1955; 2nd edn 1964) *Geen tijd: op zoek naar oorzaken en gevolgen van het moderne tijdgebrek*, Amsterdam: Scheltema and Holkema.

Höjer, M. and Mattsson, L.-G. (2000) 'Determinism and backcasting in future studies', *Futures*, 32: 613–634.

Hokanson, D. (1999) *The Lincoln Highway: Main Street across America*, Iowa City: University of Iowa Press.

Holtz Kay, J. (1997) *Asphalt nation: how the automobile took over America and how we can get it back*, New York: Crown Publishers.

Hommels, A. M. (2001) *Unbuilding cities: obduracy in urban sociotechnical change*, Maastricht: Universitaire Pers Maastricht.

Hood, C. (1993) *722 miles: the building of the subways and how they transformed New York*, New York: Simon & Schuster.

Hoogma, R., Kemp, R., Schot, J. and Truffer, B. (2002) *Experimenting for sustainable transport: the approach of strategic niche management*, London: Spon Press.

Hörning, K. H., Ahrens, D. and Gerhard, A. (1997) *Zeitpraktiken: Experimentierfelder der Spätmoderne*, Frankfurt am Main: Suhrkamp.

Hörning, K. H., Ahrens, D. and Gerhard, A. (1999) 'Do technologies have time?: new practices of time and the transformation of communication technologies', *Time & Society*, 8(2): 293–308.

Hörning, K. H., Gerhard, A. and Michailow, M. (1995) *Time pioneers: flexible working time and new lifestyles*, London: Polity Press.

Hout, T. van der and Werkgroep Evaluatie Verkeerslichtenregelingen (1990) *Verlies en winst bij verkeerslichtenregelingen*, Ede: CROW.

Howse, D. (1980) *Greenwich time and the discovery of the longitude*, Oxford: Oxford University Press.

Hoyle, B. S. and Knowles, R. (eds) (1998) *Modern transport geography*, Chichester: John Wiley & Sons.

Hughes, T. P. (1983) *Networks of power: electrification in western society, 1880–1930*, Baltimore, MD: Johns Hopkins University Press.

—— (1989) *American genesis: a century of invention and technological enthusiasm 1870–1970*, New York: Viking Penguin.

Hupkes, G. (1977) *Gasgeven of afremmen: toekomstscenario's voor ons vervoer-systeem*, Deventer: Kluwer.

—— (1979) 'Nieuwe ontwikkelingen rond de BREVER-wet', *Verkeerskunde*, 30(8): 363–369.

Hutchins, E. (1991) 'Organizing work by adaptation', *Organizational science*, 2: 14–29.

—— (1995) *Cognition in the wild*, Cambridge, MA: MIT Press.

Huth, H. (1990) *Nature and the American: three centuries of changing attitudes*, Lincoln: University of Nebraska Press.

Illich, I. (1974) *Energy and equity*, London: Marion Boyars.

Illich, I., Rieger, M. and Trapp, S. (1998) 'Speed? What speed?' in J. Millar and M. Schwarz (eds) *Speed – visions of an accelerated age*, London: Photographers' Gallery.

Imrie, R. (2000) 'Disability and discourses of mobility and movement', *Environment and planning*, 32(9): 1641–1656.

Jacobs, J. (1961) *The death and life of great American cities*, New York: Vintage Books.

Jakle, J. A. (1985) *The tourist: travel in twentieth-century North America*, Lincoln: University of Nebraska Press.

—— (1990) 'Landscapes redesigned for the automobile', in M. P. Conzen (ed.) *The making of the American landscape*, Boston, MA: Unwin Hyman, pp. 293–310.

Jakle, J. A. and Sculle, K. A. (1994) *The gas station in America*, Baltimore, MD: The Johns Hopkins University Press.

—— (1999) *Fast food: roadside restaurants in the automobile age*, Baltimore, MD: Johns Hopkins University Press.

Jakle, J. A., Sculle, K. A. and Rogers, J. S. (1996) *The motel in America*, Baltimore, MD: The Johns Hopkins University Press.

Janelle, D. G. (1968) 'Central place development in a time-space framework', *Professional Geographer*, 20: 5–10.

—— (1991) 'Global interdependence and its consequences', in S. D. Brunn and T. R. Leinbach (eds) *Collapsing space and time: geographic aspects of communications and information*, London: HarperCollins Academic, pp. 49–81.

Jarvis, R. (1997) *Romantic writing and pedestrian travel*, Basingstoke: Macmillan.

Joerges, B. (1994) 'How to recombine large technical systems: the case of European organ transplantation', in J. Summerton (ed.) *The development of large technical systems*, San Francisco, CA: Westview Press, pp. 25–51.

—— (1999) 'Do politics have artefacts?' *Social studies of science*, 29(3): 411–431.

Jonasson, M. (2000) *The creation of places in traffic through performative action*, Gothenburg: Economics and Commercial Law University of Gothenburg.

Juhlin, O. (1997) *Prometheus at the wheel: representations of road transport informatics*, Linköping: Institute of Tema Research, Linköping University.

Kampen, L. T. B. van (1992) *De veiligheid van de fiets in het wegverkeer: een literatuurstudie als onderdeel A van het project 'Veilige fiets en letselpreventie' van het Masterplan Fiets*, Leidschendam: Stichting SWOV.

Kaplan, C. (1996) *Questions of travel: postmodern discourses of displacement*, Durham, NC: Duke University Press.

Kaschuba, W. (1991) 'Die Fußreise – von der Arbeitswanderung zur bürgerlichen Bildungsbewegung', in H. Bausinger, K. Beyrer and G. Korff. (eds) *Reisekultur:*

von der Pilgerfahrt zum modernen Tourismus, Munich: Verlag C. H. Beck, pp. 165–173.

Katz, J. E. and Aakhus, M. A. (2002) *Perpetual contact: mobile communication, private talk, public performance*, Cambridge: Cambridge University Press.

Kaufmann, V. (2002) *Re-thinking mobility*, Aldershot: Ashgate.

Kelly, K. (1995) *Out of control: the new biology of machines, social systems and the economic world*, Reading, MA: Addison Wesley.

Kern, S. (1983) *The culture of time and space 1880–1918*, London: Weidenfeld and Nicholson.

Kesselring, S. (2001) *Mobile Politik: ein soziologischer Blick auf Verkehrspolitik in München*, Berlin: Edition Sigma.

Kirsch, G., Nijkamp, P. and Zimmermann, K. (eds) (1988) *The formulation of time preferences in a multidisciplinary perspective: their consequences for individual behaviour and collective decision-making*, Aldershot/Brookfield, VT: Avebury.

Kirsch, S. (1995) 'The incredible shrinking world? Technology and the production of space', *Environment and planning D: society and space*, 13: 529–555.

Klant, J. J. (1954) *De fiets*, 's-Gravenhage: Bert Bakker.

Kline, R. and Pinch, T. (1996) 'Users as agents of technological change: the social construction of the automobile in the rural United States', *Technology and culture*, 37: 763–795.

Kloos, M. and Maar, B. de (1996) *Schiphol architecture: innovative airport design*, Amsterdam: Architectura and Natura Press.

Knippenberg, H. and Nauta, B. (1989) 'Naar eenheid van tijd in Nederland 1835–1909', *Tijdschrift voor sociale geschiedenis*, 15(4): 325–344.

Knippenberg, H. and Pater, B. de (1988) *De eenwording van Nederland*, Nijmegen: SUN.

Knippenberg-Den Brinker, C. W. F. (1987) *Time in travel*, Groningen: Rijksuniversiteit Groningen.

Knoke, W. (1996) *Bold new world: the essential road map to the twenty-first century*, New York: Kodansha America.

Koenig, G. M. (1996) *Eine kulturgeschichte des spazierganges: spuren einer buergerlichen praktik 1780–1850*, Wien: Boehlau.

Kraan, M. E. (1996) *Time to travel?: a model for the allocation of time and money*, Enschede: Universiteit Twente.

Kramarae, C. (ed.) (1988) *Technology and women's voices: keeping in touch*, London: Routledge.

Kuhn, T. S. (1962) *The structure of scientific revolutions*, Chicago, IL: University of Chicago Press.

Kuipers, L. (1998) *Kruispuntontwerp*, Alkmaar: G.C.T.

Kunstler, J. H. (1994) *The geography of nowhere: the rise and decline of America's man-made landscape*, New York: Simon & Schuster.

La Porte, T. (1988) 'The United States air traffic system: increasing reliability in the midst of growth', in R. Mayntz and T. P. Hughes (eds) *The development of large technical systems*, Frankfurt am Main: Campus Verlag, pp. 215–244.

Lackey, K. (1997) *RoadFrames: the American highway narrative*, Lincoln: University of Nebraska Press.

Lakoff, G. and Johnson, M. (1980) *Metaphors we live by*, Chicago, IL: University of Chicago Press.

Lammers, J. (1995) *Cities make room for cyclists: examples from towns in the Netherlands, Denmark, Germany and Switzerland*, 's Gravenhage: Ministry of Transport, Public Works and Water Management.

Landes, D. S. (1983) *Revolution in time: clocks and the making of the modern world*, Cambridge, MA: Harvard University Press.

Langeweg, F. (ed.) (1988) *Zorgen voor morgen: nationale milieuverkenning*, Alphen aan den Rijn: Samsom H. D. Tjeenk Willink.

Lash, S. and Urry, J. (1994) *Economies of signs and space*, London: Sage Publications.

Latour, B. (1993) *La clef de Berlin et autres leçons d'un amateur de sciences*, Paris: La Découverte.

—— (1996a) *Aramis, or, the love of technology*, trans. C. Porter, Cambridge, MA: Harvard University Press.

—— (1996b) 'Social theory and the study of computerized work sites', in W. J. Orlikowski (ed.) *Information technology and changes in organizational work*, London: Chapman & Hall.

—— (1997) 'Trains of thought: Piaget, formalism, and the fifth dimension', *Common knowledge*, 6(3): 170–191.

Laurier, E. (2001) 'Why people say where they are during mobile phone calls', *Environment and planning D: society & space*, 19(4): 485–504.

Law, J. (1987) 'Technology and heterogeneous engineering: the case of Portuguese expansion', in W. E. Bijker and T. P. Hughes (eds) *The social construction of technology: new directions in the sociology and history of technology*, Cambridge, MA: MIT Press, pp. 111–134.

—— (1994) *Organizing modernity*, Oxford: Blackwell.

Lay, M. G. (1992) *Ways of the world: a history of the world's roads and of the vehicles that used them*, New Brunswick, NJ: Rutgers University Press.

Le Corbusier (1924) *Urbanisme*, Paris: Flammarion.

Least Heat Moon, W. (1984) *Blue highways: a journey into America*, London: Picador.

Leed, E. J. (1991) *The mind of the traveller: from gilgamesh to global tourism*, New York: Basic Books.

Lefebvre, H. (1991) *The production of space*, Oxford: Blackwell.

Lemaire, T. (1970) *Filosofie van het landschap*, Baarn: Uitgeverij Ambo.

Levin, M. R. (2000) *Cultures of control*, Amsterdam: Harwood Academic Publishers.

Levin, T. Y., Frohne, U. and Clift, S. (2002) *CTRL [SPACE]: rhetorics of surveillance from Bentham to Big Brother*, Cambridge, MA: MIT Press.

Levine, R. V. (1998) *A geography of time: the temporal misadventures of a social psychologist, or how every culture keeps time just a little bit differently*, New York: Basic Books.

Lewis, D. L. and Goldstein, L. (eds) (1983) *The automobile and American culture*, Ann Arbor: University of Michigan Press.

Lewis, T. (1997) *Divided highways: building the interstate highways, transforming American life*, New York: Viking.

Lichtenstein, C. and Engler, F. (1992) *Streamlined: a metaphor for progress: the esthetics of minimized drag*, Baden: Lars Mueller.

Ligtermoet, D. M. (1990) *Beleid en planning in de wegenbouw: de relatie tussen beleidsvorming en planning in de geschiedenis van de aanleg en verbetering van rijkswegen*, Amsterdam: Vrije Universiteit.

Ling, P. J. (1990) *America and the automobile: technology, reform and social change, 1893–1923*, Manchester: Manchester University Press.

Lippincott, K. and Eco, U. (1999) *The story of time*, London: Merrell Holberton.

Löfgren, O. (1999) *On holiday: a history of vacationing*, Berkeley: University of California Press.

Loos, A. and Kropman, J. (1993) 'Reistijd cruciaal voor keuze vervoerwijze', *Verkeerskunde*, 44(5): 26–29.

Lowe, J. C. and Moryadas, S. (1975) *The geography of movement*, Boston, MA: Houghton Mifflin Company.

Lowe, M. D. (1989) *The bicycle: vehicle for a small planet*, Washington, DC: Worldwatch Institute.

Lyall, S. (2005) 'Road design? He calls it a revolution', *New York Times Magazine*, 22 January 2005, available online <http://www.hamilton-baillie.co.uk/papers/ NewYorkTimes230105.doc> (accessed 18 August 2005).

Lyon, D. (1994) *The electronic eye: the rise of the surveillance society*, Cambridge: Polity Press.

—— (2001) *Surveillance society: monitoring everyday life*, Buckingham: Open University Press.

—— (ed.) (2003) *Surveillance as social sorting: privacy, risk and digital discrimination*, London: Routledge.

McClelland, L. F. (1997) *Building the national parks: historic landscape design and construction*, Baltimore, MD: Johns Hopkins University Press.

McClintock, H. (ed.) (1992) *The bicycle and city traffic: principles and practice*, London: Belhaven Press.

McGrath, J. E. (1988) *The social psychology of time: new perspectives*, London: Sage Publications.

McKean, J. R., Johnson, D. M. and Walsh, R. G. (1995) 'Valuing time in travel cost demand analysis: an empirical investigation', *Land economics*, 71(1): 96–105.

MacKenzie, D. and Wajcman, J. (1999) *The social shaping of technology*, Buckingham: Open University Press.

Macnaghten, P. and Urry, J. (1998) *Contested natures*, London: Sage Publications.

McQuire, S. (1998) *Visions of modernity: representation, memory, time and space in the age of the camera*, London: Sage Publications.

McShane, C. (1994) *Down the asphalt path: the automobile and the American city*, New York: Columbia University Press.

—— (1997) *The automobile: a chronology of its antecedents, development, and impact*, Westport, CT: Greenwood Publishing Group.

Mączak, A. (1995) *Travel in early modern Europe*, trans. U. Phillips, Cambridge: Polity Press.

Makimoto, T. and Manners, D. (1997) *Digital nomad*, Chichester: John Wiley & Sons.

Malen, K. van der and Pama, G. (1994) 'Minister De Boer over de spanning tussen milieu en economie. "Laat mensen in de file staan, dan kiezen ze voor openbaar vervoer"' in *NRC Handelsblad*, 22 October 1994.

Marchetti, C. (1994) 'Anthropological invariants in travel behavior', *Technological forecasting and social change: an international journal*, 47(1): 75–88.

Margolies, J. (1995) *Home away from home: motels in America*, New York: Bulfinch Press.

Marx, K. (1858; edn 1973) *Grundrisse: foundations of the critique of political economy*, trans. M. Nicolaus, New York: Random House.

Marx, L. (1964) *The machine in the garden: technology and the pastoral ideal in America*, Oxford: Oxford University Press.

Massey, D. and Jess, P. (1995) *A place in the world?: places, cultures and globalization*, Oxford: Oxford University Press.

May, J. and Thrift, N. (eds) (2001) *Timespace: geographies of temporality*, London: Routledge.

Mayinger, F. (ed.) (2001) *Mobility and traffic in the 21st century*, Berlin: Springer.

Mayntz, R. and Hughes, T. P. (eds) (1988) *The development of large technical systems*, Frankfurt am Main: Campus Verlag.

Meadows, D. H., Meadows, D. L., Randers, J. and Behrens, W. (1972) *The limits to growth: a report for the Club of Rome's project on the predicament of mankind*, London: Earth Island Limited.

Meeuse, P. (ed.) (2000) *Lopen*, Amsterdam: De Bezige Bij.

Merriman, P. (2004) 'Driving places: Marc Augé, non-places, and the geographies of England's M1 motorway', *Theory, culture & society*, 21(4): 145–167.

Michael, M. (1998) 'Co(a)gency and the car: attributing agency in the case of the "road rage"', in B. Brenna, J. Law and I. Moser (eds) *Machines, agency and desire*, Oslo: Centre for Technology and Culture, pp. 125–141.

Michels, T. (ed.) (1993) *Cycling in the city, pedalling in the polder: recent developments in policy and research for bicycle facilities in the Netherlands*, Ede: CROW.

Mierlo, J. G. A. van (2000) *De wereld gaat aan beleid ten onder...: over beleidsfalen in de publieke sector en wat daar aan te doen*, Maastricht: Universitaire Pers Maastricht.

Millar, J. and Schwarz, M. (eds) (1998) *Speed – visions of an accelerated age*, London: Photographers' Gallery.

Miller, D. (ed.) (2001) *Car cultures*, Oxford: Berg.

Ministerie van Verkeer en Waterstaat (Ministry of Transport, Public Works and Water Management) (1971) *TP 2000: op weg naar 2000, een toekomstprojectie van Verkeer en Waterstaat*, The Hague: Sdu.

—— (1973) *TP 2000: eerste deel antwoordnota: methodologie*, The Hague, Staatsuitgeverij.

—— (1975) *TP 2000: tweede deel antwoordnota*, 's-Gravenhage, Staatsuitgeverij.

Ministerie van Verkeer en Waterstaat (1996) *Samen werken aan bereikbaarheid*, 's-Gravenhage: Ministerie van Verkeer en Waterstaat.

—— (1997) *Evaluatierapport Masterplan Fiets*, The Hague: Ministerie van Verkeer en Waterstaat.

Ministerie van Verkeer en Waterstaat/Ministerie van Volkshuisvesting en Ruimtelijke Ordening (1977) *Structuurschema verkeer en vervoer*, 's-Gravenhage, Staatsuitgeverij. [a. Beleidsvoornemen. (1977) b. Hoofdlijnen uit de inspraak. (1978) c. Adviezen. (1978) c1. Aanvullend advies. (1979) d. Regeringsbeslissing. (1979)]

Ministerie van Verkeer en Waterstaat/Ministerie van Volkshuisvesting Ruimtelijke Ordening en Milieubeheer (1988–1990) *Tweede struktuurschema verkeer en vervoer*, 's-Gravenhage: Sdu. [Dl. A: Beleidsvoornemen. – Dl. C: Adviezen. – Dl. D: Regeringsbeslissing. – Dl. E: Tweede structuurschema...: tekst van de na parlementaire behandeling vastgestelde planologische kernbeslissing.]

Ministerie van Verkeer en Waterstaat, Projectdirectie Nationaal Verkeers en

Vervoersplan (2001) *Van A naar Beter: Nationaal Verkeers- en Vervoersplan 2001–2020: kabinetsstandpunt en resultaten inspraak en advies*, The Hague: Ministerie van Verkeer en Waterstaat.

Minnen, J. van (1995) *Rotondes en voorrangsregelingen*, Leidschendam: Stichting Wetenschappelijk Onderzoek Verkeersveiligheid SWOV.

Misa, T. J., Brey, P. and Feenberg, A. (2003) *Modernity and technology*, Cambridge, MA: MIT Press.

Mokhtarian, P. L. and Chen, C. (2004) 'TTB or not TTB, that is the question: a review and analysis of the empirical literature on travel time (and money) budgets', *Transportation research: Part A – policy and practice*, 38(9–10), pp. 643–675.

Mol, A. (1997) *Wat is kiezen: een empirisch-filosofische verkenning*, Enschede: Universiteit Twente.

Molin, E. J. E. and Timmermans, L. (1998) *De snelheid begrensd: een onderzoek naar het draagvlak voor de intelligente snelheidsadapter voor personenauto's*, Delft: Technische Universiteit Delft.

Molz, J. G. (2004) ' "Watch us wander": negotiating the public and the private in round-the-world travel websites', paper presented at the Alternative Mobility Futures Conference, 8–11 January 2004, Lancaster.

Mom, G. (1999) *Schiphol: haven, station, knooppunt sinds 1916*, Zutphen: Walburg Pers.

Mom, G. and Kirsch, D. A. (2001) 'Technologies in tension: horses, electric trucks, and the motorization of American cities, 1900–1925', *Technology and culture: the international quarterly of the society for the history of technology*, 42(3): 489–518.

Mom, G., Schot, J. W. and Staal, P. E. (2002) 'Werken aan mobiliteit: de inburgering van de auto', in *Techniek in Nederland in de twintigste eeuw: transport en communicatie*, vol. 5, Zutphen: Walburg Pers, pp. 45–74.

Monkkonen, E. H. (1988) *America becomes urban: the development of US and towns 1780–1980*, Berkeley: University of California Press.

Moorman, C. and Miner, A. S. (1998) 'Organizational improvisation and organizational memory', *The academy of management review*, 23(4): 698–723.

Moors, E. H. M. and Geels, F. W. (2001) *Dynamics of sociotechnical change in transport and mobility: opportunities for governance*, Bilthoven: National Institute of Public Health and the Environment.

Morris, M. (1988) 'At Henry Parkes Motel', *Cultural studies*, 2: 1–47.

Moser, I. and Law, J. (1999) 'Good passages, bad passages', in J. Law and J. Hassard (eds) *Actor-network-theory and after*, Oxford: Blackwell, pp. 196–219.

MuConsult (1995) *Tijdsbestedingsonderzoek: ontwikkelingen in tijdsbestedingen in mobiliteit tussen 1975 en 1995*, Amersfoort: MuConsult BV.

Mumford, L. (1963) *Technics and civilization*, San Diego, CA: Harcourt Brace Jovanovich.

—— (1964) *The highway and the city*, New York: New American Library.

Nash, R. (1982) *Wilderness and the American mind*, New Haven, CT and London: Yale University Press.

National Park Service (1956) *Our heritage: a plan for its protection and use, MISSION 66*, Washington, DC: National Park Service, US Department of the Interior.

Nelson, D. (1980) *Frederick W. Taylor and the rise of scientific management*, Madison: University of Wisconsin Press.

Niewold, R. and Paarlberg, B. (1997) *Gehoorzaamt de signalen…: 65 jaar verkeerslichten in Amsterdam*, Amsterdam: Gemeente Amsterdam Dienst Infrastructuur Verkeer en Vervoer.

Nijkamp, P. (2001) *Modern nomadisme, het milieu en de stad*, Amsterdam: Vrije Universiteit.

Norris, C. and Armstrong, G. (1999) *The maximum surveillance society: the rise of CCTV*, Oxford: Berg.

Nowotny, H. (1989) *Eigenzeit: Entstehung und Strukturierung eines Zeitgefühls*, Frankfurt am Main: Suhrkamp.

Nye, D. E. (1994) *American technological sublime*, Cambridge, MA: MIT Press.

—— (1997) *Narratives and spaces: technology and the construction of American culture*, Exeter: University of Exeter Press.

O'Dea, W. P. (1994) 'The value of a travel time saving to an individual', *International journal of transport economics*, 21(3): 255–268.

Ohler, N. (1986) *Reisen im Mittelalter*, Munich: Artemis.

Orlikowski, W. J. (1996) 'Improvising organizational transformation over time: a situated change perspective', *Information systems research: a journal of the Institute of Management Sciences*, 7(1): 63–92.

Osborne, P. (2000) *Travelling light: photography, travel and visual culture*, Manchester: Manchester University Press.

Östör, Á. (1993) *Vessels of time: an essay on temporal change and social transformation*, New Delhi: Oxford University Press.

Otte, M. (1993) *Het stelsel van gedragsregels in het wegverkeer*, Arnhem: Gouda Quint.

—— (1994) *Verkeersregels in Revisie: pleidooi voor een uitputtend RVV*, Arnhem: Gouda Quint.

Pacey, A. (1983) *The culture of technology*, Oxford: Basil Blackwell.

Parkes, D. and Thrift, N. (1980) *Times, spaces, and places: a chronogeographic perspective*, Chichester: John Wiley & Sons.

Pascoe, D. (2001) *Airspaces*, London: Reaktion.

Pater, B. C. D. and Schmal, H. (1982) *Reistijden, reiskosten en forensisme op Amsterdam in de periode 1855–1980: een tijdgeografische studie*, Amsterdam: Vrije Universiteit.

Patin, T. (1999) 'Exhibitions and empire: national parks and the performance of manifest destiny', *Journal of American culture*, 22(1): 41–60.

Patton, P. (1986) *Open road: a celebration of the American highway*, New York: Simon & Schuster.

Peeters, P. M. (1988) *Schoon op weg: naar een trendbreuk in het personenverkeer: rapport*, Amsterdam: Vereniging Milieudefensie.

Perrow, C. (1984; 2nd edn 1999) *Normal accidents: living with high-risk technologies; with a new afterword and a postscript on the Y2K problem* (2nd edn), Princeton, NJ: Princeton University Press.

Peters, P. F. (1990) 'Hoe bekeer je een automobilist?', *Intermediair*, 1990(1–2): 15–19.

—— (1994) *De verdwenen horizon: over de anatomie van de reis in 2050*, The Hague: Rijksplanologische Dienst.

—— (1995a) 'De verdwenen horizon: over de anatomie van de reis in 2050', *Kennis en Methode*, 19(1): 64–80.

—— (1995b) 'Leve de auto', in K. Waagmeester (ed.) *Ontstolen welvaart: kroniek van duurzaam Nederland*, Utrecht: Platform voor Duurzame Ontwikkeling/Jan Mets, pp. 36–59.

—— (1997a) 'De haast van Albertine: fysieke mobiliteit, snelheid en de herontdekking van het langzame', in M. A. Hajer and F. Halsema (eds) *Land in zicht!: Een cultuurpolitieke visie op de ruimtelijke inrichting*, Amsterdam: Bert Bakker, pp. 29–43.

—— (1997b) 'Reistijd in de dagen van Thomas Cook: de co-evolutie van snelheid en temporele precisie in verplaatsingspraktijken', *Kennis en Methode*, XXI(3): 178–191.

—— (1997c) 'De toekomst volgens de Club van Rome', in K. Waagmeester (ed.) *Houdbare economie*, Kampen: Kok Agora, pp. 15–37.

—— (1998a) 'De smalle marges van de politiek', in H. Achterhuis and B. Elzen (eds) *Cultuur en mobiliteit*, The Hague: Sdu, pp. 38–63.

—— (1998b) 'Verkeersethiek op straat', *Filosofie & praktijk*, 19(3): 149–159.

—— (1998c) 'Lopen in Schuberts Winterreise', *Hollands Maandblad*, 1998(6–7): 5–13.

—— (1999) *In de praktijk: naar een andere conceptualisering van verplaatsingen*, Delft: Connekt.

—— (2000) 'Parallel velocities', in *Theory, culture & society*, 17(6): 131–138.

—— (2002) 'De cultuur van de verplaatsing', in H. Geerlings, W. Hafkamp and G. Peters (eds) *Mobiliteit als uitdaging: een integrale benadering*, Rotterdam: Uitgeverij 010, pp. 63–75.

—— (2003) *De haast van Albertine. Reizen in de technologische cultuur: naar een theorie van passages*, Amsterdam: Uitgeverij De Balie.

Peters, P. F. and Hajer, M. A. (2001) *Paying in the polder: urban road pricing and Dutch cultures of deliberation*, Amsterdam: Amsterdam Research Centre for the Metropolitan Environment (AME).

Peters, P. F., Heuvel, M. van den and Renssen, H. van (1997) *Tijd in relatie tot duurzaam consumeren*, The Hague: Ministerie van Volkshuisvesting, Ruimtelijke Ordening en Milieubeheer/Directie Industrie- en Consumentenbeleid.

Peters, P. F., Peeters, P. M., Wilde, R. de and Clement, B. (2001) *Een constante in beweging?: reistijd, vrituele mobiliteit en de BREVER-wet*, Rotterdam: Adviesdient Verkeer en Vervoer.

Pinch, T. and Bijker, W. E. (1987) 'The social construction of facts and artifacts: or how the sociology of science and the sociology of technology might benefit each other', in W. E. Bijker, Th. P. Hughes and T. Pinch (eds) *The social construction of technological systems: new directions in the sociology and history of technology*, Cambridge, MA: MIT Press, pp. 17–50.

Ploeger, J. (1997) 'Designing for cycling: the new Dutch design manual', in R. Tolley (ed.) *The greening of urban transport: planning for walking and cycling in Western cities*, Chichester: John Wiley & Sons, pp. 397–402.

Ploeger, J., Botma, H., Michels, T. and Stichting CROW (1993) *Sign up for the bike: design manual for a cycle-friendly infrastructure*, Ede: Centre for Research and Contract Standardization in Civil and Traffic Engineering (CROW).

Poidevin, R. L. and MacBeath, M. (eds) (1993) *The philosophy of time*, Oxford: Oxford University Press.

Pope, N. (2001) 'Dickens's "The Signalman" and information problems in the Railway Age', *Technology and culture: the international quarterly of the Society for the History of Technology*, 42(3): 436–488.

Porter, T. M. (1994) 'Making things quantitative', *Science in context*, 7(3): 389–408.

—— (1995) *Trust in numbers: the pursuit of objectivity in science and public life*, Princeton, NJ: Princeton University Press.

Pratt, M. L. (1992) *Imperial eyes: travel writing and transculturation*, London: Routledge.

Projectteam Nationaal Verkeer- en Vervoerplan. (1999) *Perspectievennota verkeer en vervoer*, The Hague: Projectteam Nationaal Verkeer- en Vervoerplan.

Proust, M. (1989) *Remembrance of things past*, Vol. 2, *The Guermantes Way. Cities of the plain*, trans. C. K. Scott-Moncrieff and T. Kilmartin, London: Penguin Books.

Provoost, M. (1996) *Asfalt: automobiliteit in de Rotterdamse stedebouw*, Rotterdam: Uitgeverij 010.

Pudney, J. (1953) *The Thomas Cook story*, London: Joseph.

Rae, J. B. (1971) *The road and the car in American life*, London: MIT Press.

Raitz, K. (1998) 'American roads, roadside America', *The geographical review*, 88(3): 363–387.

Reheis, F. (1996) *Die Kreativität der Langsamkeit: neuer Wohlstand durch Entschleunigung*, Darmstadt: Wissenschaftliche Buchgesellschaft.

Reichert, F. (ed.) (1998) *Fernreisen im Mittelalter*, Berlin: Akademie Verlag.

Reijnders, L. (2000) *Reislust: op weg naar het paradijs en andere bestemmingen*, Amsterdam: Van Gennep.

Rheingold, H. (1993; 2nd edn 2000) *The virtual community: homesteading on the electronic frontier*, London: MIT Press.

Richards, J. and MacKenzie, J. M. (1988) *The railway station: a social history*, Oxford: Oxford University Press.

Richardson, E. (1973) *Dams, parks and politics: resource, development and preservation in the Truman-Eisenhower era*, Lexington: University Press of Kentucky.

Rietdijk, J. W. and Spoelstra, F. A. (2001) *Smartcards in de reële en virtuele wereld*, The Hague: Ten Hagen & Stam.

Rietveld, P. (2000a) 'De latente vraag naar mobiliteit', *Rooilijn: mededelingen van het planologisch en demografisch Instituut*, 5: 222–228 (227).

—— (2000b) *Snelheid en bereikbaarheid: snelheidsverlaging tussen feit en fictie*, Amsterdam: Vrije Universiteit.

Rifkin, J. (1987) *Time wars: the primary conflict in human history*, New York: Henry Holt and Company.

—— (2000) *The age of access: the new culture of hypercapitalism, where all of life is a paid-for experience*, New York: Jeremy P. Tarcher/Putnam.

Robinson, J. C. (1989) *The walk: notes on a romantic image*, Norman: University of Oklahoma Press.

Rokach, A. and Millman, A. (1992) *Focus on travel: photographing memorable pictures of journeys to new places*, New York: Abbeville Press.

Rosen, C. (1995) *The romantic generation*, Cambridge, MA: Harvard University Press.

Rosen, P. (1999) *Towards sustainable urban transport: constructivism, planning and policy*, Cambridge: Anglia Polytechnic University.

—— (2002) *Framing production: technology, culture, and change in the British bicycle industry*, Cambridge, MA: MIT Press.

Rosseel, E. (2000) *Monaden, nomaden en pelgrims: nomadisering en het utopisch ideaal*, Kampen: Agora.

Rothman, H. K. (1998) *Devil's bargains: tourism in the twentieth-century American west*, Lawrence: Kansas University Press.

Rotteveel, K. (ed.) (1992) *Grenzen aan de snelheid: verslag van de studiedag over effectieve snelheidsbegrenzing*, Amersfoort: Initiatiefgroep Wijs op Weg.

Runte, A. (1979) *National parks: the American experience*, Lincoln: University of Nebraska Press.

—— (1990) *Trains of discovery: western railroads and the national parks*, Niwot, CO: Roberts Rineharts.

Rutz, H. J. (1992) *The politics of time*, Washington, DC: American Anthropological Association.

Sachs, W. (1992) *For love of the automobile: looking back into the history of our desires*, Berkeley: University of California Press.

—— (1999) *Planet dialectics: explorations in environment and development*, London: Zed Books.

Safdie, M. and Kohn, W. (1998) *The city after the automobile: an architect's vision*, Boulder, CO: Westview Press.

Sassen, S. and Appiah, K. A. (1999) *Globalization and its discontents: essays on the new mobility of people and money*, New York: New Press.

Sax, J. L. (1980) *Mountains without handrails: reflections on the national parks*, Ann Arbor: University of Michigan Press.

Schafer, A. (1998) 'The global demand for motorized mobility', *Transportation research, Part A: policy and practice*, 32(6): 455–477.

Schafer, A. and Victor, D. G. (1997) 'The past and future of global mobility', *Scientific American*, 277(4): 36–39.

—— (2000) 'The future mobility of the world population', *Transportation research Part A, policy and practice*, 34(3): 171–206.

Scharfe, M. (1991) 'Die alte Straße: Fragmente', in H. Bausinger, K. Beyrer and G. Korff (eds) (1991) *Reisekultur: von der Pilgerfahrt zum modernen Tourismus*, Munich: Verlag C. H. Beck, pp. 20–27.

Scharff, V. (1991) *Taking the wheel: women and the coming of the motor age*, New York: Free Press.

Schatzki, T. R. (1996) *Social practices: a Wittgensteinian approach to human activity and the social*, Cambridge: Cambridge University Press.

Schatzki, T. R., Knorr-Cetina, K. and Savigny, E. von (eds) (2001) *The practice turn in contemporary theory*, London: Routledge.

Schivelbusch, W. (1986) *The railway journey: the industrialization of time and space in the nineteenth century*, Leamington Spa: Berg.

Schlesinger, A. M. and Israel, F. L. (eds) (1999) *Touring America seventy-five years ago: how the automobile and the railroad changed the nation: chronicles from National Geographic*, Philadelphia, PA: Chelsea House Publishers.

Schmied, G. (1985) *Soziale Zeit: Umfang, 'Geschwindigkeit' und Evolution*, Berlin: Duncker und Humblot.

Schön, D. A. (1983) *The reflective practitioner: how professionals think in action*, New York: Basic Books.

Schot, J. W. (2002a) 'De mobiliteitsexplosie in de twintigste eeuw', *Techniek in Nederland in de twintigste eeuw: transport en communicatie*, vol. 5, Zutphen: Walburg Pers, 13–18.

—— (2002b) 'Begrensde mobiliteit', *Techniek in Nederland in de twintigste eeuw: transport en communicatie*, vol. 5, Zutphen: Walburg Pers, pp. 145–149.

Schot, J. W., Mom, G. P. A., Filarski, R. and Staal, P. E. (2002) 'Concurrentie en afstemming: water, rails, weg en lucht', *Techniek in Nederland in de twintigste eeuw: transport en communicatie*, vol. 5, Zutphen: Walburg Pers, pp. 19–44.

Schuyt, K. and Taverne, E. (2000) *1950: welvaart in zwart-wit*, The Hague: Sdu Uitgevers.

Schwarz, H. (2004) 'The rhetoric of locatibility – envisioning locative media and technologies of mobility', paper presented at the 4S & EASST Conference 'Public proofs. Science, technology and democracy', 25–28 August 2004, Paris.

Segal, H. P. (1994) *Future imperfect: the mixed blessings of technology in America*, Amherst: The University of Massachusetts Press.

Sellars, R. W. (1997) *Preserving nature in the national parks: a history*, New Haven, CT and London: Yale University Press.

Sennett, R. (1994) *Flesh and stone: the body and the city in western civilization*, New York: W. W. Norton & Company.

Serres, M. (1980) *Le passage du Nord-Ouest*, Paris: Éditions de Minuit.

Seume, J. G., Drews, J. and Kyora, S. (1993) *Mein Leben; Spaziergang nach Syrakus im Jahre 1802; Mein Sommer 1805* (1st edn), Frankfurt am Main: Deutscher Klassiker Verlag.

Shackle, G. L. S. (1983) *Time in economics*, Westport, CT: Greenwood Press.

Sharp, C. (1981) *The economics of time*, Oxford: Robertson.

Shaw, J. (1994) 'Punctuality and the everyday ethics of time: some evidence from the mass observation archive', *Time & society*, 3: 79–97.

Shields, R. (1991) *Places on the margin: alternative geographies of modernity*, London: Routledge.

Simpson, L. C. (1995) *Technology, time and the conversations of modernity*, New York and London: Routledge.

Sloterdijk, P. (1987) *Kopernikanische Mobilmachung und ptolemaeische Abruestung: aesthetischer Versuch*, Frankfurt am Main: Suhrkamp.

—— (1989) *Eurotaoismus: zur Kritik der politischen Kinetik*, Frankfurt am Main: Suhrkamp.

—— (1998) 'Modernity as mobilisation', in J. Millar and M. Schwarz (eds) *Speed – visions of an accelerated age*, London: Photographer's Gallery, pp. 43–52.

Smeets, R. (1999) *Groen licht voor de fietsers in Breda: een onderzoek naar de effecten van fietsvriendelijke verkeerslichten in Breda*, Breda: Nationale Hogeschool voor Toerisme en Verkeer.

Smith, M. R. and Marx, L. (eds) (1994) *Does technology drive history?: the dilemma of technological determinism*, Cambridge, MA: MIT Press.

Smith, P. (ed.) (1998) *The history of tourism: Thomas Cook and the origins of leisure travel*, vol. 3, *Letters from the sea and from foreign lands: descriptive of a tour round the world*, London: Routledge.

Sobel, D. (1995) *Longitude: the true story of a lone genius who solved the greatest scientific problem of his time*, New York: Penguin Books.

Sociaal en Cultureel Planbureau (1976) *Autogebruiksbeperking: mogelijkheden en aanvaardbaarheid*, Rijswijk: Sociaal en Cultureel Planbureau.

Solnit, R. (2001) *Wanderlust: a history of walking*, New York: Viking.

Sorokin, P. A. and Berger, C. Q. (1939) *Time-budgets of human behavior*, Cambridge, MA: Harvard University Press.

Spaulding, J. (1995) *Ansel Adams and the American landscape: a biography*, Berkeley: University of California Press.

Spee, J. (1991) *Ik rij als een scheermes: gedrag en wangedrag in het verkeer*, Amsterdam: Balans.

Spence, M. D. (1999) *Dispossessing the wilderness: Indian removal and the making of the national parks*, New York and Oxford: Oxford University Press.

Spiekermann, K. and Wegener, M. (1994) 'The shrinking continent: new time-space maps for Europe', *Environment and planning B*, 21: 653–673.

Stagl, J. (1995) *A history of curiosity: the theory of travel, 1550–1800*, Chur: Harwood.

Standage, T. (1998) *The Victorian internet: the remarkable story of the telegraph and the nineteenth century's on-line pioneers*, New York: Walker & Company.

Steg, L. and Sievers, I. (1996) *Milieuproblemen als sociale dilemma's: factoren die van invloed zijn op het ontstaan van en mogelijke oplossingen voor grootschalige sociale dilemma's*, The Hague: Raad voor het Milieubeheer.

Stein, J. (2001) 'Reflections on time, time-space compression and technology in the nineteenth century', in J. May and N. Thrift (eds) *Timespace: geographies of temporality*, London: Routledge, pp. 106–119.

Stephens, C. (1989) 'The most reliable time: William Bond, the New England railroads, and time awareness in nineteenth-century America', *Technology and Culture*, 30(1): 1–24.

Stommer, R. and Philipp, C. G. (1982) *Reichsautobahn: Pyramiden des Dritten Reichs: Analysen zur Aesthetik eines unbewaeltigten Mythos*, Marburg: Jonas Verlag.

Studiecentrum Verkeerstechniek (1981) *Fietsers, bromfietsers en verkeerslichten: enkele aspecten ten aanzien van fiets- en bromfietsvoorzieningen op met verkeerslichten geregelde kruispunten*, Driebergen-Rijsenburg: Studiecentrum Verkeerstechniek.

Suchman, L. A. (1987) *Plans and situated actions: the problem of human-machine communication*, Cambridge: Cambridge University Press.

—— (1993) 'Technologies of accountability: of lizards and airplanes', in G. Button (ed.) *Technology in working order: studies of work, interaction, and technology*, London: Routledge, pp. 113–126.

—— (1997) 'Centers of coordination: a case and some themes', in L. B. Resnick (ed.) *Discourse, tools, and reasoning: essays on situated cognition*, Berlin: Springer.

Summerton, J. (ed.) (1994) *Changing large technical systems*, Boulder, CO: Westview Press.

Sundquist, J. L. (1969) *Politics and policy: the Eisenhower-Kennedy, and Johnson years*, Washington: Brookings Institution.

Susman, W. I. (1984) *Culture as history: the transformation of American society in the twentieth century*, New York: Pantheon Books.

Swinglehurst, E. (1974) *The romantic journey: the story of Thomas Cook and Victorian travel*, London: Pica Editions.

Szalai, A. and Converse, P. E. (1972) *The use of time: daily activities of urban and suburban populations in twelve countries*, The Hague: Mouton.

Tabboni, S. (2001) 'The idea of social time in Norbert Elias', *Time & society*, 10(1): 5–27.

Teenstra, A. (1942) *De fiets: plezier ervan, pech ermee*, Zwolle: La Rivière & Voorhoeve.

Tenner, E. (1996) *Why things bite back: technology and the revenge of unintended consequences*, New York: Knopf.

Theroux, P. (2002) *Dark star safari: overland from Cairo to Cape Town*, London: Hamish Hamilton.

Thompson, E. P. (1967) 'Time, work-discipline and industrial capitalism', *Past and present*, 38(December): 56–97.

Thoms, D., Holden, L. and Claydon, T. (eds) (1997) *The motor car and popular culture in the twentieth century*, Aldershot: Ashgate.

Thrift, N. J. (1990) 'Transport and communications, 1730–1914', in R. A. Dodgshon and R. A. Butlin (eds) *Historical geography of England and Wales*, London: Academic Press, 453–486.

—— (1996) *Spatial formations*, London: Sage Publications.

—— (2004) 'Remembering the technological unconscious by foregrounding knowledges of position', *Environment and planning D*, 22(1): 175–190.

Tolley, R. (1989) *Calming traffic in residential areas*, Llanddewi Brefi: Brefi.

—— (ed.) (1997) *The greening of urban transport: planning for walking and cycling in Western cities*, Chichester: John Wiley & Sons.

Untermann, R. K. (1984) *Accommodating the pedestrian: adapting towns and neighborhoods for walking and bicyling*, New York: Van Nostrand Reinhold Company.

Urry, J. (1990) *The tourist gaze: leisure and travel in contemporary societies*. London: Sage Publications.

—— (1995) *Consuming places*, London: Routledge.

—— (2000a) *Sociology beyond societies: mobilities for the twenty-first century*, London: Routledge.

—— (2000b) 'Mobile sociology', *British journal of sociology*, 51(1): 185–203.

—— (2004) 'The "system" of automobility', *Theory, culture & society*, 21(4): 25–39.

Urry, J. and Rojek, C. (eds) (1997) *Touring cultures: transformations of travel and theory*, London: Routledge.

Van den Abbeele, G. (1992) *Travel as metaphor: from Montaigne to Rousseau*, Minneapolis: University of Minnesota Press.

Van der Ploeg, I. (2003) 'Biometrics and the body as information', in D. Lyon (ed.) *Surveillance as social sorting: privacy, risk and digital discrimination*, London: Routledge.

Vance, J. E. (1986) *Capturing the horizon. The historical geography of transportation since the transportation revolution of the sixteenth century*, New York: Harper and Row.

Vegesack, A. von and Kries, M. (1999) *Automobility*, Weil am Rein: Vitra Design Museum.

Veraart, F. C. A. (1995) *Geschiedenis van de fiets in Nederland, 1870–1940*, Eindhoven: Technische Universiteit Eindhoven.

Vermeulen, J., Kampman, B., Janse, P. and Centrum voor Energiebesparing en Schone Technologie (2000) *Fietsbeleid beloond*, Delft: Centrum voor Energiebesparing en Schone Technologie.

Verstraete, G. (2001) *Verstrooide burgers: Europese cultuur in een tijdperk van globalisering*, Amsterdam: Vossiuspers UvA.

Verstraete, G. and Cresswell, T. (eds) *Mobilizing place, placing mobility: the politics of representation in a globalized world*, Amsterdam: Rodopi.

Vester, F. (1995) *Crashtest mobilität: die Zukunft des Verkehrs; Fakten, Strategien, Lösungen*, Munich: Heyne.

Vigar, G. (2002) *The politics of mobility: transport, the environment and public policy*, London: Spon Press.

Virilio, P. (1977) *Vitesse et politique*, Paris: Editions Galilée.

—— (1984) *L'espace critique*, Paris: Christian Bourgois Editeur.

—— (1993a) *L'art du moteur*, Paris: Editions Galilée.

—— (1993b) *Revolutionen der Geschwindigheit*, Berlin: Merve Verlag Berlin.

Vries, G. de (1999) *Zeppelins: over filosofie, technologie en cultuur*, Amsterdam: Van Gennep.

—— (2001) 'Wetenschaps- en techniekonderzoekers: waar is de geest gebleven?', *Krisis: tijdschrift voor empirische filosofie*, 2(1): 62–78.

Vries, J. de (1981) *Barges and capitalism: passenger transportation in the Dutch economy, 1632–1839*, Utrecht: HES.

VROM-raad (1999) *Mobiliteit met beleid*, The Hague: VROM-raad.

Wachs, M., Crawford, M. and Wirka, S. M. (1992) *The car and the city: the automobile, the built environment and daily urban life*, Ann Arbor: University of Michigan Press.

Wajcman, J. (1991) *Feminism confronts technology*, Cambridge: Polity Press.

Wallace, A. D. (1993) *Walking, literature, and English culture: the origins and uses of peripatetic in the nineteenth century*, Oxford: Clarendon Press.

Wallis, M. (1993) *Route 66: the mother road*, New York: St Martin's Press.

Wee, B. van (1999) 'Hoe wetmatig is de BREVER-wet', *Verkeerskunde*, 50(9): 16–17.

Weick, K. E. (1993) 'The collapse of sensemaking in organizations: the Mann Gulch disaster', *Administrative science quarterly*, 38: 628–652.

—— (1998) 'Introductory essay – improvisation as a mindset for organizational analysis', *Organization science: a journal of the Institute of Management Sciences*, 9(5): 543–555.

Weilenmann, A. (2003) *Doing mobility*, unpublished thesis, Göteborg University.

Wellmann, A. (1991) *Der Spaziergang: stationen eines poetischen codes*, Würzburg: Königshausen & Neumann.

—— (1992) *Der Spaziergang: ein literarisches Lesebuch*, Hildesheim: Georg Olms.

Wells, H. G. (1999; 1st edn 1902) *Anticipations of the reaction of mechanical and scientific progress upon human life and thought*, Mineola, NY: Dover Publications, Inc.

Wendorff, R. (1980) *Zeit und Kultur: Geschichte des Zeitbewußtseins in Europa*, Wiesbaden: Westdeutscher Verlag.

—— (ed.) (1989) *Im Netz der Zeit: menschliches Zeiterleben interdisziplinaer*, Stuttgart: S. Hirzel Wissenschaftliche Verlagsgesellschaft Stuttgart.

White, R. B. (2000) *Home on the road: the motor home in America*, Washington, DC: Smithsonian Institution Press.

Whitelegg, J. (1993) 'Time pollution', *The ecologist: the journal of the post industrial age*, 23(4): 132–134.

—— (1997) *Critical mass: transport, environment and society in the twenty-first century*, London: Pluto Press.

—— (1998) 'The rickshaw irony', *The ecologist: the journal of the post industrial age*, 28(3): 138–139.

Wilde, R. de (1997) 'Op de klippen', *K & M: tijdschrift voor empirische filosofie*, 21(3): 254–261.

—— (2000a) *De voorspellers: een kritiek op de toekomstindustrie*, Amsterdam: De Balie.

—— (2000b) 'Innovating innovation: a contribution to the philosophy of the future', paper read at 'Policy agendas for sustainable technological innovation', 1–3 December 2000, London.

Wilde, R. de and Peters, P. F. (2000) 'Verstrikt in het net: review van Castells' "The information age: economy, society and culture"', *Krisis: tijdschrift voor empirische filosofie*, 1(3): 57–67.

Wilkinson, B. (1997) 'Nonmotorized transportation: the forgotten modes', *The annals of the American Academy of Political and Social Science*, 1997: 87–93.

Williams, C. T. (ed.) (1998) *Travel culture: essays on what makes us go*, New York: Praeger.

Wilson, A. (1992) *The culture of nature: North American landscape from Disney to the Exxon Valdez*, Cambridge, MA: Blackwell.

Wilson, A. and Middelham, F. (2000) 'Wordt Nederland goed geregeld?', *Verkeerskunde*, 51(1): 14–19.

Winner, L. (1977) *Autonomous technology*, Cambridge, MA: MIT Press.

—— (1986) *The whale and the reactor: a search for limits in an age of high technology*, Chicago, IL: University of Chicago Press.

—— (1999) 'Do artifacts have politics?', in D. MacKenzie and J. Wajcman (eds) *The social shaping of technology*, Buckingham: Open University Press, pp. 28–40.

Wirth, C. L. (1980) *Parks, politics, and the people*, Norman: University of Oklahoma Press.

Wit, J. G. de (1980) 'De wettelijke aanspraken van BREVER', *Verkeerskunde*, 31: 354–357; 415–418.

Withey, L. (1997) *Grand tours and Cook's tours: a history of leisure travel, 1750–1915*, New York: William Morrow.

Woerdman, E. (1999) *Politiek en politicologie*, Groningen: Wolters-Noordhoff.

Woolgar, S. and Cooper, G. (1999) 'Do artefacts have ambivalence? Moses' bridges, winner bridges and other urban legends in S&TS', *Social studies of science*, 29(3): 433–449.

Woud, A. van der (1987) *Het lege land: de ruimtelijke orde van Nederland, 1798–1848*, Amsterdam: Meulenhoff.

Wright, F. L. (1958) *The living city*, New York: Horizon Press.

Wupertal Institut (ed.) (1996) *Zukunftsfahiges Deutschland: ein Beitrag zu einer global nachhaltigen Entwicklung*, Basel: Birkhauser Verlag.

Wyatt, J. (1999) *Wordsworth's poems of travel, 1819–42: such sweet wayfaring*, Basingstoke: MacMillan.

Yates, J. (1989) *Control through communication: the rise of system in American management*, Baltimore, MD: Johns Hopkins University Press.

Yorke, D. A. and Margolies, J. (1996) *Hitting the road: the art of the American road map*, San Francisco, CA: Chronicle Books.

Young, M. (1988) *The metronomic society*, London: Thames and Hudson.

Young, M. and Schüller, T. (1988) *The rhythms of society*, London: Routledge.

Zahavi, Y. (1979) 'Travel behaviour in transportation systems', paper presented at the conference on 'Research directives in computer control of urban traffic systems', Pacific Grove, California, 1979.

Zerubavel, E. (1981) *Hidden rhythms: schedules and calendars in social life*, Chicago, IL: University of Chicago Press.

Zimmerli, W. C. and Sandbothe, M. (eds) (1993) *Klassiker der modernen Zeitphilosophie*, Darmstadt: Wissenschaftliche Buchgesellschaft.

Zoll, R. (1988) 'Krise der Zeiterfahrung', in R. Zoll (ed.) *Zerstörung und Wiederaneignung der Zeit*, Frankfurt am Main: Suhrkamp.

Zuckermann, W. (1991) *End of the road: from world car crisis to sustainable transportation*, Post Mills, VT: Chelsea Green Publishing Company.

Index

Blaise, C. 190n7, 191n18
Bloemen, Y. 189n1
blue highways 6
Bombay 68, 71
Boomen, T. van den 133
Boorstin, D. 36
Borst, A. 46
Boston 100, 191n1
Braque, G. 60
Brendon, P. 63–6, 71, 190n11
'BREVER' law 21–2, 24, 186n17; *see also*
  hypothesis of constant travel time
Brilli, A. 30, 33–4
Brune, T. 32
Brussels 65, 116, 194n9
Bruzelius, N. 188n17
Bryce Canyon National Park 85
Bryman, A. 95
Buckminster Fuller, R. 186n16
Buiter, H. 12
Bullard, R.D. 151
Bunce, M.F. 94
Bureau of Public Roads 77
Bush, J.D. 38

Caesar 43
Cairo 162
Calcutta 68, 71
calendars: as timekeeping devices 46–7
Calfee, J. 166
California State Automobile Association 90
Callon, M. 4
camp grounds 81, 83, 88
canals 12, 37, 61, 191n16
Canton 68
Capetown 162
car hops 80
car kilometres 4, 10, 13, 16, 25, 195n1
car manufacturers, 18, 38, 76, 87, 157
car pooling 16
car sharing 199n9
car system 16, 25
car-free Sundays 16, 186n13
Carr, E., 87, 89, 90, 132, 193n18
cars 2–4, 6–7, 9–12, 14, 16, 18, 20, 25,
  41–2, 73–6, 80, 82–91, 93, 95, 97–8, 102,
  128–31, 133, 136–7, 139, 141, 143, 145,
  149, 154, 160, 165, 172, 185n7, 191n1,
  195n1
car-sons 196n10
Castells, M. 3, 163
Cawnpore 68
cell phones 162
Central Flow Management Unit 116, 194n9
centres of coordination 111
Chen, C. 186n18
Chicago 67
children: in urban traffic 130, 138–9, 143,
  150–1, 155, 157–8

China 66, 71
Chrysler 38, 157, 198n1
CIAM 131
Ciborra, C.U. 118, 195n13
circular notes 66
city planning 195n1
Clark, P. 80
Clift, S. 167
Clingman's Dome Tower, 92–3
closed circuit television (CCTV) 167, 168
Club of Rome 12, 185n8
co-evolution: of physical transportation and
  information networks 111; of time
  practices and travel practices 45, 51, 63,
  177, 180
Cohan, S. 85
Cohen, B. 38
Cohn, D.L. 78
Cologne 65
communication 52, 57, 59, 60, 109, 110,
  127, 135, 153, 157, 163, 167–8, 171,
  178, 188n19, 194n7
communication technologies 60, 72, 126,
  198n5
comparative perspective: on modes of
  transport 11, 24, 26, 48, 149, 176,
  197n15
congestion 4, 8–10, 13–17, 19, 26, 44, 55,
  100, 101, 132, 145, 146, 159–61,
  164–6, 170–76, 195n9; *see also* traffic
  jams
congestion charge 10, 170, 172; *see also*
  road pricing
connecting strategies 182, *183*
connections 6–7, 32, 65, 66, 83, 84, 97, 101,
  107, 163, 170, 182, *183*, 190n13, 194n3
containerization 61
Continental Railway Guide 34
contingencies 2, 6, 7, 51, 70, 72, 74, 85, 97,
  99, 101, 109, 117–18, 124, 126, 157, 182
control centre 9, 107, 110–11, 126, 129; *see
  also* operations control centre
Cooke, J. 86
Cook, J.M. 190n10
Cook, T. 2, 6, 36, 49, 50, 52, 63–72, 75, 83,
  93, 162, 177, 182, 190n10
Cookism 190n10
Cook's: the man from 70, 83
corridor 190n14
Crawford, M. 191n1
Crossan, M.M. 195n12
crossings 8, 129; pedestrian 128, 133, 155,
  157, 196n4
Crystal Palace 65
Cunard Line 190n11
cyclists 10, 76, 128, 130, 133, 136, 138–48,
  150–52, 198n17

Daimler 136, 157, 198

For Product Safety Concerns and Information please contact our EU
representative GPSR@taylorandfrancis.com
Taylor & Francis Verlag GmbH, Kaufingerstraße 24, 80331 München, Germany

www.ingramcontent.com/pod-product-compliance
Lightning Source LLC
Chambersburg PA
CBHW050423280326
41932CB00013BA/1967